Hope with Eating Disorders

A self-help guide for parents, carers and friends of sufferers

Second edition

Lynn Crilly

With a Foreword by Professor Janet Treasure

BOOKS

Hammersmith Health Books
London, UK

First published in 2012 by Hay House
This second edition first published in 2019 by Hammersmith Health Books –
an imprint of Hammersmith Books Limited
4/4A Bloomsbury Square, London WC1A 2RP, UK
www.hammersmithbooks.co.uk

The information contained in this book is for educational purposes only. It is
the result of the study and the experience of the author. Whilst the information
and advice offered are believed to be true and accurate at the time of going to
press, neither the author nor the publisher can accept any legal responsibility or
liability for any errors or omissions that may have been made or for any adverse
effects which may occur as a result of following the recommendations given
herein. Always consult a qualified medical practitioner if you have any concerns
regarding your health.

British Library Cataloguing in Publication Data: A CIP record of this book is
available from the British Library.

Print ISBN 978-1-78161-147-0
Ebook ISBN 978-1-78161-148-7

Commissioning editor: Georgina Bentliff
Designed and typeset by: Julie Bennett, Bespoke Publishing
Cover design by: Julie Bennett, Bespoke Publishing
Index: Dr Laurence Errington
Production: Helen Whitehorn, Pathmedia
Printed and bound by: TJ International, Cornwall, UK
Cover Image: 123RF/© sunshinesmile

Contents

About Lynn Crilly

Lynn Crilly is an award-winning counsellor and mother of twin girls. When one of her twin daughters, Samantha, struggled with OCD and anorexia nervosa, having followed the conventional therapy routes to no avail, Lynn took the decision to follow her gut instincts and rehabilitate Samantha herself. She subsequently developed her unique form of counselling to support sufferers and their families going through similar experiences.

Lynn continues to work with families every day, battling mental health issues at her clinic in Surrey, UK. She uses the knowledge and experience she has gained to write self-help books covering an array of mental health issues, with the aim to help combat stigma and destructive myths whilst also providing a positive and constructive way forward for families and carers affected. She is admired for her passion and understanding – something she attributes to the strength and loyalty of her family and friends, with whom she spends as much time as possible. www.lynncrilly.com

Acknowledgements

First and foremost, I would like to say a *BIG* thank you to my wonderful husband, Kevin, who has always given me his unconditional love and support. His unquestioning belief in me has given me the strength to achieve all I have so far … I love you more with every new day.

Also, thank you to our beautiful twin daughters, Charlotte and Samantha. I am so proud of the gorgeous young ladies you have become and love you both very much!

A big thank you to Callum and Jay for loving my girls unconditionally and making my family complete – love you both loads.

Much love to my mum and dad, who have always been there for me, with the kettle on and ready to listen, with their constant love and support.

To my brother, Steve, and sister-in-law, Sue, thank you for being there.

A special thank you to Kate, Wendy, Jill, Gerry, Leanne, Hannah, Dionne, Kyra, Michelle, Shauna, Neil and all my friends who continue to love me unconditionally – your friendship is a rare and valued gift.

A warm thank you to our wonderful GPs, past and present, Dr John Dalzell and Dr Sarah Benney, who over the years have given us as a family and me as a professional their unreserved support.

Thank you to all my clients, both past and present, who have put their trust and belief in me and my work, which has enabled me to help and support them to make the positive changes needed in their lives and, in doing so, changing mine.

A special thank you to Dr Russell Delderfield for all his encouragement and support over the years, and for giving his expertise and knowledge in Chapter 8 – Eating disorders in men.

A huge thank you to Mel Hunter, who has been my writing hand all the way through *Hope with Eating Disorders 2nd edition*.

I have been incredibly privileged to have been supported by so many wonderful people from all walks of life, who have all trusted and believed in me enough to make a contribution to this book – for that I thank you all.

Lastly, and by no means least, thank you to my lovely publisher, Georgina Bentliff (Hammersmith Health Books), for being so supportive, open minded and a total pleasure to work with.

Once again, a big thank you to all mentioned above and the many others who have championed, helped and supported me over the years. Without each and every one of you, I know I would not be who, and where, I am today, both personally and professionally. For this I will always be grateful.

Foreword

Working with people with eating disorders for over 36 years in order to understand the illness and to help on the way to recovery, I have often heard that one of the most important things that carers can do is maintain hope. This book encapsulates the essence of how hope can be generated and sustained. Hope can be built on understanding more about the illness, building resilience in young people and their families to withstand some of the pressures that can adversely shape development, and increasing trust that recovery is attainable.

A junior doctor described her 12-year illness in a Personal View to the *British Medical Journal*. She said she could summarise her illness in one word: 'isolation'. Although numerous paths lead to isolation, including biological and psychological factors, social factors are of key importance. The noxious influence of shame and stigma drives the individual, and their family, too, into a secret cell of loneliness bereft of the social glue of shared eating and connection.

Lynn demonstrates what can be attained through curiosity and an open mind, and the refusal to accept stigma and secrecy. This book contains the lived experience of diverse forms of eating disorders, and glimpses into the variety of ways in which recovery can be attained. Connecting with others with love and respect is key, and this book demonstrates how this can be done.

Professor Janet Treasure PhD FRCP FRCPsych
Director of the Eating Disorders Service, UK

To cut a long story short...

Anyone looking at us 14 years ago would have assumed from the outside that we were a perfectly 'normal' family: my husband Kevin and I and our beautiful twin daughters, Charlotte and Samantha, seemed to have everything anyone could possibly wish for, and more. We were in a really good place in our lives, glued together by the strong foundations of our marriage and two happy, healthy girls. Of course, we had our ups and downs like most couples, and life threw challenges our way, but we always worked together to overcome them and move forward, trying carefully to balance our scaffolding business and family life, just like any other working parents. We were doing okay... Or so we thought.

Our picture-perfect little world fell apart when Samantha was diagnosed with the early stages of anorexia nervosa at the start of her teenage years. We had had very little experience of mental illness at that time and were not prepared for what was to come. Looking back, Samantha had always exhibited a vivid imagination, creating unlikely and outlandish scenarios from a very early age, though to her, these imaginings seemed very real, leading her to repeatedly check door locks, window locks, toilet seats and light switches. We had no knowledge at all of eating disorders or OCD when the girls were young and dismissed those peculiarities as being her quirky traits, her uniqueness of character. It was something we neither encouraged, discouraged nor over-analysed – it was just Samantha being Samantha.

To cut a long story short...

Now, with the diagnosis of anorexia nervosa, we were equally and naively unaware of the condition or the precise help or treatment needed for our lovely daughter as we watched her spiral so quickly out of control and into the grip of something which affected each of us individually and our family as a whole. I had no idea how to deal with eating disorders at that time, but my husband and I believed that if we entrusted Samantha's health to the 'system' she would get better – we had no reason to think otherwise at this point. However, in hindsight, and knowing what I know now, had we had the knowledge and understanding to enable us to identify and address what we now know was OCD in Samantha's childhood, I feel we might have been in a stronger position to intervene at a much earlier stage. Who knows, we might have even nipped it all in the bud...

Over the next three devastating years we tried everything we could to get her the help she so desperately needed, from our local (very supportive) GP to both NHS and private clinics and therapists, but sadly nothing appeared to be working for Samantha. As things progressed from bad to worse we all felt completely helpless as we watched our beautiful daughter become a shadow of her former self, the trauma fragmenting the family with each of us suffering in our own particular way.

Like any parent, I wanted to do the best I could to help my daughter to recover both mentally and physically and support my family to have a better understanding of her illness. I read many books and scoured the internet for as much information and guidance as I could get my hands on, but could not find anything that I or my family could truly relate to or which gave me any real hope that there was a light at the end of the tunnel for Samantha and us as a family. It seemed to me that we were all feeling around in the dark, not knowing what we were supposed to say or do. Every website, book or support group I found seemed to focus mainly on the actual person experiencing the illness and not the family, friends and/or carers who I felt needed help and support just as much as the sufferer. I desperately needed answers and wanted to reach out to others, anybody with a genuine understanding of what was happening to us, to help us stop Samantha's condition in its tracks, but to no avail. There was nothing.

I was also deeply troubled by the fact that my husband, my other daughter, Charlotte, and myself were at times all made to feel that Samantha's illness had somehow been our fault. We were living in what felt like a pressure cooker, thinking we were going to explode at any given moment, constantly scrutinising ourselves, which in itself was only adding to the overall tension. It seemed like there was so much blame being flung around while answers were thin on the ground and those closest to the sufferer were often an easy target.

After having exhausted all the options available to us, the painful truth was that Samantha was not getting any better – if anything, she was becoming more and more unwell both physically and mentally. So, in a moment of desperation and with my family falling apart, as radical as it may have been, I let my intuition guide me and took the decision to rehabilitate her myself. Thankfully, with the full support of our GP, the girls' school and our family and friends, I was able to dedicate myself completely to Samantha, injecting positive thinking, love and hope, whilst trying to show her a life outside of the eating disorder, never giving up on my belief that she would get better no matter how difficult the situation became. I worked closely with Samantha's school, knowing it was important to keep her in as normal an environment as possible, and everyone involved worked as a team throughout the recovery process.

There were no set rules to follow, no specific path to guide me, but by committing myself fully to Samantha's recovery and trying my utmost to understand things from her troubled perspective, I slowly encouraged her to start communicating with me. She began sharing her distorted and, at times, highly irrational view of her world and her innermost thoughts, her head engaged in constant battle with itself. Patience, love and open-mindedness were paramount, not just for Samantha but for the family as a unit, ensuring the lines of communication were left open at all times between us. We needed to all be on the same page so we could help Samantha and heal together. It turned out to be the steepest learning curve I could have ever imagined.

Looking back, it was quite a controversial thing to do, I suppose, but at the time my instinct told me it was the right and only way to get my daughter better as nothing appeared to have had an impact so far. Step by step over the following year or so, Samantha slowly found her way back to us and began to leave behind the eating disorder that had had such a profound and devastating effect, not only on her but on all of us. However, we were not completely out of the woods yet and if I am honest I still had my suspicions that there was something else, some underlying factor that was stalling Samantha's recovery. She was still very vulnerable, and being exposed to outside influences, including an intense relationship with a friend who was also suffering from OCD, had a negative impact on her progress. She inadvertently began to copy some of this friend's traits and habits relating to food, which was both her weakness and her catalyst, and she subsequently suffered a major setback as OCD began to manifest itself in place of the eating disorder. Control was once again the core element for her, although she was more out of control than she realised. That is the illusion with mental illnesses such as eating disorders and OCD – the sufferer believes that they have full control, when in reality it is completely the opposite and the mental illness has complete control over them. Food and everything associated with it was pivotal in Samantha's mental illness, so it seemed a fairly predictable and inevitable progression that OCD would come to the forefront once again and latch onto this weakness, making her recovery even more difficult and challenging. This time Samantha was more comfortable about opening up to me and began to explain why she felt a certain way and why she had to carry out certain acts and rituals. This helped me to accept and understand the OCD much more clearly this time around. With Samantha's determination to get better, we ploughed on together, a united team against OCD, gently rebuilding our family life into a new and stronger version of what it had previously been.

Kevin, my husband, has never really understood mental illness, and has never pretended to, but the pressure and the enormity of it all took its toll on us briefly at the height of Samantha's illness, to the point that I once asked him to leave. Thankfully he ignored my request and stayed, continuing to provide his powerful and unconditional love and support, without which we could never have survived. He used to think Samantha was intentionally behaving as she did for attention, but now he readily accepts things for what they are, supporting Samantha unconditionally, even though, sometimes, he struggles to get his head around her quirky ways of thinking.

Samantha's twin sister, Charlotte, has also been pivotal in her recovery and now works alongside me at my practice, with an empathy that can only come from first-hand experience. She has forfeited pieces of her own life so that Samantha could be given the full-on care that she needed and the bond between my two girls is now unbelievably strong. Their mutual respect for one another, as a result of the journey they have shared, is testament to that.

I have learnt through all of this the importance of constant communication, patience, non-judgement, unconditional love and most of all HOPE, and that in fact there is no such thing as the 'perfect' family. Trying to be perfect is not only unrealistic; it can be dangerous.

Sometime into Samantha's recovery, I was contacted by the mother of a 17-year-old girl who was suffering from an eating disorder. She asked me if I could help as they were finding, as we had, that none of the conventional routes was making any difference. Encouraged by my husband, I approached their situation just as I had approached Samantha's, looking beyond her illness to the person within and giving them the unconditional and non-judgemental support that I realised from our experience had been so beneficial. Having been able to help her, and her family, successfully, I made the decision to build my own counselling practice based on everything I had read, learnt and experienced from our own journey with Samantha. I then went on to do some studying of my own, including training as a Master of NLP (Neuro-linguistic Programming – see page 120) and a Psy-TaP practitioner (see page 134). I was keen to work with other sufferers and their families, giving them the unreserved support and complete lack of judgement that my own experience had taught me were vital. I tentatively opened my doors to people from all walks of life struggling to deal with mental illness, be it the sufferer or a supportive loved one. My little successes were never shouted from the rooftops but from then on people seemed to find me through recommendation and word of mouth. I am now contacted on a daily basis by frantic and frightened parents, carers, siblings and friends from all over the country, all of whom have concerns about children, some as young as nine years old, most just wanting to talk to me, desperate for a glimmer of hope. I now help people suffering from eating disorders, OCD, anxiety, depression and low self-esteem.

The way I interact with my clients may seem a little unorthodox to some. However, I feel it is important to get to know the person as a whole rather than just seeing them through the lens of their illness, and working alongside the family rather than with just one person helps to build a united front against the illness. No two people who enter my office are ever the same and all experience the issues in a way that is unique to them; hence, the way I approach their treatment is similarly unique to each client. I am learning about each individual case as it naturally unfolds so I can give as much time and attention as we need both in and outside our sessions to build a mutual trust within our relationship which enables me to be one step ahead of the illness, in turn facilitating a quicker and more effective recovery for all concerned; we may do puzzles together while we chat, or make jewellery or do other arts and crafts projects. The atmosphere tends to be much less intense than the traditional image of the patient-therapist relationship and can even be fun! I have certainly learnt a lot from working with people in this way, and I focus on maintaining a positive environment, so from the minute they walk in they feel comfortable and at ease and from the very start they know they can get better and that they are in control of their own recovery. I also respond on an emotional level rather than a clinical one to the things they tell me. I do not always get it right, and I do not pretend to; sometimes there may be the need for additional assistance and input from other avenues, but my practical and down-to-earth approach has earned me the endearing handle of 'Fairy Godmother'.

So here I am, many years later. If you had told me over 10 years ago that I would be doing what I am doing today I would not have believed you. Nor could I have foreseen that our future as a family would be so much healthier and happier – our dynamics have changed in a way I did not think possible. During these rewarding years I have had the privilege of working with some wonderful people and their families, each and every one of them unique. Whilst I have been able to support and guide them through their journeys, I too have learnt from them. My clients have said that they find my practical and down-to-earth approach really refreshing and even compared me to the therapist in the film *The King's Speech* on more than one occasion! His methods were unconventional and unorthodox – but they got results. I never expected my practice to expand to the scale it has, but through this I have been able to share my ever-growing knowledge of many kinds of mental illness and help clients to find the best route towards recovery, not just for the sufferer but for those close to them.

My ever-increasing client list highlighted just how little emotional support or real empathy there was available for the carers, friends and families of those suffering from mental illness and having had first-hand experience of the destruction it can cause within the family unit, I felt compelled to write my first book – *Hope with Eating Disorders*, published in 2012. I was keen to share what I had learnt from our journey with Samantha in the hope that it would bring some guidance, comfort, strength and hope to others. Outwardly it was impossible to identify families who were going through similar experiences, yet when I spoke openly about what we had experienced within our family, I learnt that most people I knew were struggling with something behind closed doors. They had been too afraid to talk about it for fear of the stigma or judgement which sadly still surrounds mental health issues, even in today's society, though a staggering one in four of us will experience or suffer from some form of mental illness at one time in our lives. It was then I realised how widespread issues like self-harm, anxiety, depression, OCD and eating disorders were, and how confusing the wealth of information available on these subjects could be to the reader. Despite many high-profile initiatives by the Government and various celebrities making mental health awareness a target, there are still countless people of all ages suffering in silence, in need of help and support, and many loved ones, friends and carers, confused, frightened and unsure of how to help them.

Looking back, although Samantha had left most of her issues behind, she never truly felt comfortable in her own skin until recently, when she reignited her love for drama and the arts. Consequently, we have watched her grow into a beautiful, confident and vibrant young lady, pursuing a passion that allows her to express herself. Her passion and desire for life have been strengthened by the encouragement of her supportive and loving fiancé, Jay. Charlotte also has a wonderful, understanding fiancé, Callum, who has been on this journey with us since the beginning, so I am hugely relieved – being happy and healthy is all I have ever wanted for both of my girls.

Which brings us to *Hope with Eating Disorders 2nd edition...* Having experienced at first hand some of what you are going through, my main aim in writing the first edition of this book was to help you understand eating disorders and identify the symptoms of this destructive mental illness as early as you possibly could, allowing you to intervene swiftly and with more insight into the different treatments available, both of which are paramount for a quicker and more effective long-term recovery.

That first edition was published in 2012 and, I am proud to say, was very well received by sufferers, carers and those who work within the eating disorders world. I went on to write three more books: *Fundamentals: A Guide For Parents, Teachers and Carers on Mental Health and Self-Esteem*, with co-author Natasha Devon; a teenage novel, *Snap Out Of It*, with Donna Iliffe-Pollard; and in 2017, drawing on my knowledge of obsessive compulsive disorder, *Hope with OCD* with the publisher of this edition, Hammersmith Health Books.

In the seven years since the first edition of *Hope with Eating Disorders* was published, many things have moved on and changed. The wider public's understanding of eating disorders and body image has in many ways grown, but at the same time the pressures that society faces are evolving at such a pace that it can be difficult to keep up. The media landscape has altered, with the internet and social media exerting a stronger influence than ever before, and the repercussions of so-called health regimes, such as clean eating and obsessive exercising, are more apparent than ever. I felt it was the right time to bring out a second edition of this book, to reflect those changes and make sure *Hope with Eating Disorders* remains relevant to as many families coping with this illness as possible.

To cut a long story short...

Furthermore, my own understanding and experience have also grown, thanks to my clients who continue to teach me so much. No two people who walk through my door are the same, and every single one of their experiences has allowed me to grow my knowledge of eating disorders and other mental illnesses, and how they affect individuals and the people caring for them. Writing this second edition gives me the opportunity to pass on all that I have learnt from them to you.

In the chapters that follow, I will try to answer some of the questions that I am frequently asked, and my objective is to give you, the reader, the hope and belief that you have the strength and courage not only to support and guide your child / friend / loved-one through these turbulent waters, but to be able to see them safely to the other side, where they, and indeed everyone closely involved with them, will be able to move forward with their lives. I would like this book to act as a road map not only for those who simply do not know where to turn for help, but also for those who would like to have a clearer understanding of eating disorders in general.

I hope to relieve you of some of the burden, confusion and pain you may be feeling, as you enter the unknown, and to arm you with as much knowledge, guidance and strength as I can, to enable you to continue your journey with courage, trusting in your own personal skills and instinct, just as I did, remembering always that communication is the key, along with unconditional love, perseverance, non-judgement, patience and hope.

This book emphasises that each eating disorder sufferer is individual and unique and there is no 'right' or 'wrong' path to recovery. My own professional experience demonstrates that each family or support network must take whatever action is right for them; if one option proves ineffective, try another – never buy into the myth that eating disorder sufferers cannot recover, never give up hope and never give up trying.

With hope, perseverance, love and a lot of effort from us all, my family has reached a very positive place. Samantha has recently graduated with a 2:1 in performing arts. She is now engaged to Jay, who I know will continue to love and support her through any difficult times that may lie ahead. And, above all, she is happy and healthy – bubbly, funny and waking with a smile on her face. Her sister, Charlotte, is forging her own path with a loving partner, Callum, and a bright future ahead, and my husband and I can look forward to the next phase in our lives, finally content that our girls are happy and surrounded by love. The experience we have been through with Samantha's illness has brought us to where we are now: wiser, more appreciative of each other, and with more understanding of others. I never stopped hoping we would one day reach this point, and now I am able to hand that hope on to you. Anything is possible ... my family is living proof of that.

Ana

by Samantha Crilly

Sitting down to my family dinner,
Everyone staring as I become thinner.
Ana slowly creeping into my thoughts
Telling me to put down my knife and fork.
There's nothing I can do to make her eat, Mum whispers
to Dad,
Ana smiles all smug and glad.
I don't understand why she won't eat, Dad mutters to Mum.
Secret is I do, I'm just wrapped around Ana's thumb.
Feeling my bones rub against the chair
Even through all the layers I wear
Running upstairs and locking my door
Drained and exhausted I collapse on the floor.
Ana, you're killing me, I can't let you win.
I take off my top and see my heart beat through my skin.
Mum and Dad banging on the door,
I whisper to Ana I don't want you anymore –
I'm going to die if you win this war!
You're nothing without me Ana cries,
Another one of her crazy lies.
Ana will always find a way of creeping into your mind,
Brainwashing you, making you blind
Unable to see what you are doing to your body,
To her it is just an evil hobby.
To those she has touched and lived within,
Please, please, do not let her win.
Hers is a corrupt and vicious mind.
To make yourself happy, it is not her but you, you must find.

This book is dedicated to...

the memory of my Auntie Babs – thank you for giving me the strength

to start writing the first edition of this book;

and to my wonderful husband, Kevin, and our beautiful daughters,

Charlotte and Samantha, for giving me the strength to finish it and go

on to write many more.

Chapter 1

What is an eating disorder?

Disordered eating, and the mentality which fuels it, appears to make no sense at all. After all, what would possess someone to deny themselves the most basic of human needs – a healthy and balanced diet?

Furthermore, it can be difficult to determine where 'fussiness' stops and disordered eating begins (and therefore when a cause for concern arises). It can be hard to know if someone is genuinely particular about the foods they like and dislike, or whether this desire to control their food intake has wandered into more dangerous territory. For example, anorexia sufferers can claim suddenly and inexplicably (to those around them) to have embraced vegetarianism or veganism. This could be a ploy to further restrict their food intake. However, it could equally be a perfectly sincere desire to give up certain foods and herald a happy, healthy life as a vegetarian or vegan.

Think of the number of people you know who are either on a diet or declaring that they should embark on one. Equally, I am sure you know many people who are slightly overweight. Statistics show that the Western world is rapidly heading towards widespread obesity – but how do you determine the difference between someone simply enjoying their food or using it as a coping mechanism?

It has been argued that what we would now be quick to brand

1

as 'eating disorders' have in fact been around for centuries, and that our modern obsession and the recent meteoric rise in diagnoses arise less out of a growing trend and more out of our desire to label everything. Of course, the same logic could be applied to diabetes and many other illnesses, so this line of reasoning does not quite stand up to scrutiny.

When behaviour surrounding food becomes extreme, it can then be classed as an eating disorder, but often the patterns of thinking which have informed that behaviour have begun much earlier. What's more, the individual habits of a sufferer might not wholly conform to one recognised disorder but take some traits from several, and because the term 'eating disorder' covers a multitude of different abuses of food, they can affect people in a multitude of different ways. Therefore, diagnosis can be very difficult. Completely healthy but naturally slender people are often accused of having an eating disorder, while most of the people with bulimia nervosa caught in a binge/purge cycle have a 'normal' body mass index (BMI) or are even slightly overweight. The simple lesson is that, however tempting it might be, it is not possible to make a conclusive diagnosis simply from looking at someone.

Instead, we should be on the alert for the signs of an eating disorder when someone displays anxiety in a situation where food will be (a) present and (b) unavoidable. People can become anxious around food for any number of reasons, but this anxiety can grow to the extent that it dominates every waking thought. It can sometimes even seep into a person's subconscious while they sleep. I have known sufferers who say they dream about food.

Hannah, who is now recovered from anorexia nervosa and binge eating disorder, looks back:

My eating disorder took over my life. It is all I thought about. Everything I looked at I saw differently e.g. my friends' meals at

2

Chapter 1

> school, food packages, people's bodies... it stopped me from
> going to events and to school.

Disordered eating goes hand in hand with disordered thinking. This is not just because of the underlying emotional and low self-esteem issues which can infuse the disorder, but because nutrition – or lack of it – affects the delicate balance of chemicals in the brain. Lack of nutrients consequently interrupts reasoned thought. That is exactly why a carer's attempts to confront the problem may prove utterly ineffectual: the logic that someone without an eating disorder might apply to the situation is usually just not accessible to the sufferer. For instance, most sufferers believe that they are in control of their eating disorder when, in reality, it is often the other way round, as Antalia demonstrates below:

> It is weird – I felt like I was in control. I chose what to eat and I
> chose when to purge. However, after a couple of years with this
> constant voice urging me to go to the toilet, I realised it was *it*
> that controlled me.

Hannah Rushbrooke reiterates this in describing how her eating disorder made her feel:

> Weirdly, I grew to feel very safe as my eating disorder developed.
> I was in this bubble where all the horrible side effects I
> experienced actually made me feel so happy because I believed
> they brought me total control; the hunger pains and dizziness
> told me I was doing it right and I was that bit closer to what I was
> aiming for... to be that bit thinner and to feel happy and in control.
> In reality I was anything but in control. It also made me feel
> very lonely. Very few people understood my disorder so people
> would get angry and frustrated with me and my behaviours. I
> grew depressed and hopeless that I'd ever be 'normal' again... I
> wished to have a normal attitude towards food and to not be the
> 'sick' one at school; it was a very difficult journey of recovery.

The carer's perspective

Eating disorder sufferers cannot simply be told to 'pull themselves together', to 'stop doing that' or to 'just eat or not eat'. Many carers and friends can become incredibly frustrated and frightened as they perceive an eating disorder as something the sufferer may choose to inflict upon themselves, of their own volition. This is just not the case. My daughter Samantha's twin sister, Charlotte, recalls:

> What pulled me through was knowing that Sam was still inside, and it was not her talking and acting at that time, it was the eating disorder.

Samantha adds:

> We always look at someone with a mental illness as if they are the illness, as if the illness has completely possessed them. It likes to blind you from seeing that your loved one is still there, right in front of you. You must find them within the fog, reconnect with them and stand by their side and help them fight their darkness.

In refusing to eat and exercise in a healthy way, we logically know that eating disorder sufferers are running the risk of causing untold harm to their bodies and minds, both temporarily and in the long term. It is therefore very hard for a carer or friend to understand what might trigger someone to starve and deny themselves nutrients, or to binge and purge on a regular basis, or to consume such large quantities of calories that they become clinically obese.

For any loving parent or carer, used to providing everything their loved one needs, the feelings of frustration, uselessness and despair as their loved one destroys their health and happiness with an eating disorder can be hard to bear. It is not only

Chapter 1

extremely painful to watch but also incredibly difficult to deal
with, affecting not just the sufferer, but also the family as a whole.

Debbie, mother of Hannah, who is now recovered, shares her
feelings of frustration at the time:

> I was frustrated and impatient. I wanted to shake her and say,
> 'please just eat'. I prayed for her to be overweight again. It was
> better than her being underweight! It took time and patience to
> learn about anorexia. I was frightened.

While the focus rightly falls on the person with the eating
disorder, the needs of their loved ones and other family members
and friends can often go inadvertently unacknowledged. I know
at first hand how hard it is, and how helpless you can feel as
you watch your once happy-go-lucky child, friend or loved one,
disappear before your very eyes, as you lose them to the clutches
of an eating disorder.

However, I also know what an important and vital role
parents, siblings and carers can play in the recovery of someone
with an eating disorder. Not only through my own family's
journey, but also that of many families I have met and worked
with, I have seen the power of a parent or carer's love, and the
unquestionable lengths they will go to, to help and support their
loved ones through to recovery.

Paige, who is in recovery from anorexia nervosa, talks of the
support her family have given her through her journey:

> It has affected my relationship with my Mum and Dad. They
> always worry about me and what I'm eating. They also can
> sometimes get frustrated about what foods I can and can't eat.
> Despite these odd moments, we have grown closer as a family.
> They are both so supportive of me and help me through any
> tough times I have, and I couldn't have imagined coping with
> this without them.

Working through all the information available on eating disorders, and on mental health issues in general, can often leave us utterly baffled and vaguely hysterical – it can seem like a veritable minefield and an impossible all-consuming situation.

Throughout the course of this book, you will discover that as a parent or carer you are not alone. I hope you will learn that some of the mixed thoughts and feelings you and your family may be experiencing, inevitably including concern, worry, sadness, frustration and even resentment and anger at times, are normal and natural; and most importantly, I hope that you will arm yourself with a real understanding of your loved one's illness and discover some of the most effective ways to help them and the rest of the family towards recovery.

From my own experience, one of the most important things I have learnt, and would like to share with you at this point in the book, is that you cannot apply logic to something illogical, in the same way you cannot apply reason to something unreasonable and you cannot make sense out of something nonsensical. In other words, 'you simply have to accept what is, to enable you to understand'.

For families, it can be almost unbearable to witness what your loved one is doing, not only to themselves but also the effect their behaviour is having on the wider family and friendship circle. It is not a weakness to admit that caring for someone with an eating disorder can be both maddening and exhausting. It can cause a lot of anxiety and disruption and may lead to a terrifying unravelling of the norms of family life.

However difficult eating disorders are to understand, they are sadly becoming more, rather than less, common. Hospital admissions for eating disorders have gone up by around seven per cent annually since 2005,[1] with 'eating disorders' now being used as an umbrella term for a wide number of separate – but interlinked – conditions. Anorexia nervosa, bulimia nervosa and over-eating are the most widely known, while others, including orthorexia, where the sufferer pursues an obsessively healthy diet, and compulsive exercise, where the need to burn calories through exercise becomes an obsession, are slowly gaining more understanding and recognition.

Within this book I will explore the above eating disorders as well as some of the lesser known ones, with the aim of giving you, the reader, more of an insight and understanding of these conditions, both individually and how they can link and overlap. It can also be quite common for people with one recognised eating disorder also to show the symptoms of another, or indeed for their issues around food to be interlinked with another mental illness.

What causes an eating disorder?

Is it nature, or nurture, or both? Can we fairly blame popular culture (magazines, advertising, the internet and social media) and the pressures of today's society? The truth is that for each individual it may be all or none of these things. Every sufferer has a unique set of reasons for their disordered eating, fuelled by their disordered thinking.

So, it is not exactly clear what causes an eating disorder and, although there are various theories surrounding its development, it is currently thought that eating disorders stem from a combination of biological, genetic, cognitive and/or environmental factors acting together or alone as a trigger.

Genetic vulnerability

In the seven years since I wrote the first edition of this book, the evidence that some people's genes make them more vulnerable than others to an eating disorder has grown. That is not to say that there is a specific 'eating disorders' gene that causes the illness, but that a complex interaction between different genes could play a part. Furthermore, certain chemicals in the brain that control hunger, appetite and digestion have been found to be unbalanced in those with eating disorders.[2]

More studies and research have been done with individuals, siblings, twins and families which appear to show that people born with specific genotypes have a higher risk of developing an eating disorder. Those who have a family member with an eating disorder, are thought to be at least seven times more likely to develop an eating disorder.[3]

That is not to say that families, and parents in particular, are to blame for eating disorders. In fact, there is NO evidence that particular parenting styles are a direct cause of eating disorders. What is clear though is that loved ones can have a huge role to play in the care and recovery of sufferers and the most successful treatments now actively encourage families to play a part, not least in reminding their loved ones that they are more than just the illness that they are battling.

Psychological factors

Some evidence shows that someone's personality traits can also play a part. Research into anorexia nervosa and bulimia nervosa, the most well-known eating disorders, has indicated that traits such as perfectionism, obsessive-compulsiveness, negativity and low self-esteem may be involved. Sufferers can often feel, regardless of their many achievements in life, inadequate, flawed and worthless. Developing an eating disorder may be an attempt to try to take control of themselves and their lives, although ironically – as I have said – the eating disorder itself ultimately controls the sufferer rather than the other way around.

A lack of a sense of identity has also been identified as a possible trigger. People who do not have a strong sense of their own self may also be easily influenced by outside forces, and be susceptible to a number of psychological issues including eating disorders. In their own jumbled sense of self, they may look to an eating disorder as a way of defining themselves and giving themselves an identity.

Christine, mother of Ben, who is now in recovery from bulimia nervosa, says:

> Even from a very young age I noticed that Ben was very self-conscious and would often shy away from social situations. I think his eating disorder started during early secondary school, where we now know he was questioning his own sexuality. He used the eating disorder as a coping mechanism. However, since he has opened up to us and a couple of his friends as well as the counsellor he was seeing, he is now much happier within himself and feels as though he has found who he truly is. Onwards and upwards.

Socio-cultural influences

The Western beauty ideal of thinness is sometimes impossible to avoid. It permeates the media and also comes in the form of pressure from peers and, increasingly, social media. While many have the kind of personality that can shrug this off or handle the burden it poses, others find it harder to resist the lure of 'body ideals' and 'beauty'.

The most predominant images that are in our culture today suggest that beauty for females is in the form of 'thin', and for males, is in the form of 'muscular'. Some people, possibly without even realising, internalise these ideals, leaving them at a greater risk of developing an eating disorder.

Environmental factors

When we feel overwhelmed, stressed or out of control, we naturally try to find ways to manage these unpleasant and challenging feelings. For some, binge-eating or restricting food can become a way of dealing with the stress or ill feelings. This behaviour may be used as a coping mechanism, and in doing so the person suffering can regain feelings of control and contentment, even if they are just momentary.

Jan, who suffered from anorexia and OFSED (other specified feeding or eating disorder) says:

> Now I'm older, although I do not feel the need to starve myself anymore, my eating can be disordered and is greatly dependent on the levels of stress or emotion I am feeling at a particular time.

If someone is vulnerable to an eating disorder, sometimes all it can take is one comment, or a culmination of small events that come together to trigger the development of one. It could be a comment from a classmate, workmate or friend about their weight, or appearance, or just a simple personal criticism, which could trigger the disordered thoughts. It has also been known that bigger, tragic life events, such as shock, loss or abuse, can also trigger an eating disorder.

An eating disorder may develop out of another, seemingly unconnected, illness. In my daughter Samantha's case, a simple virus which led her to lose some weight was one of the triggers. As a result, she received a lot of compliments which tapped into a pre-existing insecurity she had concerning her body shape. She wanted to continue to lose weight thereafter, but it eventually got out of control. It really was as simple and as complicated as that.

Samantha herself adds:

> Looking back, I was not very comfortable in my own skin. When I was complimented for having lost a bit of weight it made me feel good about myself, so I just kept going. It spiralled out of my own control, although at the time I thought I was the one in control.

There is some early evidence that anorexia nervosa, particularly in teenage girls, may be linked to a prior viral or bacterial infection. As I say, much more research needs to be done, but this is definitely a factor to bear in mind.

Furthermore, with young people, there is some evidence to suggest that girls who reach sexual maturity ahead of their friends and peers are at an increased risk of developing an eating disorder. They, and the people around them, may wrongly interpret their new curves as 'being overweight'; this can cause feelings of shame and being uncomfortable within themselves because they no longer look like their peers who may still have childlike bodies.

Dieting

Dieting may not be the cause of an eating disorder, but it can often be a precursor. It can be a way for someone to start the process of control, counting calories, limiting types and amounts of food, and watching the numbers drop on the scales. Focusing on dieting, food and weight loss can be an escape from true emotions and issues.

Dieting can be a vulnerable time for anyone, but particular attention needs to be paid to teenagers who are trying to lose weight. At this stage in life, not only are they particularly at risk from the pressures of society, it can also be a time of great change, both physically and psychologically, leaving them more exposed to the dangers of extreme dieting. If, like Samantha, they also receive positive comments on their weight loss, this can inadvertently push the more vulnerable to make the dangerous step from 'diet' to 'disorder'.

The National Eating Disorders Association in America reports that 35 per cent of 'normal dieters' progress to uncontrolled dieting and 20 to 25 per cent of those individuals progress to an eating disorder.[4]

Other mental illnesses

Research has shown that if someone is suffering from another mental illness, such as depression, anxiety or obsessive-compulsive disorder, they could be more likely to develop an eating disorder alongside it. If more than one disorder is present at one time, the symptoms of each can significantly overlap, making the disorders intertwined and thereby causing them to feed on and exacerbate each other.

Jobs and activities

Being part of sports teams and artistic groups can put someone at an increased risk. This can also be true for members of any community that is motivated by appearance, including athletes, actors, dancers, models and television personalities. This could be due to the element of competition involved, or individuals in these communities could inadvertently contribute to eating disorders by encouraging weight loss and putting too much emphasis on appearance and weight.

Having discussed all the above possible causes, it would be worth noting that some eating disorder sufferers have no reasoning at all as to why and how their disordered thoughts and behaviour began, as Antalia, a bulimia sufferer for eight years explains below:

I was 16 and I remember I was revising for my GCSEs, but I wasn't under a lot of stress at all. I don't know why I did it really. I was on holiday with my family and my sister and we were inside, watching something on her laptop. We ate some crisps and had a diet coke each and I remember going to the toilet and trying it. I realised then how easy it was, and I suppose it was from then that it all began.

Chapter 1

Hope with eating disorders

I know the above paints a pretty bleak picture, but I cannot reiterate enough that from my own experience, both personally and professionally, contrary to popular belief, full and lasting recovery from an eating disorder *is* possible, remembering always that as every individual sufferer is unique, so is their experience and in turn their recovery.

The most common question I am asked by concerned friends and relatives of eating disorder sufferers is simply 'What can I do?' The most crucial step is to develop a better understanding of eating disorders – not just the physical symptoms, but the state of mind which infuses them. Furthermore, the earlier you can both recognise the signs for concern and in turn act on them, the quicker your loved one may be able to receive help, stopping the illness from becoming hard-wired and taking over his/her life.

If you notice something amiss, try not to adopt a 'wait and see' approach, remembering that early intervention can be key to a quicker and more effective recovery. Even if they are not ready to seek help, acknowledging your loved one's struggle and showing that you are there for them can be the first crucial step on their journey to recovery.

Amara says of her experience with her daughter:

> My daughter started showing the classic signs of anorexia aged 12. Thankfully I did already know a little bit on the subject and was able to spot these signs pretty early. I took Amaya straight to the GP where she was put on a CAMHS [Child & Adolescent Mental Health Services] waiting list. In the meantime (as I did not want to wait for a space to become available), I took her to a private therapist who started working with her straight away. Thankfully now, the eating disorder is history.

One thing I do not want carers to do is feel guilty. It is all too easy for the people around eating disorder sufferers to blame themselves. Not only is this blame often misplaced, it can actually delay recovery, placing an obstacle in the way of your loved one's journey back to health. Guilt is a destructive and ultimately pointless emotion, and one I hope to rid you of.

Fiona, mother of Katie who is now recovered from anorexia nervosa, tells us of her feelings of guilt:

> When my daughter was diagnosed I had terrible feelings of guilt as I blamed myself. I am overweight and wanted to join a slimming club and Katie came along with me for support and to lose about half a stone herself. Although I now know it was not the sole cause, at the time of her diagnosis and for about a year I felt it was, and also my fault for being an overweight parent.

All carers – whether they be family, friends, colleagues or professionals – if possible, need to work together as a team, not only to support the sufferer but each other, too. Any chink in your armour can be exploited by an eating disorder, which is why it is crucial that carers must communicate and stand united together.

Sadly, there is no miracle cure for an eating disorder. Nor can you, as a carer, simply wave a magic wand to make your loved one better. You can give all the love, support and understanding in the world, but ultimately the only person that can really make that change is the sufferer. The greatest thing you can do is stay right beside them as they take the difficult steps on that journey.

Eating disorders can be contradictory and confusing, making it difficult to see a clear path ahead. No two cases are the same, which makes every treatment journey unique to the sufferer and their carers. I hope this book will give you the clarity you need to provide consistent and coherent support to both the sufferer themselves and their wider family and friends. It is said that 'knowledge is power' and I hope that by passing on many of the lessons I have learnt, you will feel armed to deal with the journey ahead.

Chapter 1

One of the most dangerous and depressing myths surrounding eating disorders is that they are a life sentence. It is distressing to see people 'managing' their conditions, learning to cope with them on a day-by-day basis, with both the sufferer and their carers resigned to the fact that this is as good as it gets. Although for some, being able to manage their condition may be a huge achievement in itself, others will want to rid themselves of the illness completely. This can be possible. Although eating disorders are very serious and very dangerous, the statistics are overwhelmingly stacked in favour of recovery.[5] I hope to help you find the light at the end of the dark tunnel, just as my family did.

Often it will feel like you are getting nowhere. Sometimes the situation may seem to get worse. But please do not give up. Even then, your love and support will be setting down foundations for recovery in the future. With communication, perseverance, positive thinking, love and, most importantly, hope, there is always a way through the maze of eating disorders and a path back to health and happiness for both the sufferer and their carers.

Hope with Eating Disorders will show you that full and lasting recovery is possible, and that there is no right or wrong way to recover; just as a person's eating disorder is unique to them, so is their recovery. This book will also hopefully allow you to see how you and your loved one can free yourselves from the prison of eating disorders and enjoy the liberty of a life which is not dictated by food once more.

Myths and truths

Myth: Eating disorders are just an extreme diet.
Truth: Although people who diet are more likely to develop an eating disorder, it is too simplistic to brush them off as simply an extreme diet. Eating disorders are a very serious illness, characterised by considerable psychological impairment which may progress to the point of causing wide-ranging and life-

15

threatening medical issues. They are not a lifestyle choice or simply a diet that has merely gone too far.

Myth: Eating disorders are all about attention-seeking.
Truth: People with eating disorders are not simply seeking attention. By contrast, sufferers may go to extraordinary lengths to hide or deny their behaviour, or they may not even recognise that there is anything wrong. The actual causes of an eating disorder are complex and due to a whole range of factors.

Myth: Families are to blame for eating disorders.
Truth: This is an historic misconception. While there is evidence that eating disorders may have a genetic link, and people who have family members with an eating disorder may be at higher risk of developing one themselves, the link is no more significant than, say, where genetics have a role in cancer or heart disease. Nowadays it is recognised that families play a crucial part in the recovery of eating disorder sufferers.

Myth: Eating disorders only affect teenage girls.
Truth: While the peak time for the onset of eating disorders is between the ages of 12 and 25, these illnesses can actually occur at any time, among people of all ages from all cultural and socio-economic backgrounds. Furthermore, studies suggesting that men and boys make up 11 per cent of those with eating disorders are thought to only be the tip of the iceberg.[6] The number of adult men being admitted to hospital with an eating disorder has risen by 70 per cent over the past six years – the same rate of increase as among women.[7]

To conclude

However dark the outlook seems, recovery from eating disorders is absolutely possible. By working as a team and remaining hopeful even in the darkest times, friends and family can lay the foundations for real and long-lasting recovery.

Naomi Cavaday, former British tennis player, finishes this chapter with her words of hope:

> When I started recovery, I was told that this was something I would have to manage for the rest of my life. I can now say that is not true. I spent five years in recovery, but because I have made such strong decisions to look after my mental health, I can honestly say that for the past year not only have I had no symptoms, I haven't even thought about it once. I am completely healthy and happy and even when I am stressed it is not something I even consider turning to. In the last year of my five-year recovery I didn't have any symptoms at all but just knowing it was there as a crutch was important, knowing that if things did go badly I could always revert to those behaviours to cope. Getting rid of that crutch was the most difficult part of my whole recovery along with taking the initial steps in the beginning. I am incredibly proud that I can get on and enjoy my life now with nothing holding me back.

Chapter 2

Anorexia nervosa, bulimia nervosa and over-eating

Suffering from an eating disorder could be compared to having a manipulative and unkind bully residing inside your head who convinces you they are your one and only friend – your best friend and the only friend that you will ever need. With time, this 'friend' gradually unleashes its torture on the unsuspecting victim until they surrender to its voice of unreason. For the sufferer, they are fighting an internal war with themselves, but with no clear resolution. This can be utterly exhausting, and the more tired the person who has the eating disorder becomes, the more space the head creates for this 'friend' to occupy and take over. Being at war with any part of yourself can never bring peace, whether it be for the sufferer or their loved ones. Although the person suffering may feel as though they have control over this 'friendship', in reality it is the other way around.

Eve, who is now in recovery from anorexia nervosa, says:

> Anorexia is like having a 'friend' telling you how you will feel so much better when you like what you see in the mirror, like losing some weight will make your self-worth rise and confidence soar, which is totally the opposite to what happens.

Sadly, there is no severing of ties or getting rid of this 'friendship' without the sheer determination and perseverance of the sufferer and the right kind of intervention, help and support, be it professional and / or from a loved one(s).

Living with a loved one with an eating disorder, whether it be anorexia nervosa, bulimia nervosa, over-eating, OSFED (other specified feeding or eating disorder) or one of the many others, can be both extremely frightening and incredibly frustrating at the same time. It is very important to remember here that any form of eating disorder is a mental illness with physical symptoms as well as mental torment; it is not about food itself, but more about how the person feels and how they cope with these feelings. The way the person interacts with food may help them to feel more able to manage these emotions or may make them feel more in control.

Charliee says of how her eating disorder gave her conflicted emotions:

> I had a love-hate relationship with my eating disorder. I would often describe it as having a friend and also an enemy living inside me. It made me feel as though I had control, but it also made me feel out of control nearer the end of my journey.

An 'eating disorder' covers a multitude of different guises which are unique to the person suffering; this may include restricting the amount of food they eat, eating very large quantities of food at once, getting rid of food they have eaten through unnatural and unhealthy means (e.g. extreme amounts of exercise, purging, the misuse of laxatives and / or not eating), or a combination of some or all of these behaviours.

According to the UK's leading eating disorder charity, Beat, approximately 1.25 million people in the UK are affected by an eating disorder; of those, 10 per cent suffer from anorexia nervosa and 40 per cent from bulimia nervosa; between these two eating disorders they make up 50 per cent of sufferers. We must, however, bear in mind that these figures only take into consideration the people who have been officially diagnosed. I am sure there are many, many more suffering in silence.

In addition to anorexia, bulimia, over-eating and OSFED, other eating disorders are now beginning to be recognised by the medical profession, including restrictive food intake disorder, rumination disorder and pica. Orthorexia (an obsession with eating healthily) is not specifically listed as an illness in its own right; however, this ever-increasing form of eating disorder is also now being looked at by the professional community with the view to it becoming a recognised and diagnosable condition.

Each of the different eating disorders will have its own distinct behaviours associated with it. However, there will also be similarities and crossovers interlinked between them, not least in terms of the fact that they are all characterised by unhealthy and extreme behaviour around food.

Wanting to learn more, you may turn to the internet, hoping it may help you to understand a bit more. Alternatively, you may scour articles in the press on the different conditions. This could find you ending up even more baffled and frustrated. As there is so much varied information available through various channels it is very difficult to know what applies to you and your own unique situation. I hope to provide the information that I think really matters, with no agenda other than helping you to a better understanding of many of the eating disorders and the signs to look for.

Dan, whose girlfriend is now in recovery from anorexia nervosa, talks of how his first instincts were to learn more about the illness:

It took me a long time to understand how serious it was, which I believe is common for anyone in my situation. I had to research a lot of information just to understand the basics of what was happening, but more important was speaking to her about how she reacted to food and how I could help her. This was a big hurdle for me because all I wanted to do was help and a lot of the time it seemed like I was doing the opposite.

Anorexia nervosa

In its simplest form, anorexia nervosa is the severe restriction of food intake over a period of time. While there are other elements which categorise this dangerous and sometimes woefully misunderstood illness, each and every sufferer is unique, and each and every one of them experiences the disorder in a different way.

The term 'anorexia' was first coined by Sir William Gull, one of Queen Victoria's personal physicians, back in 1873. (The word is of Greek origin, 'an' being the prefix for 'little' and 'orexis' for 'appetite', meaning 'a lack of desire to eat'.) This fact in itself answers any claims that anorexia nervosa is a new phenomenon.

Anorexia nervosa is not an illness of the body; it is an illness of the mind. Sadly, it has the highest mortality rate of any mental illness. It cannot be cured simply by treating the physical symptoms alone; it is the mind that must be treated. For this reason, it terrifies and fascinates people in equal measure. However, please remember this does not mean giving up or giving in to this upsetting diagnosis. Remembering always that recovery is possible, however, I cannot stress enough at this point that this can only be achieved by treating the mind as well as the body – not forgetting at the same time that the sufferer has to really want to get better too.

If you are a carer of someone suffering from anorexia, the people around you probably will not know what to do or say in order to help. You may feel isolated, because most support networks available to you may not come to your aid in the same way they would if your loved one had a physical injury, or even a better understood illness.

Marg Oaten, mother of Gemma Oaten, a former sufferer of anorexia, reinforces this point when she says:

> In some ways, we found it a strain to explain it to family members – all cared deeply, but some just didn't get the whole eating disorder illness.

Of all the many eating disorders, anorexia nervosa undoubtedly gets the most press. This can be both a good thing, because it raises awareness of this illness, and potentially dangerous because the information out there can perpetuate myths which can actually prevent carers from seeing the signs of anorexia early on.

Sadly, anorexia can sometimes be the media's friend because, when it becomes very severe, it is visually shocking. There can also be a worrying tendency for it to be portrayed as 'glamorous', with sufferers often citing a desire to conform to society's beauty ideal as the reason behind their compulsion to starve themselves. In reality, the causal factors behind their illness are almost certainly manifold and highly complex. There is very rarely one solitary motive for disordered eating. The sufferer's numerous motivations intertwine, fuelling one another and the condition. If we persist in trying to boil anorexia down to one fundamental contributory factor, we will only continue to give rise to a number of myths and misconceptions.

We have all seen the headlines which scream 'I weighed just 4½ stone!' These stories are usually accompanied by a picture of the subject, looking shockingly skeletal, in their underwear. As a result, many people believe that the most important symptom of anorexia nervosa is weight loss, and that the lower the sufferer's weight, the more severe their condition. This is not necessarily true. For some sufferers, their weight could be seen as 'healthy'; however, their mind could be totally tormented and plagued with disordered thoughts around food and potential body issues. Again, it is always crucial for you to bear in mind that anorexia nervosa is a mental illness, not a physical one.

The trend for 'poorly pictures' (which were advised against in a set of media guidelines issued by Beat), can in reality prevent sufferers from seeking the help they need. We have been led to believe that if someone is a 'normal' weight, they cannot, by definition, have an eating disorder. Again, this is not necessarily true.

Chapter 2

The question of weight

What truly categorises anorexia nervosa is obsession. To reach the astonishingly low weights which are sometimes reported in the press, a sufferer would have required time, not to mention a fairly small frame and high metabolic rate to begin with. Some people starve for years without physically reaching a weight which is perceived as an urgent problem by the medical community. Are they still suffering from anorexia nervosa? The answer is a resounding yes.

Using weight to diagnose anorexia is like seeing how far someone can walk before determining if they have a broken leg. It simply does not take into account the issues at the source of the disorder.

It also leads us to draw the conclusion that in order to rehabilitate someone suffering from anorexia nervosa, we should force them to eat. Once their weight has reached a 'normal level' they are cured … right? … Wrong!

We must remember that the underlying emotional issue, the mind-based obsession which is at the disorder's origin, is still present.

Hope says of how the anorexia took over her mind and thoughts:

> When I was growing up, the anorexia made me feel better about life. It helped me to switch off from feelings of guilt and pain. The anorexia reassured me when I was struggling with my emotions and made life feel manageable again.

I cannot reiterate enough that this is a mental illness we are dealing with and not just a physical one. This is precisely why so many anorexia sufferers relapse almost immediately after leaving professional care.

The first and most crucial hurdle to overcome in diagnosing anorexia nervosa is the idea that you must weigh your loved one.

In doing so you are searching for physical symptoms rather than the emotional causes, which are usually at the root of the issue.

Kimberley developed anorexia after having first been diagnosed with obsessive-compulsive disorder (OCD). Interestingly, OCD and anorexia share a number of common traits and have often been shown to go hand in hand. Gail, Kimberley's mother, shares her thoughts and beliefs when she says:

> I firmly believe that, if you treat the mind, you treat the body. The majority of professionals treat the body first, leaving the mind unrecovered.

By focusing on the physical symptoms only, we are missing the emotional signs. Knowing this can be the carer's greatest ally. Obsession is a difficult thing to identify; however, with the right understanding and knowledge it can be spotted early, before the anorexia develops and becomes physically life-threatening. For example, a father I have worked with said that, looking back, the first sign of his daughter's anorexia was when she began to wear his clothes. At the time, he reasoned that she simply liked wearing them. In retrospect, of course, she was trying to cover her body and, more specifically, conceal her weight loss. Very few people wake up one morning and simply decide to stop eating, for no reason at all. Most likely there will have been a pattern of issues and maybe events that set the person on the path towards an eating disorder.

As this book progresses, we will explore the experiences of sufferers and carers from all walks of life who have been affected by eating disorders. Eva, whose battle with anorexia began in her early teens, is described by her mother, Kyra, as:

> Never being happy with her body shape. She was teased, causing a loss of confidence in her body, so that her self-esteem plummeted and she developed anorexia.

Chapter 2

What Kyra has, quite rightly, observed here is that loss of confidence and self-esteem was a precursor to her daughter's eventual condition. As we discussed in chapter one, my own daughter Samantha, developed anorexia at the same age as Eva having lost weight as a result of contracting a virus, Samantha says of how it all started for her:

> When people started to compliment me on my weight loss, how good I looked, how it suited me, it made me feel good and gave me a buzz. I thought that if I lost a bit more it would make me feel even better and so it all began...

If your loved one has a pre-existing insecurity, anorexia, or indeed any eating disorder, can begin very innocently.

Many of the parents I have worked with and spoken to have been encouraged to think that, because eating disorders are such a serious and dramatic illness, they must have arisen out of a previous traumatic incident. They then blame themselves for not having 'noticed'. In my experience, this is rarely the case. In fact, eating disorders usually arise out of something very innocent. There is always the possibility that the illness originates in something more sinister, but this is by no means a certainty.

A former anorexia sufferer appeared on a popular daytime television programme. She was asked during the interview why her eating disorder had begun. 'I just threw my sandwiches away one day,' she said. The interviewer persisted, 'Yes, but why? Why did you throw your sandwiches away?' She thought for a minute, then replied, 'I just did.' This conversational pattern was repeated at least three times before the interviewer accepted that, as far as this sufferer was concerned, the problem began on the day she threw her sandwiches away.

Some people are by their nature sensitive and prone to insecurity. It takes very little for that sensitivity to be tapped into.

There is not a great deal that unites absolutely all eating disorder sufferers, because, as discussed, each sufferer, and their story, is unique and individual. They do, however, all have one thing in common: low self-esteem.

It is this low self-worth which gives birth to a mind-based issue which, in turn, can evolve into an eating disorder. As a carer, looking out for huge quantities of weight-loss is missing a vital opportunity to address the problem at an early stage. Zoe, now 28, my daughter Samantha's best friend, talks about when she first realised how ill Sam actually was:

> At first I wasn't properly aware of what she was going through. No one was. Because we spent so much time together it was easy to ignore the weight loss. When I saw the effect Sam's illness was having on her family, that's when it hit me. It took over their lives; anorexia controls every thought at every moment, but it felt like more than anything Sam wanted to be treated like a 'normal' person.

When does the need for concern arise?

Arguably, we are all a little critical of our bodies in our seemingly image-obsessed culture. Teenagers, in particular, will go through a certain degree of worry and angst concerning their physical appearance during the normal course of growing up. So where does the need for concern arise?

Justin, who is now 27 and a friend of my daughter, reflects on his awareness of Samantha's eating disorder, during their teens:

> I'd noticed that Sam had been losing weight, but this was not uncommon, as many of the girls in my year were hitting puberty and changing physically. I felt quite ashamed that I had not noticed it before, but I suppose that it's not really the sort of thing that a 13-year-old boy looks out for.

For someone suffering from anorexia, food dominates their every waking thought, and in some cases, their dreams while they are sleeping too. They are constantly fantasising about how to avoid food, and what they will and will not eat. It is a common misconception that anorexia sufferers do not like food. The vast majority love it. They are obsessed with it. As my Samantha says, looking back:

> When I was younger, before the anorexia started, I loved food. I enjoyed cooking it, eating it and everything about it. Even through the anorexia, I never hated food. I just hated how it made me feel, and what it did to me.

They see food as a powerful and irresistible enemy, something to be physically avoided but which is omnipresent in their thoughts. It is often said that anorexia is about control, but this vastly misses the point that sufferers have actually lost control over their minds, as the illness has overpowered them.

In the early stages, signs that may concern you and that could potentially lead to the beginnings of anorexia nervosa are:

- an encyclopaedic knowledge of the calorific values of foods
- frequently weighing themselves (often more than once per day)
- displaying secretive behaviour in situations where food is unavoidable (putting food in a napkin or feeding it to the dog, for example)
- having a wide range of excuses as to why they will not be present at mealtimes ('I ate a big lunch' or 'I am going to have dinner at a friend's house')
- either constantly deflecting attention from, or drawing attention to, any resultant weight loss
- constantly picking fault with their body
- exercising excessively

- spending a lot of time on websites that revolve around food and body image
- prizing weight loss above other life interests (giving up previous hobbies and friends)
- having a sudden interest in cooking (but not eating).

This last symptom is perhaps a surprising side-effect for the early stages of anorexia; however, it is very common. Sufferers will cook huge meals, bake cakes and puddings for their friends and family, but eat nothing themselves. Perversely, they wish to test themselves, to tempt themselves by touching, handling and smelling the food, but not ingesting. It can also be symptomatic of the degree to which anorexia sufferers think about food, despite avoiding it.

Eva's best friend, Chelsea, recalls the first time she felt really concerned was when she noticed her friend undertaking this bizarre practice. She says:

> My friend had a small barbeque and invited everyone over. She cooked all this food but never touched any of it and instead had a small salad. That's when I realised it was getting really bad.

As a carer it is important to be vigilant about this – the fact that anorexia sufferers often cook and bake might fool you into believing that they are eating. It is important to take note of what they actually do eat.

Change in personality

I am giving this 'symptom' more space as these three little words may well be the biggest red flag to the development of anorexia nervosa, and with hindsight this symptom is usually what parents, siblings, friends and loved ones notice first. At the time, it may have been hard to understand why the person was suddenly short tempered or withdrawn, or why his/her emotions seemed so up and down. Later, when their loved one's illness had developed, they were able to recognise that change in personality as a sign.

Tied in with this is secrecy. Most sufferers with anorexia know – instinctively and from a fairly early stage – their condition needs to be hidden. They are aware that the people around them, who care for them, will try to stop them restricting their food intake. They may convince themselves that these people are either jealous or do not understand. Their minds house two seemingly contradictory notions: that avoiding food is the most important thing that they can do, but that it is also somehow wrong and must be hidden from others.

This is just one example of the constant internal dialogue and noise that takes place in the minds of anorexia sufferers. They are always constantly arguing with themselves, and this can be exhausting. They may appear tired and seem withdrawn and preoccupied. As a result, a large proportion of a sufferer's time is spent attempting to cover his/her tracks. Sufferers may become introverted. Loss of confidence, concentration or ability to interact socially are all key signs.

It is absolutely vital always to bear in mind that the anorexia sufferer's mind is not a logical place. Siblings and friends, in particular, tend to become increasingly exasperated, wondering why they simply will not or cannot eat. They can sometimes tell them to 'stop it', rationalising that their friend or loved one is starving themselves possibly to gain attention.

Again, this is because of a general lack of understanding of anorexia nervosa as an illness. It can often be perceived by the people around the sufferer as being a selfish condition. While this is true to an extent, objectively speaking, it is important always to bear in mind that the sufferer is ill and cannot always help themselves. Anorexia nervosa is not a lifestyle choice. The sufferer is possessed by their illness. Harbouring resentment and ill-feeling can cause the situation to escalate, and arguments can ensue. Mealtimes and social gatherings may be a potential battleground in any event, without these feelings of bitterness being thrown into the mix.

Suzanne Dando, former British Olympic gymnast, reflects back on the effect her anorexia had on her family:

> Recovery is a slow process. Methodical? Yes. Fraught with ups and downs? Of course. There were days when it seemed easier to let the disease win and return to abnormal behaviour, secrecy, being insular and moody, and shunning all those who are desperate to help. It's a disease that makes us selfish. Not until we are firmly on the road to recovery can we appreciate just how much pain we inflict on our parents and loved ones, who have to stand by and watch us try to destroy ourselves both physically and mentally.

While we will see in a later chapter that there have recently been much higher instances of male eating disorders, those men not directly affected often have the most trouble in comprehending an eating disorder. Fathers, brothers and male partners are not lacking in sympathy or concern; often they merely have difficulty in understanding the warped and distorted thinking of the mind of someone suffering from anorexia. By trying to tackle anorexia with logic, they can become increasingly frustrated, arguments can occur, and the sufferer could sink further into him/herself.

Charles, father to Eva, who has now recovered from anorexia nervosa, speaks of the frustration he felt during his daughter's illness:

> I watched a rapid change, as my loving, caring, bubbly and vivacious daughter turned into an obsessive, dull-eyed shell. As her father, surely I could solve this problem, as I do daily in everyday life? Successful, powerful, and without limits as to financial resources, I felt positive that I could turn this around quickly. How wrong could I be?! I entered a battle which I

wasn't prepared for, and started a learning curve that would often leave me devastated and frustrated. Over a two-year period, I watched my little girl lie, cheat, bully, manipulate, plead, cry, threaten and use any method open to her to avoid eating and to satisfy the anorexic noises constantly in her head.

Opportunities to communicate with a sufferer about how they feel can be sporadic and should be encouraged. The information you receive from them can prove vital in the recovery process. Try not to apply logic; as hard as it may be, try to accept that their mind is a confused place and that, in talking, they are providing you with an important glimpse into its inner workings.

David, whose girlfriend of four years suffered from an eating disorder, says that the best piece of advice he could extend to carers is 'not to judge'. He says:

There were times when my girlfriend was very open with me about her eating disorder. I realised it was important not to act shocked, or create conflict, because then she'd stop communicating with me.

Which brings us onto another notable fact: the brain requires energy. In many cases, the effect that malnutrition has on the mind is not only more immediate, but much easier to detect, than the physical symptoms. However, becoming forgetful or irritable is commonplace in the early stages of anorexia nervosa. If a sufferer is known for being highly efficient in their job, then suddenly begins to report that their colleagues are 'picking on them' because they 'forgot something', this could mean they have lost the ability to concentrate. The same can apply to a sudden plummeting in school grades.

Starving the brain can also lead to a lack of creative ability. It is important to be aware of a sudden unwillingness or inability to undertake creative endeavours which were previously a pleasure, such as art, writing or music.

Forgetting to lock the front door, leaving the iron on, losing their personal possessions – these are all signs of the inattentiveness which can accompany the brain not being fed enough. Of course, some people are naturally forgetful so, again, I must emphasise that the most crucial symptom is a drastic change in personality.

In these early stages, and indeed throughout the course of your loved one's illness and recovery, communication is your most powerful tool; this not only benefits the sufferer, but the carers as well. It can be the best way for you and your loved one to negotiate yourselves out of the maze.

My daughter's friend Justin gives his thoughts on how communication helped to turn things around for us:

> Sam started to become more and more withdrawn, spending more time in her room than she had done before. It was quite strange as this withdrawal seemed to gradually lead to the whole family spending less time with each other. It was frustrating for me at the time, as I could just see that they needed to talk to each other. Once they had realised this, looking back that's the point at which they started to make progress. It was great when they started talking and spending more time with each other again.

Physical signs

Of course, these subtle emotional signs can be easy to miss, or can be mistaken for the more common-or-garden teenage angst or mild depression. If anorexia nervosa has developed to a stage where the physical symptoms become more prominent, you may notice:

- Unexplained weight loss
- Erratic, sparse or non-existent periods in girls and women
- Fine downy hair growing on the body (and in particular on the back)

- Hair loss/thinning of hair on the head
- The sufferer often complains they feel cold, even in warm temperatures, and their nose, fingertips and toes are cold to the touch
- The sufferer becomes pale and looks drawn
- Bad posture – either because they do not have the energy to hold themselves upright or because they want to apologise for their bodies
- Fainting/dizzy spells
- Frequent episodes of crying or tearfulness
- Anger/mood swings
- Wearing baggy clothes or layering to hide the weight loss.

The biggest tell-tale sign is, however, in my experience, the appearance of the eyes. The difference between someone who is naturally very slender and someone who has starved themselves into that state can be ascertained simply by looking them in the eye. The sufferer's eyes can be sunken and vacant and look 'haunted', because the sufferer is literally haunted by their condition. Their mind is consumed by their disorder and so they have retreated into themselves. Their energy is used up in self-analysis and they have nothing left to give the outside world.

If your loved one exhibits the psychological and physical signs and symptoms of anorexia nervosa, try not to plough your time and energy into blaming yourself. Instead, take the opportunity to learn about the illness itself and the various treatments and options available to you when they do reach out to you for help. We will explore some of these later on.

It is also important to separate fact from fiction and to try to understand fully what is happening in the mind of your loved one.

Sarah wrote the following, which highlights the contradictions in her thinking when she suffered from anorexia:

At my lowest weight during my anorexia, looking in the mirror became an obsession. Many people have a misconception of what anorexics see; when I looked in the mirror I didn't see a fat person in front of me, it wasn't the image that kept me from not eating. I knew I was thin. I just wasn't thin enough. It also wasn't about how I was perceived by other people. I didn't care if I had a typically good body. I wanted a thin body. It isn't what anorexics see in the mirror which makes them continue to starve themselves, but the feeling that anorexia gives them. It's the same as giving a drug addict drugs or giving alcoholics a drink. It takes a certain type of person to develop anorexia – they have to be slightly depressed and insecure. When people feel like something is missing inside them, they try to fill it with something. To me, not eating filled that hole; it made me feel I had something, which is why it is so hard to beat as you cling on to the feeling of losing weight.

Sarah has identified here the single biggest and most all-pervading myth which surrounds anorexia – namely, that anorexics see a large person when they look in the mirror. They usually know they are thin, they simply do not think they are thin enough – and they will never be thin enough while they continue in this mind-set.

Someone suffering from anorexia might pick out a single perceived 'flaw' and focus on it (for example, their thighs, bottom or stomach). Because of their unrelenting belief that this 'problem area' is disproportionate or ugly, they are then less aware of how slender the other areas of their body have become. They do not always do this, but this, I believe, is where the idea that sufferers see a 'fat person' in the mirror could have arisen from.

Many carers reason that they are counteracting their loved one's condition by encouraging them to see how truly thin they have become. This can sometimes be counterproductive, firstly because a sufferer usually knows how thin they are, and secondly because they are perversely proud of it and thrive on any mention of it.

An anorexia sufferer sees weight-loss as an achievement, their sole life-goal. Drawing attention to it can be the equivalent of patting them on the back and saying, 'Well done!'.

Tamsin, who is now recovered, demonstrates this when she remembers:

> I was in a queue at school, waiting to use the pay-phone to call my mum (these were the days before mobiles). A girl who was in my class turned around to face me, with a look of absolute disgust, and said, 'Tamsin, eat something, put some weight on, you look revoltingly skinny.' I spent the rest of the day floating on air, so proud of myself that I really must, at last, be thin. I resolved to eat even less from then on.

Myths and truths about anorexia nervosa

Below is a summary of the familiar 'facts' which are often quoted in relation to anorexia. They are, as we have discovered, myths which can prevent us from really understanding the illness.

Myth: If an anorexia sufferer gains weight, they are recovering.
Truth: Anorexia (and, indeed, any other eating disorder) is a mental illness, like depression. While there are physical symptoms, it is the mind-based issues which need to be addressed. Remember: if you treat the mind, the mind will treat the body.

Myth: Anorexia is ultimately about 'control'.
Truth: A lot of sufferers refer to 'control' because that is how their condition appears to them. However, from an outside perspective, they have lost control totally.

Myth: Anorexia sufferers have always experienced a significant and traumatic event.
Truth: Anorexia can arise in response to trauma; however, this

varies from person to person. A significant or dramatic past event is by no means a certainty.

Myth: Anorexia sufferers see a 'fat' person when they look in the mirror.
Truth: Often, sufferers are aware of how thin they have become; they simply do not consider it to be thin enough. (This myth arises from the fact that, often, sufferers pick and focus on one perceived 'flaw', such as their stomach or thighs, and obsess about it, rather than seeing their body as a whole.)

Myth: Anorexia sufferers always try to conceal their weight loss.
Truth: Some sufferers will wear baggy clothes in a bid to hide their weight loss. Others will try to draw attention to their slimmer frame. Again, this varies from person to person.

Myth: Anorexia sufferers only eat lettuce leaves.
Truth: A sufferer will restrict their food intake. However, they might allow themselves a very small amount of chocolate each day. The food stuff they choose is irrelevant; it is the restriction that is important.

Myth: Anorexia only affects teenage girls.
Truth: As we will discover throughout the course of this book, anorexia and other eating disorders affect both genders and all age ranges, races and social backgrounds.

Myth: Anorexia sufferers are classic over-achievers and/or perfectionists.
Truth: Just as sufferers of anorexia come from all walks of life, they also have a variety of different personalities.

Chapter 2

Hope with anorexia

It is important to emphasise at this stage that my motive for dispelling the common myths surrounding anorexia nervosa is not to paint a bleak picture, or to suggest that the condition is a life sentence, or beyond treatment. Sadly, there is no quick fix; it takes time, patience and understanding. However, please remember that anorexia nervosa can be overcome. The example of my own daughter, as well as of the others described in this book and countless more, proves this. However, this illness needs to be respected and correctly understood.

It is important to bear in mind when the recovery process begins that any step forward, however small objectively, will seem momentous in the mind of the sufferer. Often, the person suffering may believe they are 'doing really well' because they are eating enough to sustain their weight and stabilise, when your ultimate aim, of course, is for them to put on weight. You may feel frustrated with them at this point and wish that they would try harder. Be patient. Bear in mind they have gone from actively wanting to become thinner and thinner to eating enough so that they do not lose any more weight; it is important to acknowledge that this is a positive step in the right direction. After all, most people like to be praised, and a person suffering from an eating disorder is usually no different. If anything, I have found, in most cases, that compliments and praise can help to combat the negative feelings and thoughts in the sufferer's mind, fuelling them to try harder, as they are often keen to please those around them. This then helps to break the negative cycle shared between the sufferer and carers and can lead to a more positive environment for all concerned.

Bear in mind also, however, that simply because they are eating enough to sustain their body, that does not mean that they are consuming sufficient calories to heal their mind. Feeding the brain is what can silence the internal urgings of anorexia and allows the sufferer to let go of their illness. The body prioritises the vital internal organs over the mind, so this may take some time. Emotional progress usually follows physical progress. Food intake can stabilise the sufferer, but to recover they must want to get better themselves. It takes time, patience, perseverance, understanding and unconditional love to exorcise these demons.

My daughter Samantha reinforces this point when she says:

> The key to my recovery was my mum and finding my own willpower within me to make myself get better. Mum made me realise that there was more to life than my illness, and helped me come to terms with the fact that I had a problem and must get better or be ill and waste my life.

At this stage, I would like to emphasise that, from my experience, you cannot define recovery; recovery is different for every person and unique to them. I will come back to that later.

Bulimia nervosa

The word 'bulimia' derives from the Greek 'boulimia', meaning 'appetite of an ox'. While it is fairly common for anorexia sufferers to practise some bulimic behaviour in addition to starving themselves, and for bulimia sufferers to starve for periods of time as a form of purging, anorexia nervosa and bulimia nervosa are two very distinct illnesses, with the latter actually more closely linked with compulsive eating, addiction and even self-harm.

Victoire, a former model, who is now recovered from anorexia and bulimia, shares her different mind-sets when suffering from the two illnesses:

> I felt very powerful while I was anorexic because I thought I was in control of everything and this is the danger with this illness. At the same time, my back was hurting all the time, I couldn't sleep on my front as I was in constant pain, I saw myself huge in the

mirror whereas, in reality, I was terribly skinny and felt down. It was a daily battle in my head with this bitchy voice telling me I was fat. I thought I was becoming crazy. It was different with bulimia, I felt lonely and ashamed most of the time, really diminished as a human being because I was not able to control myself anymore.

Bulimia shares some characteristics with self-harm, the binge-and-purge cycle providing a release for emotional tension and a way to inflict punishment on the body for feelings of guilt or inadequacy. Again, as with anorexia nervosa, it is not certain that significant trauma has occurred in the sufferer's past. The contingent factor is the person's sensitivity and innate inability to cope with difficult situations, rather than the severity of their life circumstances.

There are, though, some common factors between the two conditions: just as with anorexia, there are many different ways to suffer from bulimia. Like anorexia, bulimia is a mental illness with physical symptoms. Also, like anorexia, it is sadly still woefully misunderstood, although steps are now being taken to raise awareness.

Bulimia nervosa is distinguished by the act of bingeing and purging. Sufferers first gorge on a huge amount of food (either objectively speaking, or what they consider to be a huge portion), and this is followed by what are known as 'compensatory behaviours'. These 'behaviours' most commonly involve sufferers forcing themselves to vomit, taking laxatives, or a combination of the two. This is often coupled with periods of starvation, excessive exercising or even sleeping for large quantities of time to 'work off' the calories consumed.

A great deal of this misunderstanding arises out of the idea that it is the binge that the sufferer 'enjoys', and the purge which they feel they must undertake because they do not want to gain weight. This is overly simplistic. As bulimia progresses, the sufferer might binge on foods they do not even like – or on frozen or out-of-date foods – just to give them the opportunity to purge. It is normally the act of purging – the physical release, the punishment of the body and mind – which the bulimia sufferer craves.

William talks of his experience:

> When its intensity was extremely mild, it tended to help me feel relaxed and reduce feelings of anxiety and tension. However, when intense, the feelings varied between rejuvenation, confidence and relaxation after purging, fear of being 'caught' whilst eating and subsequently purging. The greatest fear was that of admitting to myself that I had a 'problem'.

For a bulimia sufferer, the desire to binge and purge consumes their every waking thought. Social meals become a military-style operation: they have to check out their surroundings to see where the toilets are and how they will plan their escape from the table. Like anorexia sufferers, these social occasions are rare because both types of sufferer actually fear food, but for totally different reasons. Bulimia sufferers see food as a best friend and a mortal enemy. They look forward to being alone with it, but they hate it and themselves for what that will inevitably entail.

Contrary to popular belief, bulimia does not always lead the sufferer to lose a lot of weight. This is because it is physically impossible to purge the body of everything eaten during a binge; sufferers are often a 'normal' weight, or even slightly overweight, and indeed their weight may fluctuate wildly. However, it is important to note that the lack of obvious external physical symptoms does not detract from the severity of the illness. The appearance of most bulimia sufferers does not always reflect the extent of the damage they are doing to themselves internally, and both physically and mentally, and this is one of the disorder's most dangerous factors. Bulimia shows us very clearly that eating disorders are not just related to body image. It is clear from the person's behaviour that this disordered attitude towards food arises out of a truly disordered mind. This alone can be, in part, what makes the illness so confusing for the carers around them.

Naturally, people are more likely to understand an illness they can see, which may explain why both sufferers of bulimia nervosa and their loved ones may find that other people are less sympathetic towards their situation than if they were suffering from an illness whose damage they can see. You may find that, as a carer, you are isolated. Your loved one probably appears physically healthy, but, as we will see later, he/she is likely to behave strangely, becoming moody, withdrawn and/or prone to emotional outbursts.

It can be hard to talk about bulimia with others when it feels there is such a stigma attached to it, as there is with most mental illnesses – the illness is intrinsically linked with feelings of shame and disgust, both for the sufferers themselves and for their carers. This combination of factors can isolate them from the outside world. After all, the idea of someone overindulging and then disappearing to the toilet does not make for easy conversation. People fear what they cannot understand, and, like alcoholism or drug abuse, it can sometimes be easier for people to sweep the issue to one side or whisper about it behind closed doors rather than to confront it.

William, who has suffered for many years from bulimia nervosa, talks of the 'elephant in the room':

> Prior to 'coming out', the biggest impact was the issue of secrecy. My wife, son and I all knew that I had a disorder but none of us would talk about the 'elephant in the room'.

Like anorexia nervosa, media coverage of bulimia can often be misleading. While talking about it in magazines, newspapers or online can help reduce the stigma of this eating disorder, but some reporting can often undermine real understanding of what the illness entails. The need to match interviews with dramatic images means that often those we read about are the few who have lost a dramatic amount of weight. As this is less often the case for sufferers of bulimia, the picture painted in the media can often be skewed and perhaps contribute to some of the misunderstanding surrounding this illness.

Looking beyond appearance

To be able to identify bulimia nervosa in the early stages of the illness, some of the crucial signs to look out for revolve around evidence of the cycle of binging and purging. These can include:

- becoming more reclusive, rejecting invitations to social occasions and avoiding company
- if the person still lives at home, noticing large quantities of food disappearing mysteriously
- having a secret stash of food somewhere in their home
- eating very quickly, without seeming to enjoy the food
- suddenly seeming to have much less money (because it has been spent on food)
- having an excuse to go to the bathroom directly after meals
- showing signs of dehydration
- showing constant signs of cold or flu-like symptoms – runny nose, streaming eyes, sore throat; this is because forcing oneself to be sick causes mucus to build up, leading to the nose and eyes streaming.

The shame of bulimia

One of the biggest hurdles to overcome on a bulimia sufferer's road to recovery is conquering the feelings of shame and guilt which can give rise to the urgent need for secrecy which is a key feature of the illness.

Lizzie, who is now fully recovered from bulimia, when asked how it made her feel, says:

Chapter 2

> I guess the word that comes to mind is shameful. I also felt that it controlled me and was more powerful than me. Thankfully now that's no longer the case.

As I have already discussed, it is often hard to recognise when someone is suffering from bulimia nervosa. It is also very difficult for sufferers to confront their issues with food, let alone talk about them with others. Often people with bulimia believe they will be labelled as 'greedy' by their friends and loved ones, or viewed as having no self-control, whereas sufferers of anorexia can often feel 'proud' of their abilities to starve, and wear their weight loss like a badge of honour; bulimia sufferers are often plagued with constant feelings of self-disgust. They also often fear judgement and criticism, and this fear can permeate all areas of their lives, so that eventually they over-react to even the smallest criticism of their work, personality or appearance in their professional and private lives.

The most effective way to approach bulimia, therefore, is with sympathy and without judgement. Most bulimia sufferers often long for, above all else, an acknowledgement of what they are going through. They need to feel that the people around them are open to understanding without judgement.

As time goes on, the sufferer often lives with the knowledge that, in all probability, everyone around them knows, and even this can make them feel like a failure. They often see themselves as a failed anorexia sufferer, too lacking in willpower to starve; they can become paranoid, imagining that everyone is laughing at them. As a carer, it is important to try to provide your loved one with your unconditional support and strength, with the aim of counteracting these damaging feelings.

It is also important to note that a large part of bulimia can be a habit. Often sufferers are not exactly sure how or why their condition started, but they find themselves unable to stop, despite wanting to. For example, a bulimia sufferer might always binge and purge in the evening when they come home from school or work. They do not want to, but they have become so practised in doing it they find themselves unable to stop, much like a smoker. Studies show it takes as little as a few weeks for a habit to develop. The good news is, it takes a similarly short time to break those habits – however, it is important for long-term recovery that the underlying emotional factors and low self-esteem also need to be addressed.

You will often hear a bulimia sufferer say 'If only I could lose two stone, my life would be so much better.' The important part of that sentence is not that they wish to lose two stone; it is that they feel their lives could be better.

Emily, a former sufferer, says:

> My father drummed it into me from a young age that I was overweight and unpleasant to look at. At around the age of 20 I heard about bulimia through a radio programme and thought it sounded like a good way to control my weight.

Emily battled with bulimia for the next 25 years. It would have been easy for her to reconcile herself to her fate. However, brilliantly, she is now well into recovery. The crucial change happened when she realised she needed help. She says:

> It got to the point where I was really fed up with myself and my behaviour, leading to a strong desire to want to change. It was a gradual process, for me, which occurred over time, like a layering effect, enabling me to grow stronger and stronger. Until one day I realised I had detached myself from my old behaviours and had moved on, leaving them behind me in my past.

It is important to note, at this stage, that communication with bulimia sufferers does not always yield the reaction you would like or expect. With someone in such physical and emotional turmoil, they may lash out, or say things that they do not mean, blame you, their loved one, for interfering or tell you they do not need you. It is important for you to keep in mind that this is often the mental illness talking, and that your loved one probably does not mean this. As their carer, try to find the strength to continue plugging away at the channels of communication and to distinguish between when it is the sufferer and when it is their illness talking.

Richard, whose partner was a bulimia sufferer, says:

> The scariest thing was the effect my girlfriend's eating disorder had on her mind. Looking back, there were a lot of times when she didn't treat me particularly well, and I was always left questioning whether it was her, or her eating disorder, that made her behave that way.

Carers of all eating disorder sufferers often require a thick skin as it can be difficult not to take personal comments, or anger, from your loved one to heart. However, this is also an essential part of the person you love's recovery.

Physical and emotional signs

The thought and behaviour patterns of someone suffering from bulimia often mirror the extremes of their eating habits. The first and most important sign that someone might be suffering from bulimia is, without doubt, mood swings. These will become more and more severe as the sufferer's condition worsens.

It is no surprise when you try to imagine what they are up against. Due to purging on a regular basis, their body is likely to be deficient in key minerals, such as iron and potassium, which are essential for balancing the workings of the brain; a deficiency in these minerals can cause erratic and unpredictable behaviour. What is more, they are under constant siege from negative thoughts, which will inevitably be reflected in how they relate to others. Finally, because the extent to which the desire to binge and purge takes over the sufferer's mind and life, it can lead, in some cases, to depression.

Depression and eating disorders are often part and parcel of one another, with research suggesting that 50 to 75 per cent of those with eating disorders also experience major depressive disorder,[8] and this is never more true than of a bulimia sufferer. The binge-and-purge process is a physical expression of inner turmoil. It is a cry for help, aimed at the self. The longer someone has suffered from bulimia, the more fragile and volatile their mental state will most likely be.

Bulimia suffers can experience:

- Feelings of depression or anxiety
- Mood swings
- Irritability
- Tearfulness
- Expressions of wild elation, or anger, for no apparent reason
- Inability to concentrate
- Frequently feeling sleepy.

In addition, the imbalance in their nutrition, while not necessarily resulting in weight loss, can lead to the following:

- Thinning of hair/hair loss
- Poor circulation
- Weak nails
- Dry/flaky skin
- Weakening of the immune system: being prone to picking up colds, flu, etc
- Puffiness around the jaw line (as the glands become swollen)
- Erosion of the teeth, from making themselves sick
- Red or raw knuckles if they are using their fingers to force themselves to vomit.

Myths and truths about bulimia nervosa

As we have seen, there are many myths and misconceptions surrounding bulimia; sadly, it is still a deeply misunderstood illness. Below is a summary of the most common myths, and the facts:

Myth: Bulimia sufferers are underweight.
Truth: Sufferers are often slightly overweight, or what is considered a 'normal' weight. It is even less possible to diagnose bulimia by weighing the patient than it is for anorexia nervosa.

Myth: Bulimia and anorexia are interchangeable.
Truth: Bulimia and anorexia are two distinct illnesses. While they may borrow specific behaviours from one another, they manifest themselves in totally different ways, physically and psychologically.

Myth: Bulimia is ultimately about losing weight.
Truth: Bulimia sufferers might be labouring under the false idea that their condition will lead to weight loss, but this is also accompanied by feelings of inadequacy, guilt, shame and self-loathing. It is these emotions which ultimately fuel the illness.

Myth: Bulimia is less dangerous than anorexia.
Truth: While anorexia statistically has a higher mortality than bulimia, bulimia can be deadly (most often bulimia-related deaths are caused by a heart attack, resulting from the strain vomiting places on the heart). There are also a myriad of serious physical and psychological symptoms, as listed above.

Myth: Bulimia is about vanity.
Truth: Bulimia is akin to self-harm. It develops as a coping mechanism for difficult emotions and is fuelled by low self-

esteem. While a person might act confidently, it is simply that: an act.

Myth: There is a certain type of person who is more likely to suffer from bulimia.
Truth: Bulimia affects people of all ages, races, walks of life and genders.

Hope with bulimia nervosa

Bulimia can be conquered. The most important thing is that the sufferer must want to get better. Bulimia sufferers invariably reach a stage where they are physically and emotionally tired of their illness. They may not know why they are doing it anymore and want to stop, but they may believe that they are unable to. This can be the prime time for them to receive treatment. Over the chapters that follow, I will show you that it is possible for them and their carers to go on to lead happy and healthy lives. As Ivett's testimonial demonstrates – she has recovered from bulimia and says:

> After having bulimia for 10 years, I realised it wasn't making me slim! I was eating a lot and getting bigger. The problem was that when I started to eat I couldn't stop. I spent so much money on food – literally money down the toilet! So I decided one day to stop doing it. I now have breakfast, lunch and dinner. I never miss them. I have lost weight! I am so much happier now – and cannot believe that I ever made myself sick.

Over-eating: Binge eating disorder and emotional eating

When eating disorders are discussed, over-eating is often overlooked. It is not always seen as being in the same 'league' as anorexia nervosa or bulimia nervosa. Over-eating can be as much a disordered way of eating as anorexia and bulimia, and just as dangerous. Yet, in a society experiencing an 'obesity epidemic', it is rarely identified in that way. In some cases, sufferers are victimised and perceived as villains. Public opinion rarely seems to take into account that a person may not be over-eating through pure greed, but because of a complex set of psychological issues, including low self-esteem or a life event, which could lead them to seek solace in food. People find different ways to deal with their emotions and certain situations – some eat less, some eat more; equally, some drink to excess, take drugs or smoke.

A large proportion of the UK population is overweight or obese – 58 per cent of women and 68 per cent of men in 2015[9] – however, most do not perceive themselves as having an eating disorder, and in fact, many do not. So, we ask, where is the line drawn between enjoying your food and using it as an emotional crutch?

The answer lies in the notion of 'mindful eating'. Over-eating becomes a problem when the sufferer is not aware of what they consume. Over-eaters tend not to chew, and to eat while engaging in other everyday activities (such as watching television, social networking on their computers, texting or speaking on the telephone, or working at their desks). Many tend to 'graze' constantly, eating sweets and other bite-sized snacks consistently throughout the day.

Someone suffering from over-eating is also likely to be in genuine denial about how much they eat. Sufferers will often say 'I don't eat all day' because they instantly forget what they have, in reality, consumed.

Over-eating most commonly falls into one of two disorders: binge eating disorder and emotional over-eating. While these two have characteristics of their own, they also share many similarities.

The eating/emotion connection

It is a popular theory among psychologists that over-eating has its roots in childhood. When we are young we become so accustomed to being rewarded with food – going out to dinner to celebrate good grades, having a special cake on our birthday, or being consoled with 'treats' when things go wrong – that we could carry this habit into our adult lives.

However, while being 'treated' to and comforted by food in childhood is pretty much universal, not everyone ultimately develops an eating disorder. Add in very low self-esteem or another mental illness, such as depression or anxiety, and the chances of a disordered relationship with food increase.

Food often masks the real problems in the life of a sufferer from over-eating. Sufferers believe their life would be better if they could conquer their over-eating and lose weight, but this is, in actuality, a red herring.

Tara, who has suffered from compulsive eating since the age of 7, says:

> When it first started, food made me feel comforted and numbed the painful emotions that I had. Then I became scared and angry because I couldn't stop compulsively over-eating.

Sufferers are often dissatisfied or frustrated with their love lives, careers or other life circumstances. They eat as a means of coping with this and, as they gain weight, they sink further into their unhappiness. So, the situation becomes a vicious circle.

Melanie, 24, describes how over-eating can arise out of feelings of boredom and inadequacy:

> I turned to eating after the breakdown of my parents' marriage. I had a full year of not doing a lot and sat around at home with just my part-time job to keep me busy, and spent hours on end

> with food as my only comfort. It gave me something to do. I was bored and down about everything and I felt that crisps and sweets would make me feel better. They didn't at all. But when there is nothing, and your family and friends are busy, food is always there. I look back now, as I am really trying hard to lose the weight I gained, wishing I had found comfort in something else. But at the time, it was all I felt I really had.

Over-eaters will often tell you they feel 'hungry', but it is an emotional hunger as opposed to a physical one. The two have become confused in the sufferer's mind. Cravings for food in response to uncomfortable emotions, like boredom or loneliness, feel so powerful it is difficult to distinguish them from genuine hunger.

Sufferers are also often so keen not to repeat the food mistakes of the previous day, they will often go through short periods of starvation. This can, of course, be counterproductive, because starvation causes the body to binge when food is reintroduced.

It is also worth noting that the over-eater may be dehydrated. Often, thirst is mistaken for hunger. Very few of us drink enough water, and over-eaters, with their tendency not to look after their more general health, are no exception.

Signs that differentiate over-eating as an issue are:

- eating in response to an upsetting event
- having low confidence
- having general dissatisfaction with life
- eating quickly, without chewing
- eating 'mindlessly', while doing something else
- using their weight as an excuse for putting off taking steps to improve their lives.

As well as creating a destructive cycle around food and exacerbating the negative emotional responses of sufferers, over-eating – like all eating disorders – can also have an impact on their physical health. The most common health implications of over-eating include obesity, high blood pressure and cholesterol, heart disease, Type 2 diabetes, joint and back pain, and fertility problems.

The difference between binge eating disorder and emotional over-eating

Binge eating disorder

Binge eating is, as you would expect, very closely linked to bulimia, the difference being that the sufferer will not purge after they have binged. The two disorders also share the unfortunate similarity of being shrouded in secrecy. Just as bulimia sufferers often wish they had the 'willpower' to be thinner, it is not uncommon to hear a binge eater express a desire to be 'better' at purging.

Those who binge on food often have a hidden stash of food, stockpiled by numerous visits to different supermarkets so as not to arouse suspicion. Binge eating does not take place in response to physical hunger. In fact, the person might not be able to recognise the signs of physical hunger, because they are so used to eating in response to their emotions.

In some cases, because society can teach us to be ashamed of our urge to eat, and because of the huge and unusual quantities they consume, binge eating disorder sufferers often feel a constant sense of embarrassment, sometimes driving them to even greater lengths to conceal their behaviour. Often perceived as anti-social, their tendency to hide themselves away results from the dual factors of a) never wanting to be too far from food, and b) not wishing to put themselves in a situation where a friend or loved one might uncover their terrible secret.

Alternatively, the sufferer may adopt a 'larger than life' persona, again in an attempt to hide their illness and persuade the people they encounter (and perhaps even themselves) that they are happy with their size. Jennifer's story, below, demonstrates this:

I'd been friends with Sally for years and always thought of her as the 'jolly' overweight girl, who was perfectly at ease with her size. She was always giggling, flirting and showing off her oversized curves in short skirts. Gradually, as I spent more time with her, however, I noticed the mood swings. If she had a bit too much to drink, one minute she'd be the life and soul of the party, the next she would be sitting in the corner, sulking or sometimes crying and no one could ever work out what had caused the switch. Once, someone asked her if she was upset because she was bigger than the other women in the bar. She denied it, but responded by becoming incredibly angry, so we could see a nerve had been touched. We later discovered that she was eating a full large takeaway pizza, a tub of ice cream and drinking a bottle of wine every single night in her flat, alone. She was desperate to stop but didn't know how. I don't see her much anymore. Her mood swings isolated her from most of her mates. But I believe that her eating habits were at the root of them.

Bingeing can escalate rapidly, or it can be a habit which develops gradually over a number of years. Other than weight gain, as the story above demonstrates it can be difficult for the sufferer's family and friends to pinpoint the problem, or to know what action to take when they do. There are also 'occasional binge eaters' – the constant yearning to eat is present but the sufferer will set limits on themselves, yo-yoing between what they consider to be acceptable 'limits'. Physically there may be no symptoms at all for an occasional binge eater, but psychologically there are still issues which need to be addressed.

Having said that, 'emotional hunger' (which we touched on above) is something most of us will have experienced at some point. Part of the issue is the attachment of a moral judgement in our perception of food (advertising can have a lot to answer for in this regard) – it is somehow considered 'naughty' to eat chocolate, so we persuade ourselves that we 'deserve' it for whatever reason. Every time you have bought yourself a high-calorie but delicious snack on your way home from school or work because you have had a 'hard day', you have had a glimpse into the mentality of someone suffering from binge eating.

Emotional over-eating

Emotional over-eating does share many similarities with binge eating, in terms of the shame and embarrassment for sufferers, but it differs slightly in that food is used as an emotional crutch, the only thing a sufferer turns to when they need comfort and help to deal with their feelings. Often, the feel-good chemicals released by high-calorie foods have become so addictive that the sufferer seeks a further 'hit' each time the feeling begins to fade. (They are similar to smokers in this regard.)

Of course, we all use food as a pick-me-up at times, tearing open a box of chocolates to make ourselves feel better (often only to find it actually makes us feel worse). For someone who cannot control their emotional over-eating, they will turn to food so often to cope with their feelings that ultimately it will make them feel like they are not in control.

Emotional hunger is an urgent need for food, a craving generally for something unhealthy and high in fat. Simply becoming full will not satisfy that hunger and it causes feelings of shame, guilt and powerlessness.

Mikyla Dodd, an actress most famous for her role in 'Hollyoaks' and her later appearance in 'Celebrity Fit Club', has battled with compulsive eating and is passionate about changing attitudes and approaches to it. She sums up the most common misconception surrounding over-eating and how she believes it should be tackled:

> The biology of the situation is simple but the cause is far more complex and requires a much more in-depth approach to achieve lasting success and to like/value yourself more than you do food.

Chapter 2

> I think we should be able to discuss [eating disorders] openly as an issue instead of being so afraid to address it in case we cause further damage. To ignore it actually exacerbates the feelings of loneliness and isolation that then, in turn, create a bigger problem.

Myths and truths about emotional over-eating

As we have already discovered, there are many misconceptions surrounding anorexia nervosa and bulimia nervosa; emotional over-eating and binge eating disorder are no different.

Myth: People who over-eat need to go on a diet.
Truth: Losing weight merely treats one of the most common outcomes of over-eating. What it does not tackle is the emotional issues that lie at the root of the disorder.

Furthermore, a falling number on the scales is very hard to achieve unless the issues driving the eating disorder are successfully tackled. An all-round approach, where psychological help goes hand in hand with nutritional support, is more likely to change the behaviour that drives compulsive eating.

Myth: Emotional over-eating and Binge Eating Disorder are not dangerous.
Truth: Those who over-eat are very likely to have underlying emotional or mental health issues, such as depression or anxiety, which can have a debilitating and devastating effect on people's lives. Furthermore, the physical impact of over-eating is very real. Those who are overweight or obese are at increased risk of dangerous conditions, including heart disease, high blood pressure and Type 2 diabetes.

Myth: Sufferers of binge eating or compulsive eating are trying to satisfy their hunger.

Truth: Bingeing and over-eating are not linked to physical hunger or even a desire for food. In fact, those who over-eat consume excessive quantities of food as a way to soothe and comfort themselves in times of stress, sadness, depression, loneliness and/or anger. Their behaviour is compulsive, often secretive, and feels out of their control. This is why tackling the cause of these negative emotions is vital if sufferers are to gain some control over their illness.

Myth: Sufferers of binge eating or compulsive eating are overweight.
Truth: Some binge eaters are overweight, but not all. While they have periods when they eat far more than the recommended number of calories, they may then balance this out by strict dieting in between the binges. You cannot tell who has a problem with over-eating by what people look like.

Myth: Sufferers of binge eating or compulsive eating just don't know when to stop.
Truth: Many binge eaters are fully aware of what they should eat, and how big their portions should be. However, their illness compels them to ignore this, to eat beyond the point where they feel full, to lose control over the amount they consume. They often know what they are doing but are unable to stop.

Hope with over-eating

While anorexia nervosa and bulimia nervosa stand out as very stark illnesses, binge eating, and emotional over-eating are more insidious. The behaviours seem to creep into the whole person, leading over-eaters to take on the identity of an overweight person, which affects the whole lifestyle they lead and often the personality they project.

However, sufferers can of course get better. Recovery

essentially hinges on breaking the associations the sufferer has made between positive emotions and certain foods and conquering the food cravings that fuel their binges. For that to happen, food needs to be taken off its pedestal. It needs to be given a much more minor role in the sufferer's life. They must learn to eat to live and stop living to eat.

As a carer, your most effective weapons will be compassion, understanding and communication. It is important not to make the sufferer feel 'greedy', and to not restrict their food intake. It is also important in the recovery journey that the sufferer does not feel as though eating is 'wrong'. This can only lead to secretive behaviour and, perversely, the desire to eat even more. Instead, it is helpful to let them know that they are entitled to eat, while at the same time exploring the underlying emotions which are fuelling their over-eating.

It should be noted that there is a difference between restricting food intake and actively 'enabling' the sufferer's over-eating. It is a fine line that can be difficult to tread successfully.

Once again, communication is absolutely vital – however, it is not your job as a carer to draw attention to the sufferer's eating habits. They will already know they are over-eating, and they will already be riddled with guilt and shame because of this. As a carer, it is essential to help the sufferer explore the reasons behind their condition, to find out what holes in their emotional, professional and private lives they are attempting to fill with food.

As a carer, it is important to be careful not to fuel the over-eating yourself. Be aware of the words and phrases you use with respect to the person suffering; try not to describe them as 'always being big' or 'loving their food' as messages like this can subtly embed themselves in the sufferer's identity, making them unable to see how their life could be different. Allow them to explore who they are outside food. Encourage them to think about what they are good at and what they want from their lives.

Often, when they feel happier and more fulfilled, the over-eating will stop of its own accord.

To conclude

Caring for someone with an eating disorder can push everyone involved to their limits and beyond. However, I would like to reiterate, that, with the right support, understanding, unconditional love, patience, time and the sufferer's own determination, *all* eating disorders can be beaten, and full recovery is possible.

Chapter 3

Other eating disorders

There are hundreds of ways to have an unhealthy relationship with food and body image; not everyone will fit the diagnostic criteria for the most widely recognised eating-related illnesses: anorexia nervosa, bulimia nervosa and binge eating disorder. In this chapter, I will endeavour to help you identify some of the other destructive behaviours which have been recognised and 'labelled'.

At this point, it is also important to stress that these 'labels' often have blurred boundaries. Your loved one may show signs of more than one of them, or may exhibit different behaviour around eating altogether. So, while labels can be helpful, it is important to keep in mind that everyone displays their signs and symptoms differently.

Even if they do not fit the criteria that doctors use to diagnose eating disorders, it does not make their pain any less real or less deserving of understanding and support. Nor does it make it any easier for carers to watch their loved ones suffer.

OSFED

OSFED (other specified feeding or eating disorder) is a term that has been used since 2013 and is often diagnosed when someone's symptoms do not fit the specific diagnostic criteria for anorexia nervosa, bulimia nervosa or binge eating disorder. Even though it is less widely known, it is actually the most diagnosed eating disorder, with around 30 per cent of those who seek help for eating disorders falling into this category.[10]

Before the diagnostic criteria changed in 2013, OSFED would have fallen under another acronym, EDNOS (eating disorder not otherwise specified). EDNOS also included what has become binge eating disorder, which has now been identified as a separate disorder in its own right. However, binge eating that is irregular, unusual or specific may still find itself being classified under OSFED. These changes in the way the different disorders are classified were aimed at ensuring more people were able to get a diagnosis that more accurately fitted their symptoms.

To be diagnosed as having OSFED, a person's eating behaviour would be considerably interfering with their life and causing them significant distress. While their symptoms would not meet the full criteria for any of the other specified feeding and/or eating disorders, their obsessive relationship with food, exercise, shape and/or weight would be overshadowing and controlling their everyday life.

The causes of OSFED

Like other eating disorders, the causes of OSFED usually come from a complex interplay of biological, psychological and societal factors. Someone's biological make-up may put them more at risk of developing an unhealthy relationship with food, body image and/or exercise. Add in the pressure from Western society to be thin or muscular, or the media storm around clean eating and extreme exercise, along with the stresses and anxieties that some people are more susceptible to; for many, it is all too easy for their relationship with food to become wildly distorted.

Chapter 3

The signs of OSFED

The signs of OSFED are, by definition, often less clear-cut than those of other eating disorders. The fad diets which saturate today's society can also make eating disorders hard to detect. OSFED is not about dieting to fit into a party dress or suddenly becoming really keen on running. It is when someone's preoccupation with food or exercise becomes so pervasive that it starts – and if left unchecked, continues – to take over their mind and life.

Be aware if your loved one has rigid rules around food, diets and/or excessive exercise. They may binge eat, consuming large amounts, and their attitude towards food, and often life in general, may be saturated by their own poor image of their body and a lack of self-esteem.

Collin talks of his frustration at the time:

> Holly started becoming, I would say, a little obsessive about her training times and when she ate her meals during the day. It really hit me one weekend; as we spent the days together, she would not leave the house as she was afraid she would not be able to eat the right foods at the right times. It did confuse me as sometimes in the evenings we would sit and watch a movie and she would eat a bag of popcorn and chocolate bars; she would soon be cross with me for not stopping her eating it all and be unhappy within herself the next day for doing so. It seemed the only time Holly was sort of happy was when she was in complete control of her eating and lifestyle. I didn't think she was in control at all. Holly was later diagnosed with OSFED, and it all clicked into place.

Similarly, as with other eating disorders, it will most likely be changes in the person's behaviour and moods that those around them notice first, before any physical signs start to appear.

Signs to look out for may include:
- Distorted body image
- A preoccupation with the purity of food

- Shame or anxiety around food or body image
- Obsessively exercising
- Low confidence and self-esteem
- Irritability and mood swings
- Restricting calories
- Binge eating
- Purging through making themselves sick, using laxatives or excessive exercise
- Strange rituals associated with eating.

The frequency of these symptoms may be erratic or without a pattern, which is why this could lead to the diagnosis to be OSFED and not anorexia nervosa, bulimia nervosa or binge eating disorder.

Hope with OSFED

Full recovery from OSFED is possible, and there are many different treatment paths. The starting point is to get OSFED diagnosed, and that can often be a challenge in itself, not least because sufferers with OSFED may not actually recognise that they are ill enough to seek help.

Like all eating disorders, time and patience are needed to find the right combination of treatments that work. Support, love, and perseverance from loved ones have a crucial role to play in the recovery plan, as well as sufferers wanting to get better themselves. By working together, and by believing that recovery is possible, the sufferer can move forward and find a healthier and happier relationship with food.

Lesser known eating disorders

There are various practices and rituals which people may develop around food which are both physically and psychologically unhealthy. They can also be unsociable, dominate the sufferer's life and prevent them from enjoying themselves or fulfilling their potential. During the course of this chapter, I will help you to be able to identify some of these disorders.

Of course, it would be impossible to describe every single way to have disordered thinking with regards to food and exercise. However, the following are further disorders that have been identified, in addition to behaviours covered by an OSFED diagnosis.

Orthorexia

While the word 'anorexia' was first used nearly 150 years ago, 'orthorexia' is a far newer phrase, first coined by American doctor Steven Bratman in 1997. Even so, more than 20 years on, it is still not widely known and is not currently recognised as a distinct eating disorder. Awareness of this illness is starting to change, however, as the shifting cultural landscape – and the impact of social media in particular – makes orthorexia more prevalent than ever.

Orthorexia is rarely driven – at least at the start – by a desire to be thin, but rather by a craving to be healthy and pure. Someone with orthorexia will be excessively preoccupied by 'healthy' eating to the extent that it dominates every aspect of their lives. They will divide food into 'good' and 'bad' or 'pure' and 'impure' and may even scrutinise how food is prepared, rejecting it if it is not made to their exacting standards. Those with orthorexia may have an encyclopaedic knowledge of calories, vitamins and nutrients, and will often criticise the eating habits of family and friends.

Of course, healthy eating sounds like a good thing and certainly not everyone following a healthy lifestyle will develop orthorexia. Like the other eating disorders, it can be worrying when it becomes obsessive, when someone feels immense guilt if they break the rules that they have set for themselves, or if it takes over their life, preventing them enjoying social occasions with friends or family.

Alex tells us of his journey with orthorexia and his search for 'perfection':

I wish I could have accepted myself when I was younger. It could have been so different and life would have been so much more enjoyable. Growing up, I was and felt like the skinny kid. I was painfully quiet and struggled with even the most basic interactions. As I got older it became almost too much for me to take and I decided that I wanted to transform myself and go from feeling irrelevant to feeling perfect and in control.

Like so many young men do, I fell into the trap of thinking the best way to develop this was to develop my body. Whilst the gym initially began as a fun pastime, it quickly turned into an obsession that dictated all aspects of my life, damaging my relationships with people and food at the same time.

I became fixated on achieving what I perceived to be the perfect body, convincing myself that once I finally reached it everything else in my life would fall into place. I spent years obsessing over and deciding whether foods were 'clean' or 'dirty'. I began to feel uncontrollable levels of guilt anytime I ate a food that I deemed to be dirty, and on a couple of occasions I would release the food rather than deal with how I was feeling.

This then moved into an obsession with calorie counting and meticulous tracking of everything that I ate. This caused me to withdraw from people, causing relationships with friends and the opposite sex to be hugely challenged, with many not surviving. I lost track of who I was as a person and my actions became governed by whether I had enough calories left to eat.

It's been a long journey, but after some counselling, personal development and finding some balance in my life, I am now a much happier person leading a much more fulfilling life. The desire for perfection was time wasted and brought me nothing but stress.

Like any mental health condition, orthorexia is dangerous, fuelling unhealthy thought patterns and sometimes leading to, or overlapping with, other psychological illnesses. Although weight loss is not the initial intention, orthorexia has strong links with anorexia nervosa. The behaviour of someone with orthorexia may be part of anorexia, or indeed, one may lead to the other.

Orthorexia also has very immediate implications for physical health. By cutting out whole food groups, as those with orthorexia often do, sufferers are immediately cutting out huge swathes of vital vitamins and minerals, leaving them not only nutrient deficient but also unable to think logically.

The causes of orthorexia

It is quite tempting to lay the blame for orthorexia at the feet of social media, which is very effectively fuelling the current trend for 'clean eating'. However, since orthorexia was actually first defined in the mid-90s, when the internet itself was in its infancy and social media was still many years off, the roots of orthorexia are clearly not quite that simple.

After all, the internet did not create awareness about healthy eating; it merely spread the word. Long before we had 'clean eating', we were told about the negative health effects of, for example, a diet high in saturated fat or one heavy in red meat. It follows then that it is entirely reasonable that people would want to limit the amount of these foods they consume in order to be 'healthy'. However, with orthorexia, this healthy awareness can get out of control. People can become obsessed with the need to avoid 'bad foods'. What they eat becomes part of who they are and they may go to extreme lengths to pursue this identity.

The gear shift came very recently, when we suddenly had a wave of so-called experts touting the benefits of clean eating, especially on social media. With traditional media all too happy to leap on the 'pure foods' bandwagon, the right conditions for a perfect orthorexia storm suddenly came together.

Marianne, the mother of a former sufferer of orthorexia, says:

My daughter was 14 at the time I realised her 'healthy eating' had gone a bit further than my original thoughts of being just a phase. I first noticed her anxiety around food had sky rocketed overnight, pretty much, and she was beginning to lose quite a bit of weight. She used to hover around me in the kitchen and ask me so many questions about everything I was doing; in the end she decided to just cook her own meals as she did not trust what I was cooking was going to be right for her. I summoned up the courage to ask her what was going on as I was getting very concerned at her behaviour, and she finally opened up to me a bit and showed me some of the websites and YouTube videos she had been watching to get advice from. As a parent, I was shocked; in my day, if you wanted advice you would seek a professional who would look at you individually and advise on your needs. For Sara, she was watching everything and taking it all on board; it was becoming almost impossible for her to keep up with all the rules she was trying to adhere to. As part of her recovery we had to put a social media restriction on her. I never knew how influential the internet could be.

A 2017 study found that higher use of the social media channel Instagram, which has 500 million registered users worldwide, was associated with a greater tendency towards orthorexia nervosa.[11] You can see how it happened. With young, gorgeous Instagram stars telling people to cut out carbs or ditch dairy, the sage warnings from real doctors about the importance of a balanced diet would have seemed pretty dull by comparison. It is not hard to see how such glamorous role models, who nevertheless often lacked formal training in health or nutrition, made restrictive eating appear downright desirable. However, because many of the others logging onto the clean-eating sites were doing it too, this restrictive way of eating could seem like normal behaviour.

Of course, that is not to say that the intentions of these clean-eating 'gurus' were negative. Many were indeed promoting a healthy way to eat and live, even if what they were saying was often not backed by scientific fact. At the same time, it is easy to see how this overt division of foods into 'good' and 'bad' can start to spiral out of control, especially for those more vulnerable to extremes of behaviour.

Renee McGregor, performance and eating disorder specialist dietitian, and author of *Orthorexia: When Healthy Eating Goes Bad*, gives us her thoughts:

> It's hard to pin-point exactly when orthorexia became 'more prevalent' as, in actuality, it has probably been a slow build up over the last three to five years; definitely with the rise of social media and also aspects such as 'wellness' and 'fitinspiro'.
>
> Indeed, for this reason, orthorexia is one of the hardest disorders to diagnose as it can easily be hidden behind the guise of 'healthy eating'; more so since the increased interest in fitness and wellness and the rise of social media 'health' influencers.
>
> Individuals truly believe that their 'quest to eat clean' will result in a 'pure' body and everlasting health. However, the truth of the matter is that many individuals are more likely to be doing more harm than good due to the fact that many of the eating practices encouraged and followed usually involve the removal of food groups that are indeed vital for health.
>
> For someone who is already low in self-confidence and self-worth, the need to please and be 'good enough' is a relentless battle. They will go to any lengths in order to achieve what they perceive is 'perfection', the problem being that whatever they do, it is never sufficient, and the pursuit for happiness continues. The real answer of course is being able to accept oneself for who one is, faults and all.
>
> While these problems may be internal, individuals will use methods

such as 'clean eating' to project this dissatisfaction with themselves. They will often evangelise how healthy they feel on this particular path, without fully appreciating the negative impact removing food groups will be having on their health. With the rise of social media as a mode of communication, #cleaneating has become something of a 'badge of honour' with more and more people adopting the phrase and striving towards it in order to feel validated and accepted.

While I believe that social media has definitely contributed to the rise in incidence of orthorexia, we cannot go around blaming it as the main cause. It is important to highlight that orthorexia is a mental illness, like all other eating disorders. It is a method of controlling negative emotions and low self-worth. Any individual who has a poor perception of themselves will go in search of ways to help themselves feel better – the images on social media feed into this by selling the stories and lifestyles of those who claim that their method of eating has helped them to be successful and feel fantastic. These claims are what vulnerable people want, but what they do not understand is that the pursuit of happiness is not entangled in food but, actually, it is about working on themselves and learning to accept who they are as they are. Only then will they be able to be truly comfortable in their skin – not through trying to restrict or control their eating. While this gives temporary relief, it also creates a whole lot of negative health issues.

I believe that society, in general, is probably driving the increase in our dissatisfaction with ourselves, and this, of course, is then what drives individuals to want to make changes in order to help themselves feel better. Society suggests that 'success' comes from having a glamorous lifestyle and the 'perfect' career, partner, house etc. Of course, we all know that this is not true – success and happiness actually come from our own self-worth – but when we are constantly bombarded with images, new fads and trends that make us believe that they are the answer to our happiness, those of us that are susceptible will go to any lengths in order to try to achieve 'happiness'.

The signs of orthorexia

Orthorexia can initially be hard to identify, especially as it is so often disguised under the cloak of healthy eating, which is promoted and indeed encouraged by society. It can also happen incrementally, with the sufferer slowly cutting out more and more foods – or groups of food – over time in an attempt to make their eating even healthier, as they perceive it.

If you, as their carer, can see that it is getting out of control, this is perhaps when you need to be concerned. They may start criticising what others eat or begin to want to know exactly how food has been prepared or cooked. They may start avoiding going out, knowing how hard it will be to keep to their own rules around food, and they may start feeling guilt over eating foods that they believe to be unhealthy.

These kinds of behaviours will begin to have an effect on their mood, with low energy and even depression starting to take hold. As the orthorexia continues, the physical effects will start to become apparent, with weight loss, weakness and tiredness all becoming more noticeable. With their body deficient in certain nutrients, they may be more prone to getting illnesses and struggle to get over these quickly.

Hope with orthorexia

Like other eating disorders, orthorexia nervosa is a serious mental illness, and should be treated as quickly and effectively as possible to give the sufferer the best chance of full recovery. With orthorexia, those early signs can be easy to miss because the sufferer can hide behind the thought that they are actually eating healthily and benefiting from eating this way. With so much current emphasis on this way of life, it can be hard for loved ones to see when 'good' behaviour around food becomes problematic and potentially dangerous.

However, at some point that realisation should come, and if the sufferer can recognise and admit there is an issue, they will be taking the first crucial step towards recovery. With the right help and support, be it at home and/or possibly professionally, they can be helped to introduce more flexibility into their diet. By gradually relaxing the rules and letting go of the guilt, a balanced diet and a balanced mind can return.

Compulsive exercise

Health club memberships, for many, are practically mandatory in today's society. With our increasingly sedentary lifestyles, gyms are seen as providing the solution, allowing us to undertake some much-needed exercise. Away from the gym, marathons, triathlons and other extreme workouts are proving more popular than ever as people are finding more challenging ways to get fit.

Those who pound the treadmill or spend their weekends negotiating an obstacle course are often praised for their motivation and self-discipline. However, if this behaviour is taken to an extreme level, it can have serious consequences.

Issues can arise when the need to exercise becomes a compulsion and someone's drive to head to the gym or lace-up their running trainers becomes obsessive. In other words, the person no longer chooses to exercise but feels compelled to do so and struggles with guilt or anxiety if they can't.

The insight of the late Nicki Waterman, fitness expert and health writer, who generously lent her expertise and support to the first edition of this book, remains spot on:

Excessive exercise offers a built-in reinforcement. It increases endorphin levels, providing the individual with a sense of wellbeing. The endorphin levels remain high, even though the individual is seriously, and perhaps permanently, compromising their own health. Studies are currently being conducted to ascertain and better understand the addictive nature of exercise. Extreme or compulsive exercise is dangerous. The most significant dangers are overuse syndromes such as stress fractures, low heart rate, amenorrhea and osteoporosis.

Sufferers of compulsive exercise will work out for longer than advised, and sometimes continue to exercise through injuries. The constant physical strain placed on the body means that they are generally always hungry, and they can often feel guilty about this.

While excessive exercise can be a common component of various types of eating disorder, it can equally be a real issue on its own.

When exercise becomes extreme

The crux of whether the exercise has reached a problematic level is not so much how much someone exercises as the motivations behind it. If exercise is a compulsion, and feelings of guilt arise when a workout is missed, then there may well be a cause for concern.

In trying to work out whether someone's exercise levels have gone from reasonable to excessive, consider the following questions:

- Does the person feel guilty if they miss their workout or a scheduled training session?
- Does the person still exercise when they are unwell or injured?
- Would the person choose a workout over commitments with friends or family?
- Does the person become agitated and anxious if they miss a workout?
- Does the person calculate how much exercise they need to do, based on how much they eat?

If some of these questions ring true, exercise may have become problematic and both the exercise itself and the psychological underpinnings that drive it should be addressed.

Night eating syndrome

This disorder is usually caused by sufferers starving throughout the day. They long to have what they perceive as the 'willpower' to starve constantly.

Their bodies will cry out for food by the time evening arrives, resulting in powerful physical cravings, causing them to eat in secret throughout the night. This disorder is characterised by feelings of shame and of guilt. It is shrouded in secrecy.

Lucy has had first-hand experience of this, having eaten during the night for three years:

> I would starve all day and go to sleep pleased with my efforts. When I woke up in the middle of the night, sometimes it was almost as though I was sleep-walking. I would go downstairs and straight to the fridge, unaware of what I was eating. Sometimes I would even wake up halfway through eating a peanut butter sandwich, with no recollection of preparing it. The next morning, I would be aware that I had eaten the night before and say to myself, 'I won't do that again' and starve myself all day to compensate. So of course, it was a vicious circle. I broke the habit when I realised I needed to eat during the day to stop my body crying out for food at night.

As well as playing havoc with the metabolism, this disorder can result in extreme tiredness and mood swings.

Pica

Pica is Latin for 'magpie', reputedly a bird that will eat anything. Sufferers of pica disorder eat non-food substances in addition to their normal diet, such as soil, chalk, paint, plaster, glue, insects, leaves, gravel, clay, hair, soap or even laundry detergent. The sufferer will often have a craving for a specific one of these things.

This disorder is more common in children up to the age of two years and pregnant women, who may find it hard to ignore the compulsion to eat these non-food substances. It is also more common among those with disabilities such as schizophrenia or autism, although it can affect men and women of any age and background.

The consequences may include damage to the intestines or bowel, parasitic infection, poisoning or dental injury. Underlying psychological issues will need to be treated along with any nutritional deficiency arising from pica disorder.

Research suggests that pica is caused by vitamin deficiency and yet, bafflingly, the substance craved often does not contain the vitamin the sufferer is deficient in!

Another disorder, *geophagy*, mirrors the traits of pica disorder, differing only in that the sufferer eats soil and earthy substances alone.

Rumination disorder

Rumination disorder may not be well known, but as a behaviour pattern that seems to have the effect of calming the sufferer, it should be treated like any other eating disorder.

Rumination disorder entails the repeated regurgitation and re-chewing of food. Partially digested food is brought up into the mouth without apparent nausea, retching or upset. The food is then either spat out or, more frequently, chewed and re-swallowed.

It is not, as used to be thought, an illness that occurs only in children, although the number of people who suffer from this disorder is not yet clear. It may sometimes be a behaviour that runs alongside anorexia and/or bulimia nervosa.

Avoidant/restrictive food intake disorder (ARFID)

ARFID occurs when people are highly selective about the foods they eat. It is generally not related to how they see their body, but may occur because they are sensitive to the taste, texture or even colour of certain foods or perhaps they have developed anxiety around some foods.

If left untreated, it can lead to malnutrition. Sufferers may also struggle to eat enough calories for good health. Children with ARFID may not grow as they should, and sufferers of all ages may find themselves socially isolated as they avoid certain social situations because of their issues with food.

Chewing and spitting

This behaviour is not unusual in people with eating issues. Typically they crave certain types of foods but do not want to consume the calories they contain. They think – mistakenly – that by spitting out the food after chewing, that they would not be taking in those calories.

In fact, we do actually consume calories when we chew, with the sugar, fat or carbohydrates from those foods still going into our bodies, albeit at lower levels than if we swallowed the food down. Chewing food is also enough to give our brains a hit, which we may then begin to crave, and that can lead to chewing and spitting behaviour becoming compulsive.

There can be a lot of anxiety and shame associated with chewing and spitting, with sufferers feeling that they are very alone.

Bigorexia

Bigorexia is also known as 'muscle dysmorphia'. It differs from compulsive exercise in that the focus is entirely on muscle building.

Bigorexia is often described as 'anorexia in reverse' (to the outside observer it can certainly appear that way). Whereas an anorexia sufferer will never be thin enough, a bigorexia sufferer can never be as muscular as they desire. Bigorexia affects hundreds of thousands of men (and some women, too) throughout the world. Some will miss important events and work so that they can schedule in an extra workout; others will continue to train through severe pain and even broken bones.

As you might expect, bigorexia is mainly prevalent among weight-lifters, although increasingly it is affecting people in other walks of life as well. It frequently goes hand in hand with drug abuse, as sufferers are tempted to use anabolic steroids to further build muscle.

While the causes of bigorexia are not known, many have concluded that the increasing pressure on men to conform to a 'buff' physical aesthetic, combined with the increasingly normalised expectation of gym attendance, could be partly to blame.

Philippa talks of her partner's journey through suffering from bigorexia:

> Despite my partner going to the gym every day and obviously gaining size in muscle mass, he just couldn't see it. It was more than just him not being happy with himself; it became an obsession. I used to have to measure his arms and legs with a tape measure to assure him he hadn't lost size. He did finally seek help after quite a long time and things are looking slightly better each day.

Diet pill addiction

The internet has made it incredibly easy to purchase illegal, banned or prescription-only substances which promote slimming. Some are even available over the counter. These drugs can be seen as being a 'quick fix', with some claiming to increase metabolism and others to purge the body of all fat within any food consumed.

As some of these pills often contain, or emulate, recreational drugs such as speed, they may provide a chemical 'high' in addition to causing weight loss. They can be highly addictive, and sufferers of this condition may find that they need to take increasingly large quantities of the drug in order to achieve the same 'buzz'.

The suppliers of these drugs, in order to entice people into what is usually a lengthy period of taking them, often offer a 'free month-long trial', knowing that this will, in most cases, result in the person wanting or needing more. It is a psychological as opposed to a physical dependence; however, it feels very real and powerful to the person addicted to the diet pills.

Lauren, who took an illegal diet pill in increasingly high doses for almost two years, recalls how she fell into this dangerous trap:

A friend told me about a website where you could buy pills that not only made you skinny but also so you never felt like eating. I started taking two every day. They made me feel super switched-on. I never felt hungry but I also never felt tired. I was losing weight so fast – I thought it was the magic solution to all my problems. I started taking more and more. It was only when I experienced heart palpitations and passed out in college one day that I was scared into stopping.

Diet-pill addiction has all the same perils as addiction to any other illegal substance.

Extreme dieting

With an estimated 43 per cent of people in the Western world presently 'on a diet', it is little wonder that occasionally this can become both dangerous and extreme. When dieting becomes an obsession, it is usually characterised by strict rules which the sufferer believes they cannot deviate from under any circumstances.

Maria, who spent most of her twenties and thirties yo-yo dieting, remembers her mentality at the time:

> You become more and more strict with yourself. You push yourself
> to see how little you can survive on, or how 'healthy' you can be.
> And by healthy I mean no fat, no dairy, no carbs, which of course
> isn't healthy at all. In the end it becomes an obsession. And you
> become so fixated on your diet, it stops you living your life. You
> can't go out for a meal; you can't enjoy chocolate in front of the
> telly with your boyfriend. Your simple pleasures are taken away.

As Maria's testimony demonstrates, extreme dieters set themselves up to fail because the rules they impose are so unrealistic. They constantly batter their self-esteem because they have not succeeded in living up to their own strict guidelines.

You may often find the sufferer attaching a moral significance to certain foods. Some foods are 'good' and others 'bad'. This inevitably leads to the subject fantasising constantly about 'forbidden' foods. In situations where their resolve is weakened, and they eat these 'forbidden' foods – for example, a social occasion or when they have been drinking alcohol – the dieter may feel compelled to purge.

This is distinct from bulimia because the sufferer does not binge in the same way and their binge/purge behaviour is sporadic and inconsistent. However, the condition is very dangerous psychologically, not least because the sufferer is fixated on food.

Drunkorexia

This slang term originated in colleges and universities. It mostly affects the 18–25 age group and is characterised by starving all day to 'conserve' the daily calorie allowance which can then be 'used' in a drinking binge in the evening. As one ex-sufferer observed, 'It's like the Weight Watchers points system gone totally mental.'

The perceived advantage, other than avoidance of weight gain, is that drinking on an empty stomach leads to faster inebriation, hence saving money. Consequences can include liver damage, malnutrition and osteoporosis.

Routine starvation

Sufferers of this condition see periods of starvation as 'necessary' in order to maintain their physique. They will often go without food for a few days at a time. They do not consider this to be unhealthy, or worrying, but simply a way of life.

Elise, a model, says:

> In my industry it's considered totally acceptable to starve yourself totally, surviving only on black coffee and gum, for two days before a shoot or show. This was considered to be a necessary part of the job, and because I ate relatively normally the rest of the time, I had no idea I could be doing any long-term damage to my body.

As routine starvation often does not result in the more extreme physical symptoms of anorexia nervosa, such as loss of periods, sufferers would not be diagnosed as having anorexia. However, they are likely to be malnourished and have hormonal imbalances as a result of their behaviour. They also run the risk of long-term health problems, such as osteoporosis.

Purging without bingeing

This condition is categorised by eating small portions of food and then purging, either by the sufferer making themselves sick or by taking laxatives.

As sufferers do not binge on large quantities of food, they miss an essential element in the diagnosis of bulimia. The condition has more in common with anorexia, or orthorexia.

Wannarexia

'Wannarexia' was a term coined to make the distinction between the causal elements of anorexia nervosa. Increasingly over recent years, teenagers in particular cite 'fitting in' or wanting to emulate celebrities and models as their reason for hugely restricting their food intake. Many medical professionals and eating disorder sufferers would argue that this does not fit the criteria for anorexia, which is an intensely private psychological illness, often linked to OCD and feelings of control.

This is a controversial area, since most experts in the field generally conclude that anorexia arises from a combination of emotional reasons and body dissatisfaction, or at least that the illness is fuelled to some degree by super-slender beauty paradigms. The distinction between anorexia and wannarexia is, therefore, not always crystal clear.

What is certain, however, is that wannarexia is no less dangerous or deadly than anorexia – the symptoms are identical. The difference lies in the sufferer's reasons for starving themselves.

Fatorexia

'Fatorexia' is a pop culture term which describes someone who is overweight but unable or unwilling to acknowledge it. It is believed that people suffering from fatorexia see a slim figure when they look in the mirror.

Manorexia

'Manorexia' is a slang term for anorexia in men and boys. As discussed earlier, anorexia increasingly affects men and is not an exclusive term, so campaigners for male eating disorder awareness often take offence at this term being used.

In conclusion

This brief guide to terms will hopefully help you to gain a familiarity with conditions which you might see described in the press or online under the topic of eating disorders. Some are recognised medical terms; others are simply slang terms for sociological phenomena. All the disorders defined here have been diagnosed relatively recently.

Chapter 4

Recognising an eating disorder and seeking treatment

Having an understanding of how the disordered mind of someone suffering from an eating disorder works and being knowledgeable on the subject are probably the two most powerful tools you, as the carer, can have when confronting a loved one or friend that you think may be suffering from an eating disorder.

The bridge between being ill and seeking and receiving treatment in eating disorder sufferers is a precarious one to navigate, not only for sufferers themselves, but also for the people surrounding them. Leading up to and after diagnosis, many parents, partners and / or carers of eating disorder sufferers can make themselves ill by worrying, blaming themselves, raking over the past with a fine-toothed comb and frantically trying to pin-point where they went wrong. Sleepless nights, high levels of stress and even depression can ensue. From my own experience and that of others, I can honestly say that this is totally counterproductive, because the feelings of guilt can run two ways – eating disorder sufferers tend to have a hugely over-developed sense of guilt, which can be magnified when they see the effect their illness is having on their loved ones and friends. Their solution to these feelings of shame, is usually to bury themselves further in their illness, and so the situation can become a vicious cycle.

The causal reasons for eating disorders are quite often simple and seemingly insignificant. A throwaway comment or the type of teasing most children encounter at some stage in their school years can spark the beginnings of an eating disorder in one person, whereas it would have no effect whatsoever on another. It is all contingent upon a number of factors. Sometimes, of course, eating disorders can arise from trauma, abuse or violence in the home or outside it. When someone exhibits the symptoms of an eating disorder, the people around them can often assume a traumatic incident has occurred of which they are unaware and wrongly blame themselves for not having noticed or prevented it.

It is also important for parents, partners and carers to be well enough to be involved in the process of recovery. It is essential for all concerned that carers try to maintain their own physical and emotional wellbeing during this incredibly difficult time. Whether the sufferer is young and still living at home or older, the people around them will be of the utmost importance in supporting and guiding them towards health and recovery. Not isolating yourself and maintaining good relationships with friends can also help to maintain your emotional equilibrium, as a carer.

My own close friend, Kate, says:

> During this stressful time, the only way I felt able to help Lynn was to be there for her when she needed to talk or have a shoulder to cry on. I had not had any previous experience of anorexia, so I didn't feel equipped to offer advice. Hopefully, being available to talk, or just listen, at any time of day or night was some comfort.

It was!

Unfortunately, there is no quick and easy laboratory test that can give an immediate diagnosis. Focusing on the physical symptoms only can lead to maybe missing the emotional signs. Knowing this can be the parent's/carer's biggest ally, as eating disorders can often be difficult to identify in the early stages. However, there are certain patterns and tendencies that may help you to determine whether something could potentially be amiss. In my personal experience, a dramatic change in personality and behaviour can be one of the biggest warning signs. Whether your loved one is usually eccentric and quirky or insular and private, you may know them well enough to be able to recognise the differences over and above their usual mannerisms.

Recognising an eating disorder

In terms of the starting point towards recovery, often someone we know can be in very obvious need of treatment from an eating disorder. The most frustrating thing, however, is when it is obvious to everyone but the person actually suffering. Eating disorders hinge crucially on denial and self-delusion. In many cases, the conscious and unconscious parts of the sufferer's mind are at war. While they are aware, logically, that what they are subjecting their bodies to is damaging, they also believe overwhelmingly that they are in control and that they are a unique case. This is where parents, friends or partners need to be emotionally tuned-in to their loved one, as focusing on the physical symptoms alone may lead them to be missing the emotional signs that something is amiss.

My husband, Kevin, looks back at the time he realised something really was wrong:

> At the beginning of my Sam's illness I could not see that anything was wrong, to be honest. I just thought she had lost weight and slimmed down, and was going through a quiet stage. It wasn't until we were all on the beach with some friends when one of my mates asked me where Sam was, and I said she was 'over there'; he followed with, 'Oh, I didn't recognise her. She looks different.' (He had seen her only two weeks before.) Then I realised something was not right.

In my personal experience, as I have said, a dramatic change in personality and behaviour can be one of the biggest warning signs. To give you more of an idea, below is a reminder of some of the emotional and behavioural changes that may be present in someone with an eating disorder. The person may:

- show some sort of secretive behaviour around food
- have rituals either before, during or after eating, such as taking an extra interest in how it is prepared and cooked, pushing the food around the plate, cutting food into tiny piece, separating the food into food groups on the plate and/or always going to the bathroom after a meal
- make excuses to avoid family mealtimes
- push aside hobbies they once enjoyed and avoid friends and social occasions
- seem tired, stressed or preoccupied
- exhibit mood swings and a change from their normal personality – this is key.

Once your attention has been drawn to some of the initial personality changes, you may gradually start to notice other behaviours emerging, which are out of character for that person. As an eating disorder is an illness of the mind, and cannot always be seen, the person's disordered thoughts may be more difficult to detect initially. So once again, the person's behaviour and overall demeanour can play a crucial part in recognising something is not quite right, thereby potentially leading to early intervention.

Samantha looks back:

My mum noticed almost straight away that I had changed from being bubbly and talkative at the dinner table to being withdrawn and preoccupied; this was mainly due to the internal argument I was having with 'Ana' in my head, which made it difficult to hold a conversation with anyone else other than myself. I found it easier to be quiet and on my own as 'Ana' likes you to herself, and it was easier to please her at the time. Thankfully mum never gave up and eventually I gave in and told her everything, and that is when things started to change.

Some of the physical signs might include:

- Weight change, up or down (although we also know that eating disorders can be present without an obvious change in weight)
- Stomach issues
- Difficulty concentrating
- Sleep problems
- Dry skin, nails, and hair
- Feeling cold all the time
- Dental issues
- Dizziness.

It is important to say here that just because someone is showing some or all of these symptoms, it does not necessarily mean that they have an eating disorder. As a loved one or caregiver I would advise you to use your own intuition to guide you in identifying whether these symptoms are typical of the person you know or are somewhat out of character for them.

As I have emphasised, eating disorders can strike anyone at any time, and they derive from many different factors. For some people, these triggers may include events or times in their lives which have caused them particular stress or anxiety, which may contribute to their risk of developing a disordered relationship with food. These can occur at any age and to any demographic. Below is a list of possible triggers, although it is by no means exhaustive.

- Transitions at school, whether moving from one school to another or entering a new or more challenging phase at their current school.

- Starting university, as people move away from home, face deadlines and social pressures, and take responsibility for preparing their own food.
- Relationship changes, whether that is their own relationship breaking down or someone close to them, such as their parents, splitting up.
- Bereavement – for all ages, trying to make sense of losing a loved one can be a time of immense anxiety.
- Illness can cause a big upset in people's lives, leaving them feeling that their body is out of their control. They may also lose weight, receiving positive comments that spur them on to further weight loss.
- Abuse, assault or a traumatic incident may also play a part in the onset of an eating disorder.
- Puberty can be very traumatic for some young people, with the biological, psychological and social changes it brings leading to huge anxiety for some.
- Eating disorders happen at all ages, and later life events – including children leaving home, retirement and the death of a loved one – can be very traumatic. The frightening speed and life-changing nature of these events can be very hard to cope with.
- Sport, while being important for good health, can also be a very competitive environment, where a correlation is sometimes drawn between a person's weight and their sporting success.

The importance of early intervention

The way in which you, as a loved one or carer, act at this point is very important. It is of course tempting to adopt a wait-and-see approach, but the vice-like grip that eating disorders can have on a sufferer's mind-set can develop or worsen with astonishing speed. Waiting for more obvious physical signs may mean that you could underestimate the rapid psychological rampage of the eating disorder.

Chris, father of Kate who is now fully recovered, offers his advice:

> Don't kid yourself nothing is happening and get enough of the right help fast – don't skimp on it – and throw yourselves fully into the treatment.

We know that it is possible to make a full recovery from an eating disorder – there is always hope – but we also know that the earlier that sufferers are able to access treatment and receive the right help, the better chance they have of making a full recovery. At the time of writing this book, according to Beat, the eating disorder charity, on average sufferers are waiting for almost three years between their symptoms first emerging and treatment starting. This is worrying, not least because there is evidence to suggest that after around three years, it can become much harder to have a positive impact on the severity of the eating disorder.[12] Ulrike Schmidt, Professor of Eating Disorders at King's College London, which has set up a rapid early intervention service (FREED), describes eating disorders as a 'race against time'. However, for many parents, carers and friends, the reality is that the sufferer has to first acknowledge that there is an issue and, second, want to do something about it. There are few things more exasperating than watching someone we care about suffer and being unable to intervene. So what can be done in the meantime?

Again, knowledge is power and there is no better way to use this frustrating time than by increasing your knowledge. There is a huge variety of treatments available and it is important to understand what they entail and how they work. In this way, when the sufferer expresses a desire to get better, their friends and family can leap into action and find the most appropriate source of help as quickly as possible.

Jan, whose husband suffers from bulimia, talks of when he finally was ready for help:

> Trying to approach the subject without my husband 'exploding' was the biggest problem at first. It wasn't until he had a complete breakdown that we were able to talk openly about it and he sought help from his GP.

William, Jan's husband, follows with:

> I suffered a breakdown and visited my GP. Shortly before this I had been eating excessively and purging many times per day and had found that the beneficial effects that bulimia had provided, namely relieving anxiety and tension, had become ineffective. In summary, my 'friend' wasn't working any more for me!

The speed with which you, as a parent or carer, might act at this point in time is also of paramount importance. Often the sufferer might yearn for recovery in peaks and troughs, so it's important to place them in a positive and suitable environment while they are in the correct frame of mind and before any seeds of self-doubt sown by their eating disorder can begin to fester and grow. Providing consistent support throughout the recovery process will mean so much to your loved one.

Melissa, mother to Kate who is fully recovered from anorexia nervosa, speaks of how early intervention is key:

> The treatment was practical and positive and I could see it working so that's what mattered to me – that if effective help is put in place quickly and with gusto you can completely overcome psychological illness. The mind is so complex. I don't expect to understand it completely, rather remain open minded…

At the same time, it is important for carers to show that they are willing and able to help at any time. However frustrating and upsetting it is to see your loved one suffer, it is crucial to keep the lines of communication open, so they know deep down that you are always there for them. Creating opportunities to talk can be vital. A simple way to do this is to keep pursuing the activities you love doing together. Whether that is taking the dog for a walk, watching your favourite television programme or going for a trip to the shops, by continuing to maintain those opportunities for emotional closeness, you will not only be giving them the green light to turn to you for help, but you will also be maintaining some much needed normality in what may be an increasingly disordered life.

Starting the conversation

There is no specific time for a worried parent or carer to wait before they intervene, but if you are unsure about the mental state of your child or someone close to you and you have a hunch that something is not quite right, then it should be investigated further. The most effective way to intervene at this point is through communication. It is important to pick the right moment and location: it should be a time when it is just you and them, otherwise the person may feel 'ganged up on'. It should also be a place where they feel safe; phones, tablets and laptops should all be switched off, so there is nothing to distract you or them. Sometimes people worry that by telling someone, it could make things worse. You therefore need to be very clear from the start that you are there to support and help them, and that you will not do anything without discussing it with them first.

Communication should take place in a straightforward manner. Do not assume that you know what the problem is; you might be mistaken and could run the risk of talking for ages about something that they cannot relate to. Let them tell you about their feelings and fears first.

The most important thing is not to judge them, whatever they may say to you; this may cause them to clam up. Show them that you respect their emotions and also their view point, even if you do disagree with certain things that they may be telling you.

Watching for reactions is important. You can tell when you have hit on a sore point or are getting close to an uncomfortable subject by their eye contact, body language and how quick they are to defend themselves.

Remain calm. Although you are unlikely to feel calm inside, you must try to remain strong in the situation, because if you are not, the person will start to panic. If you do not act as though there is a solution to their problem, and everything will be okay, they may start to despair. They are looking to you as someone to take their pain away.

Examples of how to start a much-needed conversation with them can include:

- 'You have been very quiet lately... Is something troubling you?'
- 'Is there anything I can do to make life a bit easier for you?'
- 'Can you describe to me how you are feeling?'
- 'Would you rather write down how you are feeling on a piece of paper for me?'
- 'You have not seemed yourself recently. Is there anything wrong?'

Acknowledge that the conversation is likely to be hard for them. Tell them that you are proud of the strength they are demonstrating in telling you about their issues. They might also be reassured if you tell them that there is nothing they could say that will make you stop loving them. Tell them it is okay to be frightened and they do not have to put on a brave face, because you will work it out together.

Chapter 4

My Charlotte shares her thoughts:

> Having been around mental illness for 12 or so years, and from now working with Mum, I have seen how mental illness impacts the lives of everyone around it, not just the sufferer but also family and friends. One of the most important things I have learnt is to talk. If you think something is wrong with a family member, friend or loved one, always talk with someone you trust; try not to brush things under the carpet, and be as open and honest as you can be.

Starting the journey to recovery: the sufferer

The person suffering may well be uncharacteristically cunning, creating distractions to mask the symptoms and their excessive behaviours – anything to avoid facing their problem. They could go to extreme lengths to cover up the fact that anything is wrong, but this does not mean that they are intentionally being deceiving, calculating and/or dishonest; it is all part of their illness, challenging their usually rational thoughts.

The first and most important step towards eating disorder recovery is that the sufferer must want to get better themselves. As soul destroying as it is, attempts to rehabilitate sufferers who are not yet ready to acknowledge and deal with the problem are likely to prove fruitless. (However, with the assistance of the right kind of therapy and a positive environment, a sufferer can be stabilised, so that their condition does not worsen. Getting actively better is what requires the sufferer to engage totally with treatment and the recovery process.)

Daphne, 31, says:

> In the midst of my bulimia nervosa, I honestly felt no connection at all to other bulimics. My eating disorder was my best friend and my worst enemy rolled into one constant

companion. I knew I was doing untold damage to my body, but I honestly thought I was beyond help and that no one could ever really understand. When my friends and family attempted to intervene I was angry and irrational, because I wasn't ready to get better.

Daphne went on to make a complete recovery and has been healthy for 11 years. Her story highlights this first and most important step towards eating-disorder recovery: the sufferer must want to get better.

As discussed earlier in this book, each eating disorder manifests itself in a unique way, because each sufferer is unique. In the same way, there is sadly no 'ultimate treatment'. While one anorexia sufferer might respond incredibly well to a certain treatment, it may have little or no effect on someone else who may have also been diagnosed with anorexia nervosa. For some, a combination of therapies might be the answer. Whatever the decision, it is essential that the sufferer and their loved ones choose a course of therapy which fuels and strengthens their desire to recover.

Providing consistent support throughout the recovery process will mean so much to your loved one. As Gemma Oaten, an actress, says:

I think I got better because, as well as me taking control, my parents did too. They didn't just sit back and hand me over to all those units and hospitals. Sometimes they had no choice, especially in the early stages when we were all completely ignorant of what was going on and my life was in the balance. However, my parents pushed the boundaries and fought for the right help for me, whilst educating themselves and really understanding the illness. They also at all times remembered that I was their daughter ... a real person ... I wouldn't be here without them.

General practitioners

After having recognised that there is a problem, whether it be the sufferer themselves reaching out for help or a loved one encouraging them, the first port of call should be the local general practitioner (GP). At this stage, please remember that no one's time is ever wasted even if the diagnosis is not an eating disorder, but the earlier the condition is identified, the earlier intervention can take place, with the hope of a quicker and more effective recovery for the sufferer and their family.

Actively seeking help can be a vital first step forward towards recovery. However, it is important to remember that GPs are not miracle workers or mind readers, nor are they mental health specialists, and whilst some may have substantial knowledge and a special interest in eating disorders and/or other mental health issues, some may not. Sadly, the very limited time slot that they are allocated for each patient can sometimes be insufficient to assess all of their patients objectively. In an industry dictated by guidelines and under constant scrutiny, time is one thing most GPs are unable to offer. While awareness of eating disorders and body image is growing, there appears still to be a lack of practical medical advice available. Elisabeth, whose daughter suffered from anorexia, says:

> On the GP's surgery walls there is information on virtually every other ailment, but nothing about eating disorders. It's almost as if it's the silent time-bomb that no one wants to set off.

Ahead of the GP's appointment, it may be helpful if the sufferer (and/or the carer) makes a list highlighting their symptoms and how they feel they have changed over time. In doing so, it may help them if they become anxious during their time at the surgery and forget the crucial facts. A diagnosis is only as reliable as the information the patient provides so keeping the lines of communication as open as possible with the GP will assist greatly in their diagnosis and being able to move forward, not only in the initial appointment but in the long term. It might also be extremely helpful to arrange for someone to accompany the sufferer to their appointment; having an advocate present is beneficial to both parties and can help the sufferer understand and remember the information given to them by the GP, whilst feeling reassured that they are being supported and listened to.

It is really important, at this stage, to encourage the sufferer to be as open and honest as they feel they can be with their GP in the time frame they have, however frightening, uncomfortable and complicated the experience may be. The GP will make an initial assessment based on the information they have been given and hopefully offer both support and the relevant treatment route for their patient.

Helena, mother of Greg who is now in recovery from binge eating disorder, says of when her son first visited the GP and how not being completely honest led to difficulty in diagnosis and therefore early intervention:

I took my son to the GP when I became aware of his worrying eating cycles and emotional ups and downs. I think, looking back, I took him too soon; he was not ready to admit he needed help and was very good at covering up his emotions. During the 10-minute GP appointment Greg was able to cover up the emotional attachment he had to food that was later revealed when he got to his lowest point with the binge eating disorder, which is when he realised he needed help. On his first visit to the GP we came away feeling as though we were worried about nothing and that he just enjoyed his food a little too much. I cannot put the blame on the GP as the GP only worked with what they were told, and when we went back a few months later, the GP was wonderful and put us in the right direction for help.

Expectations of GPs can be unfairly high and unfortunately not all appointments will conclude the way the patient or carer would like, so if this is the case it would be prudent to make another appointment straight away to see either another GP in the practice or consider alternative treatments in the private healthcare system. Diagnosing eating disorders can be a difficult path for a GP to tread. Unfortunately, due to a lack of facilities and increasingly stretched budgets, GPs are frequently left in a precarious situation, unsure whether they should refer patients for specialist help. With long waiting time for that expert support, even if they do make a referral, there may be another wait before that help is made available. The situation is even worse for the over-18s, with help for adults with eating disorders being even more patchy than they are for children.

Debbie Roche, founder of the Plymouth-based eating disorder support group NotEDuk, and chairperson of Men Get Eating Disorders Too, whose son Ollie is in recovery from anorexia, summarises her experience as a carer when she says:

> I know I would do exactly the same again. However, I would have more of an understanding of the complexities of anorexia nervosa. I would be more knowledgeable of the rights of sufferers and their families and I would begin to shout for necessary changes a great deal sooner.

There is no right or wrong way at this juncture, but weighing up the advantages and disadvantages of joining an NHS waiting list as opposed to seeking private alternative help should be carefully thought through. Private treatment costs money and this may prove a stumbling block for some so my advice to parents, loved ones and caregivers would be to read and research as much as you possibly can about the diagnosis. Knowledge is power and will help you make the right choices going forward with and for the sufferer.

When our daughter Samantha was first diagnosed, our GP was very supportive, always taking time to listen, understand

and advise us to the best of his knowledge. Anything he was not too sure about he would look into after our appointment and report back to us, keen to work with us in Samantha's best interests and ours as a family unit. When he retired we thought that we would be right back to square one with a new doctor who might have little or no knowledge of mental illness, but we needn't have worried as we were blessed with yet another wonderful GP; she has been extremely helpful, so it is important to remember that there are many GPs out there who will, hopefully, be just as understanding and supportive.

Every sufferer's path to recovery is different, as are their individual experiences of the NHS, private healthcare and any alternative medical professionals they encounter; each person is unique and responds differently. If one treatment proves ineffective, it absolutely does not mean that the patient is 'incurable', it simply means that the treatment is not working for that individual, so look for another; try different avenues until you find someone or something more suitable for the person suffering.

Hannah Rushbrooke, who is now fully recovered from OSFED, gives her advice from her own experience and journey:

> I am now fully recovered from my eating disorder. I switched therapists on numerous occasions... that's one key piece of advice I'd give to anyone suffering from an eating disorder: don't just settle on one therapist; if you have the feeling they're not the right person that you feel comfortable in talking to then move on to someone else and repeat until you are comfortable.

If possible, however difficult things get, try not to allow the sufferer to fall at the first hurdle; it is important to all move forward together making a joint effort to find the right path that works for everyone. There will be ups and downs along the way and very much a 'one step forwards, two steps back' scenario for a while; it can be a long road but acceptance, understanding and perseverance are key. The sufferer needs all the encouragement you can give them to keep going until they get the help they need and deserve, so patience and open-mindedness are of the upmost importance. Propping the sufferer up for a little while is okay too, but they have to be able to walk alone at some point and take ownership of their road to recovery. For the process to flourish and be a success, they really need to want it 100 per cent for themselves. Being afraid of the unknown is a perfectly normal feeling and reaction when faced with the challenge of tackling a loved one and their mental illness. Please try not to feel daunted by the prospect of what lies ahead, have courage, be strong and stand side by side with the sufferer, standing up to the testing times that are to come by communicating and uniting to confront it head on.

Below is a selection of case studies, including our own, documenting a journey back to health. These stories have been told from the perspective of both the sufferers and their carers, to give a real insight into what this period in time entails and the emotional experience of everyone involved.

The Crilly family

In 2004, my beautiful daughter Samantha was diagnosed with anorexia. Interestingly, Sam is a twin. Her sister Charlotte has never suffered from an eating disorder. This led me to the obvious conclusion that perhaps it is not reasonable to blame parents for issues surrounding food and body image. In fact, eventually I was drawn to deduce that I, her mother, might just be able to help.

As I watched my family fall apart around me, I came to the realisation that I could not put our fate in the hands of the external therapists and medical professionals who were so clearly failing to help my daughter. I had to take action – I had to try to treat her myself. It is a common belief that mothers are 'too close' to the problem to influence their child in a positive way during eating disorder treatment. I hope that Samantha's story convinces you that this is not always the case.

Samantha was only 13 years of age when I first visited my GP, John Dalzell, to voice my concerns. She was continuing to lose weight at an alarming rate after recovering from a virus. (It is not uncommon for anorexia to begin this way.) We discussed my fears and he was incredibly supportive.

Sam, who is now fully recovered from the eating disorder, also recalls the positive reaction we had from our GP. She says, 'My doctor quickly realised my potential problem and the severity of it and gave me his support in every way possible.' He also took the time to understand the dynamics of our family, allowing Charlotte and my husband, Kevin, to be included in these early but essential stages of Samantha's recovery. Kevin says, 'I turned to our GP for a miracle cure. Of course, there isn't one, but I did get compassion and understanding.'

However, despite our good fortune in having a GP who fully comprehended the issues at stake and reacted appropriately, his hands were still tied by the inner mechanisms of the NHS. There was a 14-week wait for an appointment with the Community Mental Health Team (now known as Child and Adolescent Mental Health Services). The alternative was a private clinic – an alternative we leapt upon unreservedly, desperate for Samantha to show improvement (which sadly she did not). We also remained on the waiting list for NHS treatment.

Samantha was referred to an NHS dietitian. Charlotte remembers the dietitian as being 'very intimidating and extremely unhelpful'. Her treatment was 'cold' and textbook – she seemed reluctant to make the effort to understand Samantha as an individual, or the psychology behind her illness. Samantha remarked that she 'focused on me gaining weight quickly by using unhealthy high-fat, high-calorie foods, rather than concentrating on my thoughts and feelings towards food'.

The experience made us question the value of nutritional therapy for anorexia, at the time. As Charlotte points out, 'The eating disorder is stronger than the person's own mind' – so how much value can there be in knowing the nutritional value of foods? Equally, we worried about Sam using any knowledge she did gather to lose even more weight. However, I now believe there can be a value in nutritional therapy if the therapist has an adequate knowledge of the mentality which underlies eating disorders and, as Kevin pointed out, 'It would help if everyone had a wider knowledge of healthy eating.'

Devastatingly, not only did the other NHS treatments we tried follow suit, but so did the private treatments. During this time, Samantha underwent hypnotherapy, NHS counselling and private counselling, among other numerous and varied treatments which were recommended to us by 'experts' in the field. Sam says, 'None of the treatments in either the private or NHS hospitals were adapted to my individual needs and I felt very much like a number, with no opinion or say in anything.' She also recalls feeling 'at times, degraded'.

None of the less conventional techniques, which have been proven to be very effective in combating eating disorders, was ever offered to Sam as part of either the NHS or private systems. NLP (page 120), thought field therapy (TFT) (page 129) and Bodytalk (page 140) were never discussed with us, or even presented as an alternative route when Sam showed no signs of improvement.

It became evident to me that none of the professionals who saw Sam genuinely understood her illness. This was when I took the difficult decision to treat her myself. In retrospect, my technique relied heavily on NLP, a form of therapy which challenges negative patterns of thought and replaces them with positive and affirming ones. At the time I did not recognise that

I was using NLP, but having studied the technique since, I now realise that this is where the techniques I was using had their basis. Ultimately, however, what Sam needed, and, I believe, all eating disorder patients require, is unconditional love, time and lots of patience as well as constant support and communication. Communication is especially key, not only between therapist and patient, but between therapist, carers and families as well.

During the time when I was working to rehabilitate Samantha, she remained in what was a relatively 'normal' life. She still attended school and I had regular meetings with her teachers to discuss her progress and to ensure we were all working harmoniously towards Samantha's recovery. The school was also careful to watch over Charlotte during this time and to do whatever they could to limit the emotional effect of her sister's illness on her. I did not think it advisable for Sam to lie on our couch all day, thinking of new and innovative ways to starve herself – I felt it was important that she remained in her routine as much as possible, and was therefore able to see what life might be like after recovery.

Sam is, of course, better placed than anyone to describe the effect working with me towards recovery had on her: 'Mum worked with me to gradually build up an intake of food I felt comfortable with, so I was then able to feel at ease in social situations, which was so important in building my self-confidence and self-esteem.' Charlotte adds, 'Mum inspired Sammie to see life without her eating disorder and gave her the strength to move on, working slowly and consistently.' Kevin puts it the most succinctly: 'My wife simply loved Sam better' – by which he means I helped her get better through love.

Sam has now been recovered for 10 years.

Of course, there is no 'ultimate treatment' for eating disorders, and different techniques will be more or less effective on different patients. However, therein lies the critical point. As I continue to practise as an eating disorders therapist, it is paramount that each of my clients is treated as an individual, and their therapy is tailored to their specific needs. I learnt this from my daughter's experiences, and the principle remains true with every client I have worked with since.

The Mathers family

As my family's story demonstrates, eating disorders have a profound effect on everyone around the sufferer, like ripples from a stone thrown into a pool of water – the consequences are often subtle but far-reaching and significant. The Mathers' family story will be told from the perspective of four of its members: Eva, who, like Sam, began her battle with anorexia when she was 13 years old; her mother, Kyra; her father, Charles; and her brother Josh, who is two years older than Eva.

Eva had begun to intensely dislike her body shape from a very early age. At school, a few flippant comments were made referring to Eva's body shape. These comments were not intended with any more malice than the usual playground teasing, but they escalated in Eva's mind, causing her body confidence to plummet further. The cumulative effect was that Eva developed anorexia in her early teens.

Unfortunately for Eva, she did not fare as well as Sam in the GP lottery, and when her parents realised beyond doubt that Eva had a problem and took her to her doctor, she was met with coldness and hostility. It is Kyra's belief that her GP had no awareness of eating disorders as a mental health issue. She says: 'When I realised Eva had a serious issue with her weight we went straight to the GP. He was most unhelpful, saying it was probably a "fad" and that Eva would become bored if we just ignored it!'

Josh recalls the advice they were given at this time, which was, unbelievably, that they should ask Eva, 'Don't you think you should be eating a little more?' at family mealtimes.

Charles's recollection of these events is terrifying. He simply says, 'I firmly believe that if we had followed the first GP's advice Eva would have died.'

Eva describes being 'shipped off to join the other anorexics' in a private residential clinic. The family unanimously agree that placing sufferers with other people enduring the same condition can be incredibly detrimental. Josh says, 'Because she'd been put in a box with other like-minded patients, I felt like they fed off each other, swapping ideas and tips.'

Eva's condition deteriorated. She reflects chillingly that she wishes now that her GP 'would have listened to me when I was more in control of my mind and before the horrible twisted voices took over completely'.

Crucially for Eva's recovery, her family recognised that there is more than one path to improved health, and sought alternative options, including two dietitians and private therapists. They chose not to pursue NHS treatment further.

Eva had a mixed experience with dietitians. The first she saw did little to aid her progress; however, she then saw a different nutritional expert who was 'more knowledgeable and helpful'.

Charles adds, 'I think seeing the dietitian was beneficial for us, but I'm not sure if a wider knowledge of healthy eating helps much.' (It is interesting to note how his perspective differs from that of my husband, Kevin – further evidence for my belief that no two sufferers and their carers will necessarily think the same way.) He is shrewd enough to acknowledge that, 'with this illness, logic doesn't come into it.'

Eventually, Eva found me and my private counselling practice. I understood Eva and could get inside her mind-set and succeeded in reversing the dangerous patterns of thought and behaviour which had permeated her illness.

The family did not regret sampling a wide range of treatments, and their story is testament to the idea that eating disorder sufferers and their families should not be afraid to switch techniques if they feel that the path they are taking is not the correct one.

Eva's family were left in little doubt that, before finding the counsellor who hit upon an effective way to combat her illness, the treatments they tried were proving ineffectual. Josh was left with the impression that, while the professionals 'understood the illness on paper' they 'had no real empathy, no emotional connection to the sufferers,' which he has identified as 'vital when dealing with eating disorders'.

Many families do not have the confidence to take the decision favoured by the Mathers family and instead bow to what they perceive to be the superior knowledge of experts, persevering with ineffectual treatments. They do this for all the right reasons, because eating disorders are so incredibly difficult to comprehend from an outside perspective. Eating disorders are not like a broken leg, in which case the treatment is uniform and usually guaranteed to be successful. They require bespoke solutions, tailored to the sufferer.

Eva found her resolution in a 'treatment that was adapted to me, personally by someone I trusted'. Josh, Kyra and Charles are vocal about the importance of this bond of trust between patient and therapist. They all speak of Eva's counsellor being her 'Guardian Angel'.

Again, NLP and other alternative techniques were deployed in this instance. Kyra defines NLP as 'the best treatment' and again, as with Sam, emphasises the importance of 'lots of patience and love'.

Josh brilliantly summarises the experience of the entire Mathers family upon finding the right remedy for Eva when he says, 'It was like we could all finally breathe out after holding our breath for two years.'

Eva has now been recovered for six years.

Natasha's story

It is not only anorexia which has a dramatic impact on the people within the sufferer's life. Bulimia is an illness that the average person would not recognise unless they were looking for the very specific and subtle signs, and carers often feel completely isolated.

Natasha suffered from bulimia nervosa for eight years. Around two years into her illness, she realised she needed help and began seeking treatments. None of these treatments proved effectual until, aged 26, she underwent NLP and hypnosis. She's now been recovered for four years.

Initially, Natasha approached her GP at university, who 'actually shrugged'. She recalls, 'It was like he was saying, "What would you like me to do?" My illness escalated at that point.'

A free campus CBT service then provided some insight into Natasha's disorder. 'The campus counselling services were where for the first time I admitted to anyone the extent of my illness. From that point of view, they were useful.' CBT ultimately failed to rehabilitate Natasha, because:

It became clear to me that my counsellor had never experienced an eating disorder as severe as mine before, and I began to get the impression she was using me as a case study. She would ask me to keep food/emotion diaries. When she read them, with raised eyebrows she'd exclaim 'Gosh!' before asking if she could keep them.

Natasha describes her desire to get better as 'coming in highs and lows'. She says:

I'd make half-hearted attempts to see NHS counsellors and (after a 12-week wait) they'd make me recount everything that had ever gone wrong in my life ever, before declaring that it was little wonder I was depressed. I left feeling lower than when I went in.

Chapter 4

Throughout the duration of her illness, Natasha was unsure about the extent to which her family were aware she was suffering from bulimia. Natasha's mother, however, says:

> Once Natasha's illness became serious, there was never any guesswork. I knew my daughter had bulimia and I was completely horrified. No matter how clever bulimics think they're being, in reality they can never cover up what they are doing. It is heart-breaking to have to listen to your child cook something for themselves and throw it all up again.

There is still almost no support for carers of bulimics. And it is hardly polite social chit-chat, is it? If someone says, 'How is your daughter?' you can't say, 'She's mentally ill, actually, and spends half her life with her head in the toilet.'

In retrospect, Natasha, now aware that in fact several members of her family knew about her disorder and were extremely worried, says:

> My illness had made me so selfish, so utterly self-involved and so prone to navel-gazing, that I simply had no understanding of the impact I might be having on the people around me. I'd feel guilty, but it was a huge, all-encompassing, non-specific guilt. The kind of guilt that makes you feel like you've been punched in the stomach. I couldn't see a way free from that guilt – it didn't occur to me that I could make everyone's lives better simply by becoming well.

It was at this stage that a new person came into Natasha's life, her now step-father. Natasha's mother recalls:

> He was able to approach the situation without guilt. This was so important. As a parent you blame yourself for absolutely everything that happens to your child, whether or not it is within your control. Not embarrassing my daughter was also a huge factor. Natasha was adamant with me that she didn't

have a problem. She was deep in denial and because it is all about toilet-based functions and bodily fluids we developed a 'don't mention the war' mentality about it. When I met my now-husband, he said, 'Wow. That is awful. Let's get it sorted.' Sometimes you need someone with an outside perspective to see the bigger picture.

Natasha remembers instinctively trusting this person who was, at the time, her mother's boyfriend, and opening up to him about her illness. She says, 'He listened. He sympathised. He didn't judge. He acknowledged my problem. He made me believe I could truly get better.'

Together, with behind-the-scenes help from Natasha's mum, they found an NLP clinic which provided the key to Natasha's recovery:

NLP was ideal for me because by this stage bulimia was nothing but a habit and I just wanted rid. It is not for everyone, but I knew why I'd become ill, I'd explored my emotions to the point that I was bored of talking about them. After three sessions of NLP and hypnosis, the world seemed different. The bingeing and purging slowed down to twice per week for about a fortnight. Then one morning I woke up and suddenly thought, 'What have I been doing? What was all that about?' When I think about my eating disorder now, it is as if it happened to a friend I was once really close to but never see anymore.

Natasha's mother adds:

A lot of what bulimics are looking for is acknowledgement. I work for a well-known helpline now and when people phone me and say, 'I have an eating disorder,' I say, 'Is that bulimia? Or anorexia? Or something else?' It is nearly always bulimia, and they seem so shocked and pleased that I put it first on the list. Anorexia is seen as 'the glamorous one', but what bulimics are doing to themselves, both physically and mentally, is just as dangerous.

As a piece of advice to other carers, Natasha's mum says, 'I think, given my time again, I would have confronted my daughter earlier. But that is easy to say in hindsight.'

Once again, Natasha's story is testament to the importance of communication. Although she continues to experience a few relatively minor residual health problems, Natasha is now healthy and 'infinitely happier than I was'.

Claire's story

The majority of the advice given to us with regard to weight loss recommends going to our GPs. The reaction of medical professionals to patients who over-eat is crucial. Compulsive and binge eating are often shrouded in denial and secrecy, so an acknowledgement of the problem and the desire to seek outside help are often difficult. Pride must be swallowed, and realities checked. It is also tempting for the sufferer to attempt to rely on diet plans in magazines, on television or recommended by friends, and assume that the necessary changes can be made using willpower alone. As anyone who has ever dieted knows, this is invariably not the case. Compassion and a genuine understanding of the underlying issues are the cornerstones of obesity treatment.

Claire, who is 29 years old, approached her GP for weight loss guidance and was referred to the resident nurses. She says, 'I had tried so many ways to lose weight, so surely this had to help! No, would be the answer.'

Disappointingly, she found that the nurses concentrated solely on the physical aspects of her eating disorder, and then often with only a rudimentary understanding of nutrition. 'The only advice I got was not to eat Mars bars – Go figure! They gave me no real insight into healthy eating and meal ideas.'

Claire also recalls how she felt under immense pressure to lose a certain amount of weight each week. Obesity is characterised by feelings of shame and guilt, so to exacerbate these feelings by putting unnecessary pressure on a patient to reach certain weight targets can, ironically, promote a greater desire to eat.

In just the same way as antidepressants are often perceived as a 'quick fix' for anorexia and bulimia sufferers by medical professionals, so diet pills were offered to Claire on three separate occasions, and she claims she was 'made to feel strange for refusing'. Claire believes that, had she accepted the diet pills, her weight loss would have been accelerated to the extent that she would have met the targets set for her by the nurses. She is not specific about how much she was asked to lose each week, but is of the opinion that diet pills would have been 'the only way you could possibly lose weight at the rate they wanted you to'.

While diet pills combat the physical symptoms of obesity, the underlying emotional issues remain, meaning relapse is likely, if not inevitable.

Claire's boyfriend, Andy, was a huge source of support to her, and instrumental in her recovery. He sums up his feelings during this time when he says:

> We had tried and tried and for so long I felt as if I was between a rock and a hard place. I couldn't push for less food or more exercise without the fear of causing a downward spiral, ending with a beautiful woman feeling like she was rubbish.

Claire went on to find a counsellor who helped her address the reasons underlying her over-eating. She says, 'You can't just eat lettuce all day and expect the feelings to go away. It just doesn't work like that. All the emotions are still there, under the surface.'

Claire is careful to emphasise that she 'hasn't lost millions of pounds', yet the transformation in her attitude and mind-set has been staggering. She describes her food and exercise habits as 'sensible' now, and is losing her excess weight gradually and, more crucially, safely. She says, 'Not only have I been able to control my eating ... I don't panic if friends want to go on a long walk. Most of all, my home life is about happiness.' She cites her counselling as the reason for 'knowing I have the strength to continue on my path'.

Andy adds:

> Now, moving forward, we don't need to worry, as Claire makes her decisions not on her size this week or the weight she was last week. She makes what she thinks is a good choice. I try to remind Claire that you don't have good or bad food, you simply make an educated choice with the tools you have at your disposal.

For Claire the proof is, literally, in the pudding. She sums up her experience by saying, 'I look forward to my long and happy life. I can have pudding or not, whatever I feel like – go me!'

To conclude

As these stories show, just as no two sufferers are the same, no two paths to treatment are the same. As a carer you must not be afraid, if one form of treatment is not working for you and your loved one, to look for and try another which may work for you all. Remembering always that recovery is possible, as Paige (see page 5) shares her thoughts:

> Things will get better. There was a time early on in my recovery that I believed there was no getting better and I would be like this forever. But everyone around me was so supportive and showed me that I could live with my anorexia and not let it get in the way of my life. I would also say that recovery isn't straight-forward. There will be ups and downs and setbacks, but as long as you keep trying, your life will get better and you can live a life of hope and happiness.

In the next chapter we will explore some of the various treatments available, from the traditional to the cutting-edge, to give you an insight into how they work and what they do, and help you identify which ones may be suitable for you and your loved one.

Chapter 5

A guide to therapies

As discussed earlier in this book, each eating disorder manifests itself in a different and unique way, because each sufferer is different and unique. In the same way, there is no 'ultimate' treatment. Take, for example, the fact that one sufferer of bulimia may respond incredibly well to a certain treatment, while it may have little or no effect on someone else who has also been diagnosed with the same condition. For some, a combination of therapies can also be the answer. Whichever decision is made, it is essential that the sufferer and their carers choose a course of therapy which fuels and strengthens their desire to recover, as opposed to drowning and eventually killing it.

In order to be proactive during this frustrating time, one step which carers, parents and friends of sufferers can take is to arm themselves with a thorough knowledge of the various treatment options available. Below is an unbiased guide to many of the different therapies available, both within the NHS and outside it. I have asked specialists within each field, all of whom I know personally, to explain a bit more about their therapy, to help you understand how their individual discipline can assist in combating an eating disorder. (You may notice some approaches overlap with others or combine elements from one with another – this is all part of the wide variation in what works for different individuals.)

Cognitive behavioural therapy (CBT)

CBT is one of the most well-known forms of therapy for eating distress. CBT uses discussion-based therapy to change or reduce unhelpful thoughts about food, body shape and eating, which in turn will reduce damaging and harmful behaviours that are part of an eating disorder. CBT also helps people to set achievable, realistic treatment goals and to reinforce all the behaviours that are useful in meeting those goals.

I asked Deanne Jade, psychologist and founder of the National Centre for Eating Disorders, to describe CBT. Deanne says:

Cognitive behaviour therapy is a talking therapy for many mental health problems. It is based on the circular link between how we think and feel, and how we behave in consequence. Susan is on a diet and discovers that this week she has not lost weight. She believes that weight loss doesn't follow a straight line and tells herself let's see what happens next week. Anne also finds she has not lost weight and panics, she tells herself that the diet isn't working, or that she will never change. She is so upset she goes on a binge and decides to ditch her diet plan. CBT looks at what we think and also HOW we think. In the example above, Anne is 'catastrophising' and this is never useful. CBT helps break these patterns and is known to protect against relapse.

People with eating distress have what we describe as an 'eating disorder mind-set' which dominates their thinking, destroys their wellbeing and maintains their toxic relationship with food. The range of unhelpful thoughts is vast; there may be surface thoughts which come from having the wrong information such as 'purging keeps me thin'. There will be other unhelpful thoughts that are hidden from consciousness, such as 'People always judge me and they don't like me.' Unhelpful ways of thinking dominate the eating disorder mind-set, such as 'all or nothing' thoughts – 'unless I eat perfectly, I am useless' – which cause constant stress and vigilance. Binge eaters who eat a forbidden food may say to themselves, 'I've blown it. I might as well carry on (and start again tomorrow),' leading down a slippery slope into a full-blown binge. People with anorexia have thoughts and attitudes about food and weight which are irrational and resistant to argument. These thoughts are so strong that they can be experienced as a separate, critical and abusive Anorexic Voice.

Eating disorder values are part of the eating disorder mind-set. Needing to be the thinnest person in the hospital is an example of anorexic thinking and usually signifies that there are deeper issues, such as very poor self-regard and feelings of not being good enough in other ways.

CBT is a dual therapy. The 'B' in CBT is 'behaviour' therapy, which guides someone into more helpful behaviour through self-understanding, re-education and enhancing useful skills like flexibility, self-confidence and managing stress. We may use food monitoring together with nutritional guidance to help the therapist and their patient learn to understand and manage triggers to unwanted eating events. This tends to work well with the over-eating disorders.

The 'C' in CBT refers to 'cognitive' therapy – that is, changing the eating disorder beliefs, attitudes and values, including body image thoughts. This is not 'positive thinking'. A therapist who is fully trained in cognitive therapy can use a wide range of gentle techniques to change what and how people think, which in turn will lead to much better moods and a kinder relationship with food.

In recent times, CBT has evolved with useful add-ons known as **expanded CBT**. Cognitive-emotional behaviour therapies address the link between emotions, self-worth beliefs (known as schemas) and behaviour. There are several third wave strategies which are part of expanded CBT such as ACT (Acceptance and Commitment Therapy) and DBT (Dialectical Behaviour Therapy). Borrowing from some aspects of Zen Buddhism, these approaches strengthen your ability to take care of yourself and weather emotional turbulence in your day-to-day life. The beauty of all this is that CBT approaches can be customised to the needs of each individual person.

Does CBT work for everyone? It works more slowly for people who are very underweight and who cannot 'think clearly' and is not always suitable for people with serious issues such as severe trauma or personality disorders. Expanded CBT, however, is the treatment of choice for most eating disorders; it is associated with the greatest chance of long-term recovery, provided it is done by someone who understands 'eating disorder thinking' and who is properly trained to deliver it.

Eve, who is now in recovery from anorexia nervosa, tells us of her experience of CBT:

CBT gave me the chance to have 'me' time and, with guidance from my counsellor, open up about everything I felt and struggled with. Before having counselling, I thought that everyday worries about looks and achievement were just self-centred behaviour and not caused by deep down years of anxiety attacks where I found myself numb, breathless and slick with sweat a lot of the time. I felt paralysed, unable to escape my body. I found out coping mechanisms and felt comforted that my issues are very common and I wasn't suffering alone even if I felt I was. It gave me the time to reflect and refresh, ready to approach my life with a new perspective and grip on it to cope with things better. I still have worksheets now we did and I reflect on them whenever things feel too much and remind myself to breathe. An irreplaceable comforting calm comes from such a simple behaviour.

Dialectical behaviour therapy (DBT)

DBT has its origins in CBT and is similar in many ways. However, it differs in that it is designed to suit patients who have been diagnosed with 'borderline personality disorder' or another mental health issue which is not directly linked to their eating disorder, and are therefore less likely to respond to traditional CBT.

DBT is concerned exclusively with treating obstructive and dangerous patterns of behaviour. It does not search for, nor attempt to address, the emotional origins of an eating disorder. It is therefore only usually recommended for a specific type of patient for whom delving into their past to explore their emotions might prove counterproductive.

Lottie, who is now recovered from anorexia, believes that DBT helped her overcome her tendency to 'mentally tot up calories or plan what I would have for dinner, rather than participating in exercises'. ['Exercises' meant things like homework and housework.]

Lottie was asked to keep a food diary. She worked with a nutritionist in addition to a DBT practitioner over a period of 18 months to ensure she would complete her exercises and not give in to the temptation to relapse. She says:

> DBT was hard work and progress was slow. It required immense commitment. Although it did not completely eradicate my self-harming or disordered eating, the evidence from my diary suggests these behaviours significantly reduced whilst in DBT.

Breakthrough sessions

Deanne Jade, the psychologist and founder of the National Centre for Eating Disorders who has spoken about CBT above, goes on to tell us about her breakthrough therapy sessions and how they work:

Eating disorders are described as mental health problems, severe enough to damage health and emotional wellbeing. It is understood that there are various treatments known to be helpful, and that treatment can take a long time. Yet people can, and do, get better on their own, and therapy doesn't always work at the time when it is offered. A one-off breakthrough session can be the solution for anyone who is suffering, no matter how little they feel ready to change.

I have likened an eating disorder to an energy system, like a tornado, with the person who is suffering being trapped in the centre, unable to escape.

This energy system is fuelled by many different things, such as, fear of change, not having better ways of managing feelings, very stuck habits and unhelpful thoughts about food and weight. People with anorexia also have a voice telling them what to do. Even carers can unwittingly make the problem worse. Sometimes, a very small change can break open this vicious system and start the healing process. In a breakthrough session, we can often discover several things that will kick-start recovery and give a person hope, no matter how sick they are.

A breakthrough session is a three-hour meeting led by someone with great expertise and understanding of eating distress. It doesn't matter how sick a person is, what kind of eating disorder they have, or even how unwilling they are to see us. First, we create a life story in pictures which will bring hidden aspects of their life, good and less good, into focus and show us what has led to their difficulties with food. This is a safe experience and there is no need for us to go into detail of any trauma the person may have experienced in their life so far.

We can then build a picture of what, in that person's case, is keeping the eating disorder active in their life and show them what can be done for them so that they will be able to manage their challenges in far better ways. No matter how badly the person may feel about him/herself, we will uncover hidden resources they have which can help them to move on.

During a breakthrough session, there may be opportunities to do many things which are useful in the moment. We can change the anorexic voice; deal with unhelpful or incorrect information about food, appetite and weight; shift motivation and willingness to change; and even start the process of trauma healing via interventions such as Tapping or EMDR.

A breakthrough session is not a quick fix treatment, so we don't give people a checklist of instructions about what to do next. One thing is guaranteed. You will hear things that you probably never heard before, no matter how much therapy you have had. You will feel fully, deeply understood. Your situation will make complete sense. You may be quite tired but, you will have hope. When you wake up the next day, something will feel different.

If you want to continue having help, it will be the right help for you, but this is entirely your choice and there will be no pressure on you to continue.

Maudsley Anorexia Treatment for Adults (MANTRA)

One of the treatments recommended by the National Institute for Health and Care Excellence (NICE), MANTRA was developed by Professor Ulrike Schmidt and Professor Janet Treasure of the Eating Disorders Service at the Maudsley Hospital in London, UK.

Professor Janet Treasure explains more about how MANTRA works:

This treatment model works to try and understand the causes of the anorexia in the individual sufferer, the factors that are considered to be linked to possible underlying personality qualities, such as, being an introvert, sensitive, anxious and/or a perfectionistic. When anorexia is present, these certain personality traits can become much more magnified, causing the illness to progress further. The person suffering can then go on to develop positive beliefs that the anorexia is helping them to manage their life better.

Together with the person suffering, the therapist will explore their strengths, goals and values and in turn develop a formulation of how the above factors could be progressing or maintaining the anorexia in the individual. This formulation will then inform a treatment plan; this could include behavioural experiments to change some of these patterns and to progress new skills. The new behaviours learnt will then be linked with changes in eating behaviours.

The workbook A Cognitive Interpersonal Therapy Workbook for Treating Anorexia Nervosa: The Maudsley Model *has been published (Schmidt, 2018). This could be read alone or together with a therapist. The book has text augmented with exercises and illustrations to engage individuals in the process of recovery. The true stories from people who have recovered add to the authenticity. The book helps you transform your vicious flower of illness into a virtuous flower of recovery through chapters which teach how to increase emotional and spiritual intelligence.*

New Maudsley Model for carers

Jenny Langley, New Maudsley trainer, says of the new carer-aimed Maudsley Model:

Families of people with an eating disorder often feel unsupported and uninformed about the causes, consequences and conflicts they have to manage at home. They may feel blamed, criticised, undervalued or ignored by the care team. The New Maudsley Model reassures carers that they are an invaluable part of the solution and is based on decades of research.

The New Maudsley Model was developed by Professor Janet Treasure and her team, and shares the skills needed by clinicians within a clinical setting, with all carers, so that therapeutic work begun in treatment centres can be supported and enhanced at home, and there is a collaborative approach. Animal metaphors are used to describe common traps that carers can fall into, and also to describe the optimum approach of the unconditional love and patience of the St Bernard in the face of any avalanche, and gentle dolphin-like nudging if the sufferer is moving into difficult or dangerous waters. There is also the metaphor of the herd of elephants with all members of the caring team working together in harmony to support the sufferer.

The skills can be taught to carers of any sufferer of any age, gender or background, whatever the diagnosis, and at whatever stage the sufferer is in. Ideally, the skills should be taught to carers at the earliest opportunity, perhaps before treatment has started, or even where no treatment has been offered. Whatever treatment programme the sufferer is having, the New Maudsley Model can be taught alongside it to provide carers with skills to support their loved one throughout treatment and after discharge, all the way to recovery.

Whilst this approach is not a substitute for professional treatment, carers who attend prior to treatment commencing can be quickly empowered to navigate the care system more effectively to gain earlier access to treatment than might otherwise have been the case. At the other end of the spectrum, where sufferers have been discharged and/or have severe and enduring eating disorders, carers quickly learn how to better support their loved one and to look at other alternatives where traditional treatment pathways have not been effective.

The model is flexible and can be self-taught using Skills-Based Caring for A Loved One with an Eating Disorder *by Janet Treasure et al, and the SUCCEED DVD,* How to Care for Someone with an Eating Disorder. *Within the research setting, the model has been taught with phone sessions and also online sessions. However, the optimum platform is for carers to attend workshops with other carers. Carers learn to share ideas and in this group setting even the most disheartened carers quickly become empowered to adopt a 'can do' approach, even when their loved one appears to be totally stuck.*

Carers are given a 'health warning' to keep a close watch on medical risk and then a simple priority list:

1. *Pay attention to medical risk: Carers are reminded throughout the workshops that if they are worried that medical risk for their loved one is very high, step in and take over. 'Society expects me to look after you and step in when you are in danger.'*

2. *Reflect on your own caring responses to the eating disorder: Carers are asked the question: 'Who is the one person you can change?'*

    a) Look after yourself first: An exhausted and distressed carer cannot be an effective carer. Regularly review your support networks and coping strategies and role model to your loved one the importance of self-care.

    b) Can you change your responses to the eating disorder? Can you make small changes that might significantly improve the atmosphere for your loved one, facing their own battles with the eating disorder?

3.	*Become a change coach for your loved one. Having reflected on their own responses, and perhaps having made some changes, the carers can then turn attention to becoming an active change coach for their loved one, especially as the sufferers move around the cycle of change to the preparation and action stages.*

Carers can work on the first two steps at any time, even when their loved one is completely stuck. The first steps to becoming a change coach for their loved one involve the carer role modelling self-care, and that change is possible.

Further scientific evidence is accumulating but perhaps it is the voice of the participants themselves that is most compelling.

A helpful course in dealing with everyday situations. Gave hope in a very dark journey. Meeting with a group of people with the same problems was almost as helpful as the content of the workshop. Thank you for the opportunity.

Carer of a 22-year-old male with depression and disordered eating

Neuro linguistic programming (NLP)

NLP was created by Richard Bandler and John Grinder in California, United States, in the 1970s. It relates to the way we communicate with ourselves. 'Neuro' means 'of the mind', and 'linguistic' is the study of language. Therefore, NLP purely means that you can re-programme the language of your own mind – that is, the way that you think and the words you choose to think with.

Michele Paradise, a Harley Street personal development practitioner, NLP trainer, Havening Techniques practitioner and clinical hypnotherapist, tells us of how NLP works:

Chapter 5

Neuro-linguistic programming (NLP) is quite a mouthful but a very powerful set of techniques to enable change.

I had the privilege to be trained by Dr Richard Bandler, the co-creator of NLP, and Paul McKenna, and to assist them on their courses for 10 years so I saw a lot of change right before my eyes and I know how powerful it is in shifting behaviours, especially around eating disorders.

As Dr Bandler has said for many years, NLP is not a thing. It is the study of modelling excellence in others, using the newly learnt strategies and teaching the client how to think on purpose; not just react to their circumstances.

In 1972 in Santa Cruz, California, Dr Richard Bandler and John Grinder set out to study very successful therapists of the time, such as family therapist, Virginia Satir, the world famous hypnotherapist, Milton Erickson, and the innovative psychotherapist, Fritz Perls, to identify the strategies they used to get great results and teach others how to do it.

What they learnt is that we use our five senses to explore the world and map it. In other words, the world is so vast and rich that we have to simplify it to give it meaning and we 'chunk it down' by looking for familiarity and patterns with things and situations through what we see, hear, feel, taste and smell.

For example, every time you see a door in front of you, you have a pretty good idea how it works. You will see a door knob or handle and turn it in a direction that you've turned it many times before to open it. You don't need a set of instructions every time you see a door; they're all pretty much the same and there is a familiar, similar pattern to open them.

Our brain loves familiarity. It enables us to feel like we know about the situation, even if it's the first time we've encountered it. This is especially true with people. We are more likely to like people who are more like us, not less. You've probably met someone who reminds you of someone in your past and you think to yourself, 'They look like or remind me of Uncle John.' If you like Uncle John, you are more likely to like them and feel more comfortable around them. If you don't like Uncle John, they will be at a disadvantage with you and it may take longer for you to get to know them.

We do this in all aspects of our life, especially with behavioural patterns. We develop patterns when we need them. Some behaviours are referred to as coping strategies and we run them every time we are in a situation where we need to cope with something that may be stressful. After a while, we have learnt them so well that they are now stored in our unconscious and we don't even have to think of them anymore; they just get 'fired off' when we need them – a bit like being able to open a door without really thinking about it.

I had a client who started developing an eating disorder at the age of 9 to help her deal with bullying. She felt that her life was out of control and the only thing she could control was what she did or didn't put in her mouth. She used this as a coping strategy and taught herself very well how to do it and that behaviour became part of her life for many years; especially during times of stress.

Even after she left school and moved on to university, she still 'fired off' that behaviour when she felt stressed. It was like an old familiar friend to her and gave her comfort and control in and out of control situations. She came to me because she was now 24 years old and was in a different phase of her life and didn't want to be a slave to this behaviour and knew it was ruining her health.

The metaphor I use to describe this is that we're on a very unhealthy 'hamster wheel' in our lives that seems to serve a purpose for that time, but we hang on to these behaviours too long and they pass their sell-by date, but we're stuck on that wheel and don't know how to get off, which is where I come in. I metaphorically stick my finger in one of the spokes so that you fall off, wake up and find a new and better way to deal with an old issue.

The really good news is that we're not born with that behaviour, we learnt it. And if we can learn something, we can unlearn something; thanks to the concept of neuroplasticity, which means that the brain has the ability to form and reorganise synaptic connections, especially in response to learning. So, in a nutshell, we have the ability to relearn something and rewire our brain with the right training.

So I taught my 24-year-old client to think differently; to think on purpose instead of letting external stimuli control her emotions. I explained to her that everyone is in and out of hypnotic loops all day, every day. Driving a car, reading a book, ironing, making dinner and running behaviours, even bad ones, to name a few. We do these things on autopilot in a fairly unconscious state once we have taught ourselves how to do them.

So I got her to focus on the things that she did very well and very successfully, to model that behaviour and use that strategy for the new 'hamster wheel' she wanted to build to create freedom and growth. We anchored the new strategies to get her the results that she wanted and needed now. She 'woke up' and stopped running on autopilot. She began to think on purpose to get what she wanted and not just react to what she was presented with.

You may remember that I mentioned earlier that Bandler and Grinder modelled Milton Erickson, who was a world famous hypnotherapist of his generation, and they integrated hypnotherapy into any NLP technique for change. Therefore, every session with my client integrates hypnosis, either with eyes open or closed. This gives the practitioner the opportunity to 'speak to the unconscious' where the behaviour is stored and convince it to allow change.

A session with an NLP practitioner like myself starts with what I call an 'archaeological dig' to find out what the client's beliefs, values and strategies are. A client rarely presents with the real issue. By the time they get to me, they are manifesting a set of symptoms and it is my job to find out how the issue began. The history of the issue can be content-free if the client can't remember how it began or the memory is too painful. I then use many and varied NLP techniques until we get the client's desired outcome and finish the session with hypnotherapy so that the unconscious comes on board and allows the client to shift and change.

Havening

As mentioned earlier, Michele Paradise is a Havening techniques practitioner as well as a trainer in NLP and a clinical hypnotherapist. She tells us how the Havening techniques work:

The Havening techniques, which were developed by Dr Ronald Ruden, a neuropharmacologist in the USA, make up a psychosensory therapy; that simply means that it is a therapy that connects the mind and body when treating the client. 'Havening' is a process designed to eliminate the consequences of traumatic memories; post-Havening, the response to an emotional trigger is delinked and/or eliminated. It is extremely effective in removing phobias, stress, anxiety, grief, somatic pain, pathological emotions and many other conditions, including eating disorders.

Havening uses touch, distraction and imagination to create electrochemical changes in the brain to change the emotions around the memory. The client can leave the session with the memory but no longer having the trigger that sets off the negative thoughts and emotions.

We are electrochemical beings and when a stimulus enters the body that is distressing to us, it travels up the spinal cord and quickly passes through what is sometimes called the 'reptilian brain', also known as the autonomic nervous system, which is the life support of the body. When it is overstimulated, such as by a traumatic event or memory, our heart beats faster, we become short of breath and our hands begin to sweat, to name a few of the responses.

It then travels quickly to the 'mammalian brain' and into the limbic system where the amygdala lies. Think of the amygdala as the third eye. It is an almond shaped, grey structure roughly between the eyes. It is where trauma is stored and gets 'stuck' and sets off the all too familiar responses, such as fight, flight and freeze, and two lesser known responses, fornicate and feed. Feed very much applies to bulimia as it gives us instant, oral gratification and can lead to temporary over-eating before regurgitating what we've eaten later.

Chapter 5

When the amygdala is 'lit up', or activated, it can cause the pre-frontal cortex to go offline and 'flip its lid' and we then manifest behaviours that are out of character and harmful, or revisit old habits, such as drinking, drugs, over-eating and under-eating, even if we haven't done these for years. Until the trauma is delinked and decoded, the amygdala will get activated whenever a similar trigger or memory appears.

Havening is comprised of a series of techniques:

- Firstly, activate the traumatic event and measure it on a SUDS (subjective unit of distress) scale of 0 to 10, 0 being no emotional link to the memory and 10 being a very high emotional link.

- Applying the Havening touch, with the client's permission, on the face, shoulders to elbows and hands, releases delta waves which are what occur in deep sleep and healing states. 'Havening' is from the word 'haven', meaning a safe place; we put the client in a safe place so they can delink the negative memory from their amygdala.

- The client then counts footsteps in a place of safety, such as a beach or park. They then move their eyes laterally to the right and left and finally hum out loud two verses of a nursery rhyme. These three distraction techniques enable the client to interfere with the memory whilst being in a healing state.

We do as many rounds of this until we have the number down to 0 or 1. Often, the delinking of the traumatic memory from the amygdala can be done in one or two sessions, but every case is different.

There are four components to the perfect storm of trauma, which is referred to as EMLI:

Event – An event that has caused trauma. It can be first, second or third person so we may have experienced it, watched it, read about it or seen it on the news.

Meaning – The meaning that it has for us; it is sometimes difficult for other people to understand why it encodes traumatically.

Landscape – *What is the condition of the landscape of the brain? Is it resilient or vulnerable? This will be determined by the person's emotional health and can be affected by their socio- economic situation, their childhood, their current relationship situation and their health.*

Inescapability – *This is the feeling that you can't leave. You get stuck in the trauma and feel that there is no way out.*

The best way to demonstrate this is to use my story as an example as I was once anorexic. I grew up in the USA and my dream was to be a model on the runways of Paris and Rome, modelling haute couture. I arrived in Rome on a hot July day and went to my first model casting to a very prestigious designer full of trepidation. The designer's assistant liked my look but needed to know my measurements to see if I could fit in the clothes. I'm about 6 ft tall so have never been petite in build. She measured my bust and smiled, and then my waist and smiled but when she got to my hips she said 'too big'. My heart stopped for a minute and I just wanted to run but couldn't. I asked if I lost some weight could I come back and have another chance and she reluctantly said yes. I pretty much stopped eating from that moment.

The Event was the trauma of being told that I was too big and it encoded traumatically. The Meaning was that I was not good enough and I was fat. The Landscape of my brain was definitely vulnerable – I was thousands of miles from home and didn't speak the language and felt like a failure. The Inescapability was profound. I couldn't go back home like this. I had to stay to make enough money to get home.

The real problem was that when I did go back and get the job with the designer, I still didn't eat; I was living a life that felt completely out of control and that was the only thing I could control... what I ate. This lasted for several years and negatively affected my health.

If I met myself as a client today, I now know exactly what to do to help:

- *Firstly, I would do what I call an 'archaeological dig' to find out what the encoding trauma was. As I said before, this can be content free if the client finds it too painful to talk about.*

- *I would then, with the client's permission, 'haven' the client to delink and down regulate the trauma from the amygdala.*

- *Finally, I would get the client in an hypnotic state so that they could create a better future, finding other ways to gain control in their lives without starving themselves.*

I then teach clients how to self-haven with affirmations to support the healing process. You need no equipment, no complicated algorithms... just your hands.

Figure 1 shows what facilitated Havening looks like in session:

You now know how to self-haven so you can 'interfere' and down regulate any future negative or traumatic events and create a resilient brain landscape. The three pillars of Havening are Healing, Empowerment and Growth.

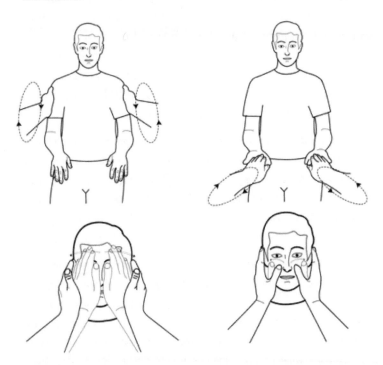

Figure 1: *The key steps of Havening. Images ©MicheleParadise*

Hypnotherapy

Largely owing to the way hypnosis is described and presented by the media, there is a great deal of myth and misconception surrounding it. For a large majority, the word 'hypnosis' conjures up visions of magician-type performers persuading unwitting volunteers that they are a chicken/can fly/have an otter in their trousers. We are led to believe that hypnosis involves the total surrender of the will to another person, who is then free to manipulate their hypnotised subject in any way they please.

In reality, hypnosis is simply a deep (and very pleasant) state of relaxation. It can be compared to when we awake on a Saturday or Sunday morning and have nothing to leap out of bed for;, we tend simply to lie still and enjoy the sensation of being somewhere between sleep and total alertness. We would still be able to jump to attention in the event of an emergency, and we are aware of the thoughts that drift in and out of our minds. It is this state which hypnosis exactly replicates.

Dionne Curtis, a hypnotherapist and NLP, TFT and Psy-TaP practitioner, explains, what hypnotherapy is:

The history of hypnosis goes back to the 1800s and has been used to better people's lives in many ways since; this is done by communicating with the sub-conscious part of your mind to effect changes that you want to happen. It is recognised that only 10 per cent of our brains' function is done consciously, which leaves 90 per cent done sub- or unconsciously. The therapist works with the subconscious mind to create positive change.

Hypnotherapy is a form of psychotherapy used to create subconscious change in a client in the form of new responses, thoughts, attitudes, behaviours or feelings. It is undertaken with a subject in hypnosis. The client is in a trance-like state where their body is deeply relaxed, but their mind is active. We all go into such states of mind naturally in daily life, for example, when daydreaming or concentrating deeply on something.

Chapter 5

The client stays in control at all times; they may have feelings of lightness or heaviness – there are various possibilities. When the client is in a relaxed state the hypnotherapist suggests things that might help the client change their behaviour or relieve their symptoms. The client's conscious mind switches off whilst they are relaxed and their subconscious mind is then open to the positive suggestions of the therapist.

A good hypnotherapist will work with the client to establish the language they use in relation to the issue they want to change, and incorporate this into the therapy session. For example, if a compulsive eater says, 'When I start to binge, it's like I've boarded a train that won't stop,' the hypnotherapist will recognise that, in the mind of the sufferer, they think of a train whenever they binge. He or she can then work with that imagery and speak directly to the patient's subconscious.

Hypnotherapy uses imagery and language to place the patient in a fictitious environment where they feel safe and secure. This will vary with each person, although it's usually set in nature – for example, on a beach or in a forest or meadow. The hypnotherapist will then work with the client to create scenarios designed to deal with their issues. For example, eating disorder sufferers who have had traumatic experiences in childhood will often harbour feelings of guilt and bitterness, which then infuse and spur on their behaviour. A hypnotherapist might encourage them to visualise a scenario in which they 'burn' something which represents their past (sometimes a pile of leaves), setting a new precedent within the brain and signalling that that portion of their life has now come to a close.

Thought field therapy (TFT)

TFT was developed by Roger Callahan in the United States. It is the practice of tapping in a set sequence (algorithm) on acupuncture pressure points to realign meridian energies within the body to promote internal healing. Dionne Curtis, a hypnotherapist and NLP, TFT and Psy-TaP practitioner, explains the technique of TFT and how it can help eating disorders:

TFT is the practice of tapping in a set sequence (algorithm) on acupuncture pressure points to realign meridian energies within the body to promote internal healing.

Roger Callahan developed TFT in the States; it then became a popular therapy in the UK and, to use the words one of the UK's first pioneers in this area, Ian Graham: when describing TFT he says that it is a 'drug free and largely talk free therapy that can resolve many emotional and psychological problems by stimulation of acupressure points on the head, upper body and hands.'

How does it work? There are set programmes within the mind of each of us that cover every emotion – even though each individual responds in a different way from the next. Some people manifest anger by repressing it; others give full vent to their anger by becoming violent or tearful. TFT interrupts the programme between experiencing the emotion and responding to the emotion; this is only necessary when the response to that emotion is inappropriate or disproportional – for example, crying when angry can be a release and healthy, but sobbing uncontrollably to a point where it is affecting life is a disproportionate response.

Having worked with clients presenting with an eating order, psychological distress it at the heart of their difficulty in trying to establish a healthy diet and weight. This distress can be varied in its origin and yet have similar characteristics: from arguments at the dinner table to more extensive and damaging origins such as various unhealthy attachment experiences and distortions.

Food addiction is the eating disorder that TFT is most effective in treating, but it can be used in conjunction with other therapies as part of a programme to combat anorexia and bulimia. TFT is not a full and final solution for eating disorders, but it can definitely help.

Difficult past experiences can resurface through similar external situations and experiences. These unresolved past events could have a triggering effect. Triggers for disordered eating can be surprisingly simple and mundane.

Chapter 5

However, where trauma has occurred, TFT can help the previously held emotion to the event to be released. With any TFT treatment, especially in conjunction with an eating disorder, a mindful exploration and understanding are vital to bring awareness to the coping behaviour.

People suffering from an eating disorder often feel restricted in their mind and subsequent behaviour. TFT is used to promote healthy and mindful behaviour, in how they feel not only around food but more importantly about themselves.

What makes TFT different from other treatments/therapies is that clients are shown how to treat themselves. They are given the correct meridian points to tap and in what order. This has two effects: the client is less inclined to become dependent on the therapist; more importantly, it gives the sufferer the realisation that they are in control of their own treatment and that they are playing a fundamental part in their own recovery. This is particularly helpful when the client faces difficult situations in the future – they have a procedure to follow and the expertise to carry out their own treatment whenever they need it, which is hugely empowering.

Whilst TFT is an extremely quick form of treatment, the client still needs to invest time and be committed to following the practice; there is no quick-fix solution.

Alice, who suffers from anxiety and an eating disorder, says how TFT has helped her:

I was apprehensive at first as I have never experienced a therapy such as TFT; however, I have found that it has been very helpful in coping with my anxiety, which in turn has definitely reduced the symptoms of my eating disorder. I was given techniques to use at home when I felt I was struggling; this in itself has been such a help.

Counselling

The word 'counselling' covers a multitude of different disciplines. Often counsellors will use an element of psychotherapy, CBT and NLP within their method. Most broadly, however, counselling offers an opportunity for patients to talk. Within an anonymous and safe environment, they are afforded the opportunity to speak about anything, while being gently guided with questions by their therapist, which allows them to come to important realisations about the origin and nature of their illness.

Counselling has a number of benefits for eating disorder patients. Firstly, it allows them to feel valued. People suffering from an eating disorder and other mental health issues often feel isolated and misunderstood. Counselling provides a forum for them to explore their feelings. Secondly, counselling is, by its very nature, tailored to the individual. There is no set format for counsellors, which means that they must, to some extent, treat everyone's case individually. As such, it is crucial in counselling – perhaps more so than with any other type of therapy – to find the right 'fit' in terms of a practitioner. A good counsellor should make their patient feel safe, secure and valued at all times. They should establish a bond of trust with their clients and make it easy for them to discuss potentially painful or difficult issues.

As a mental health counsellor myself, I ensure I have met with a sufferer's parents or carers before I commence working with them, if they are under 18. Many people are surprised that I insist on this; I have always been of the opinion, however, that rehabilitating someone with an eating disorder, or any other mental health illness, is a group effort and one which will involve constant channels of communication between clients and the people who are most influential in their lives. If a patient is over 18 and they have approached me independently, I will usually bring carers into the process a little further into therapy. Under the Data Protection Act, I of course have to obtain the client's permission to share information with carers. Once I have explained the paramount importance of trust and communication, this permission is normally granted. I like the families of my clients to understand my methods and the work I will undertake with their loved ones so they can be as helpful and supportive as possible throughout the recovery process. Recovery can sometimes be a long process, with the sufferer's mind-set changing at each stage, sometimes on a day-by-day basis.

It is important that carers are aware of the changes to help them to gain a real insight into how their loved one is thinking and feeling at each juncture. This is why I prefer to keep them in the loop. Before a client sees me for the first time, I research their interests, whether it is films, music, clothes and/or particular hobbies; this enables me to establish a rapport with them during their first session. It is important for sufferers to feel understood and accepted. It is also crucial they perceive themselves as a three-dimensional person, rather than as simply 'A Mental Health Issue'. An eating disorder can envelope the identity of the sufferer. By talking to my clients about their hobbies and passions, I am demonstrating to them that they are individuals, who are not defined by their illness. This sets in motion the journey towards my client envisaging life without their issue – a huge leap in terms of the recovery process. Encouraging clients to acknowledge their struggles and open up about the factors which might have influenced them is not always easy – it requires time, patience and perseverance.

I tend to work very intensively with my clients initially, seeing them two or three times a week. The challenge to negative emotions and feelings should be worked through as swiftly as possible. This also helps to quickly establish a bond of trust and friendship during this time. Eventually this can be maintained with less frequent sessions.

Paige says of her time and experience working with me:

I started seeing Lynn when I was suffering with severe anorexia during university and I know without Lynn I would not be here today. When I first saw Lynn, I believed that I was never going to get better, but she helped me to understand that there was hope and that I would get better. Lynn was there for me every step of the way throughout my recovery, no matter how difficult it was. She was always kind, caring and optimistic even when I was not. She helped me to understand the thoughts and feelings that I was having, and she helped me to be able to control and manage these thoughts. She also helped my mum and dad to understand what I was going through, and she supported them just as much as she did with me. Lynn has been my saving grace and she inspires me every day with the brilliant work she does. With Lynn's help, I was able to finish my degree and complete a postgraduate degree and I am now training to be a therapist. I hope I can do for other people what she did for me. Lynn helped me to get my life back and I will never be able to thank her enough. I know she will always be there for me whenever I need her, and I am so lucky to have her in my life.

Psychosensory techniques and principles (Psy-TaP)

Kevin Laye, Harley Street-based therapy practitioner, and founder of Psy-Tap, whose current work is endorsed and supported by Paul McKenna, explains to us all about Psy-TaP and how it can treat eating disorders successfully:

Having trained in many modalities over the years, from psychotherapy, hypnotherapy in many forms, EMDR, NLP, TFT, EFT, CBT and many other three-letter acronyms (TLAs), I eventually developed my own system called Psy-TaP, which stands for Psycho-sensory Techniques and Principles. It is not a therapy system per se, although many of the outcomes are of therapeutic value. Having spent much time and money learning all the previous modalities and more, I found many of them failed in the long term. Also, our patient/client profile is changing. We live in a world where we want things 'now'... next day delivery, email

Chapter 5

reply, text reply... now,now ,now...!

So the idea of long-term therapy is not that attractive for many people.

I took the mind-set of an engineer and applied it to emotional issues. People come to see us because they are out of control, or have lost control, and feel anxious or disempowered, and hope, using our therapy skills, we can rectify this.

This book, being about eating disorders, is interesting because, as I see it, the one thing the disorder is giving the client is 'control'... the client can control fully what they eat and what they choose to keep down; often it is the 'only control' they have in their life. So the idea of disabling their ability to have this control meets with resistance, fear, mistrust and dread. I believe this is why so many 'therapeutic approaches' fail. I have a good understanding of anorexia in particular, as one of my former partners had it during her teen years and taught me all about the behaviour patterns. I have also done treatments with a number of eating disorder clients over the years and have seen a common theme: in every case I have seen so far, the initial event, which was the catalyst to the behaviour, was always a trauma. In my ex-partner's case, when she was 13 her father told her that her 'arse was starting to look a bit fat'. She adored her father and had previously believed she was the apple of his eye and was a daddy's girl. The shock of this comment meant she did not sleep that night and she vowed to never be seen as 'fat' in her father's eyes again. So she began to run, do more sports at school and watch her diet until eventually the system worked and, bingo, she had control. Such was her fear of reverting back she continued, until eventually she was diagnosed as anorexic. She had 'total control' over her food and exercise, and thus total control over her father's perceptions of her. The story is obviously different with every client/patient; however, the theme is a common one.

I used also to think eating disorders sat in the APB – that is, the Addiction Pattern Behaviour grouping; however, over time my mind has changed on this. APBs often are a form of self-medication to combat stress and anxiety, and to give the person some temporary control, and thus relief from the troubling symptoms. From a neuroscience point of view, this is all based on activity in the part of the brain called the nucleus accumbens, yet it seems that this area of the brain is not activated in eating disorder behaviour. The neurology seems to be more of a limbic system response to the initiating traumatisation.

In my system, Psy-TaP, this is what we focus on. By questioning carefully and excavating the history in full, we hope to find the root of the issue... what happened just before the behaviour became a 'thing'...?

According to the model of Joseph LeDoux, it requires four things to be present simultaneously to initiate a traumatisation. These are the 'Four Is', as I refer to them.

1. *The Initial event*

2. *The Intrinsic state of being of the recipient*

3. *The Importance they attach to the event*

4. *The Inescapability (real or perceived) of the situation.*

So let's look at the earlier case as an example:

1. *The Initial event: being told her arse was getting fat by the person she loved and respected most in the world.*

2. *The Intrinsic state of being of the recipient: a girl who was in puberty, with hormones flying all over the place – an unbalanced state chemically and emotionally active.*

3. *The Importance attached to it: the person who is supposed to protect her is attacking her with words, making her feel an insecurity she had not felt before. This was perceived as unsafe and, as such, traumatic.*

4. *Inescapability: not being able to run away or escape from the event and thus feeling trapped by it.*

Result/ solution/ outcome*: Adopt a behaviour to ensure this never happens again, ergo, control food intake, and her calorific burn via exercise. This response is a pure survival mechanism, and the belief is if it is* *adopted then the situation will never happen again. Damage done. Safe...*

So, in Psy-TaP we find and uncover this 'trigger' event, and then use one of our techniques to collapse it so it becomes an inert, or de-potentiated, thought. To do this we often use a combination of meridian-based therapy, or what we refer to as 'VCART' – that is, Visual Coding and Repatterning Technique. We use eye movements in conjunction with light-based therapy to collapse the primary trauma. The technique often only takes a minute or two maximum.

'Oh no!' I hear people cry; 'you cannot collapse something like this that fast...' Okay, here's a question... How long did it take for the person to pick up the trauma? It is like picking up a bag – it takes seconds. And just because you have carried the bag for a long time does not mean the solution cannot be rapid... How long does it take to put a bag down? If you insist on saying it cannot be done that fast, what you are really saying is you are unable to do it that fast.

At this point I am always mindful of a quote from Einstein: 'To reject something without investigating it fully is surely the highest form of ignorance.'

Once the trauma has been collapsed, the rest of the work is coaching and educating the client/patient in other, better, more productive ways of achieving control.

Although I mention a system called VCART I cannot go into it in much detail as it is taught exclusively to my Psy-TaP practitioners, and only they are licensed to use it after having undergone full training and certification. So, my apologies for the tease, but it is possibly the most rapid and seemingly permanent way to eradicate traumas and phobias amongst many other things.

We do have many other techniques, though, which we use to enable our clients/patients to 'take back control'. These are also rapid, and change the usual patterns of behaviour, by breaking the pattern enough times to trigger an organic change, using the brain's capacity to evolve via something known as 'neuroplasticity'.

Neuroplasticity is the brain's ability to create new neural pathways, and also delete or prune back neural pathways that are no longer being used. Hebb's law states, 'What fires together wires together.'

So, once the trauma has been collapsed the neural pathways that were active and driving a behaviour suddenly become redundant, and a process called 'synaptic pruning' occurs in which they die back as we sleep. The new behaviour pathways fire off and get thicker and stronger, and so organically the new behaviour becomes the dominant one. The brain is simply being efficient and effective by doing this. We are simply utilising the brain's natural processing to deliver our outcomes.

So, once we have removed the trauma, how do we then direct and coach the patient/client?

One technique we use is **finger squeezing.** This is a combination of ancient TCM (Traditional Chinese Medicine) with my 21st-century twist. I looked at a system called Jin Shin jutsu and combined this with biomechanics and neurobiological processing. As shown in Figure 2, all you have to do is simply squeeze or push on a finger to collapse the negative emotional state you are feeling. Once again, this relies on neuroplasticity to organically change the brain and turn off the usual 'immediate' response to an issue that perturbs you.

Try it... it is simple, but it works!

Another technique we use often is called a **positive imagery exercise**. It goes as follows:

- Raise your right hand up and to the right of you so you are looking up at it.

- Look into your palm and create a compelling image of what you want to be like, assuming that nothing can fail.

- Then double the intensity of the picture and brighten it.

- Then double it again and again...

- When it looks amazing, and only then, take a deep breath in and

stress,
Worry tension

Fear digestion, back

Nourish everything

Panic, indecision fatigue

Sadness grief relationship breathing

Anger frustration

Figure 2: *Squeeze the finger that corresponds to the negative emotion you are feeling... (hold for up to 30 seconds, but often the collapsing of the emotional attachment is instant).*

> *as you exhale pull the image into your chest and absorb it through your heart.*

- *Then, as you breathe in, intensify the image and, as you exhale, drive the feeling through your body into every cell, muscle, nerve fibre and tissue until you are saturated with the good feeling.*

- *Then repeat with another good image.*

- *Do this as often as you like... after all, who can ever have enough good feelings?*

These processes set up new empowering behaviour patterns and the client/patient will begin to develop new thinking and behaviours, both rapidly and organically

In Psy-TaP we keep things simple... Once again, to quote Einstein:

'Things should be made simple – as simple as can be – but no simpler.'

Bodytalk

Bodytalk is a holistic therapy, meaning that it is concerned primarily with the relationship between body and mind, but is not limited to this. Understanding the significance of the part the emotions play in a person's wellbeing, Bodytalk literally works on every level of the human being and excludes nothing.

Established in the mid-1990s by Dr John Veltheim, Bodytalk describes itself as an 'integrative system' which taps into the 'innate wisdom' of the body to determine health problems that may be present and to treat them. Dr Veltheim has a background in acupuncture and chiropractic and has developed the Bodytalk system to include the best the West has to offer married with the wisdom of Eastern practices.

Bodytalk hinges on the philosophy that the body is comprised of various energy systems designed to work in harmony. During periods of sickness – physical, mental or emotional – these energies can be enormously compromised, resulting in a complete imbalance in one or all of these areas.

While this might seem a little 'alternative' to some, the success of Bodytalk as an element of eating disorder treatment is undeniable. This may be because the sufferer is encouraged to establish a bond of trust with their body once more so that, just as in NLP, they take responsibility for their own health. In eating disorder patients, the mind and body are at war, so Bodytalk is primarily attempting to open paths of communication between them, hopefully bringing harmony back to the partnership.

Kyra Mathers, whose daughter Eva was a client of mine, has gone on to train as a Bodytalk practitioner. She has an unshakeable conviction in the effectiveness of the therapy for treating eating disorders. Kyra cites one of the benefits of Bodytalk as the fact that the patient does not have to identify their issues themselves. A skilled Bodytalk practitioner is able to establish areas of the body–mind complex that are out of balance and re-establish harmony within them. Often, in the initial stages at least, eating disorder patients are reluctant to open up and discuss their lives and habits with, for example, a counsellor, yet with Bodytalk, 'You don't have to speak at all if you don't want to.'

Of course, Bodytalk may 'throw up an issue which then needs to be dealt with' (these are likely to be psychological elements of the sufferer's condition). The patient may then need to go on to use a different therapy in conjunction with Bodytalk. Kyra is of the opinion that NLP is a particularly effective companion therapy for Bodytalk, so that the body and mind are targeted simultaneously.

She summarises her experience by saying, 'In hindsight, Bodytalk helped alleviate the stress, improve the mood, so enabling Eva to respond more effectively to her counselling.'

Laura Forbes is a Bodytalk practitioner who believes the therapy to be cutting-edge, describing it as 'one of the only truly holistic forms of bodywork in the world today.' Practitioners are trained to identify 'energy blockages' in the body which signify ill-health within the 'physical, emotional, mental and spiritual layers of the human make-up.' In this way, Bodytalk could be described as a 'blend of Eastern and Western philosophies', so creating a powerful therapy.

Laura has used Bodytalk to treat eating disorder patients, but concedes that it is most effective when used 'alongside other types of therapy in a team approach to recovery.' She adds, 'It is widely recognised that [eating disorders] are linked to control, which Bodytalk can help to balance, as well as establishing the reasons for this need.'

Gastric mind band (GMB)

The 'gastric mind band' was invented and pioneered by leading psychologists and clinical hypnotherapists, Martin and Marion

Shirran, for sufferers from over-eating and binge eating. The unique combination of hypnotherapy, CBT and NLP, also incorporating their own brand of CBT, TCBT ('transdiagnostic' CBT), is now often referred to as the Gold Standard in the arena of permanent weight loss. Their combination of treatments is described as 'life architecture'; the therapy promises to help over-eaters and those with other eating disorders reprogramme their mind and create their own food rules, in essence becoming the architects of their own lives, the birth right of everyone.

The gastric mind band places the utmost importance on 'eating mindfully', which we touched upon in Chapter 2. This is the act of concentrating solely on the food being consumed, not allowing distractions (such as television) to detract from the act of eating. The over-eater is taught to 'eat slowly and to cherish each and every mouthful' focusing on 'quality rather than quantity'.

The gastric mind band takes place over the course of four sessions and has a success rate of 75 per cent. It avoids all the possible medical complications of all bariatric surgery options and, Martin says, 'enables the client to become the architect of their own life'.

Pearl underwent gastric mind band therapy at Martin's clinic in 2011. Her story is familiar, in that she saw food as controlling her life previous to undergoing treatment, and had yo-yo dieted throughout her life. She considers her gastric mind band treatment to be an unequivocal success, saying:

> The treatment worked immediately. At first I was very conscious of incorporating all of the mental and practical tools they gave me, but it quickly became a game and now is almost unconscious. It is empowerment. I am in control. Food does not control me. This is huge.

Sara Hart, who is featured on the GMB website, has been featured in the press worldwide; she has also undertaken countless TV interviews. Sara lost half her body weight following the treatment, and 10 years later has not gained a single pound. As Martin says:

> Helping someone to lose weight is relatively simple; the 'magic bullet' is in ensuring that the weight loss is permanent.

Gastric band

A gastric band is a serious medical procedure which involves the patient having their stomach 'stapled', reducing its size so that it can then only take a small amount of food (usually just a couple of spoonfuls).

Gastric bands are a last resort for overweight patients who cannot seem to stop eating using more conventional methods. Beverley, who underwent the operation, says she had tried to lose weight 'every which way you could think of. I joined every slimming club. I tried private diet clinics (who gave me appetite suppressants) and weight-loss drinks.'

Beverley says that her weight left her clinically depressed and house-bound before the operation. She opted to have a gastric band fitted privately, at a cost of £6,000. While she has since dropped five dress sizes, and says that her gastric band was '100 per cent successful, re my weight loss', she does not feel that undergoing the procedure has changed her mind-set at all. And therein lies the biggest pitfall of the gastric band (aside from the potential medical complications during surgery). It does not re-educate the over-eater; it does not allow them to love themselves and treat their body with respect. It focuses solely on the physical symptoms of over-eating.

Beverley says:

> Fifteen months on I still have bad eating habits, though the band restricts my intake. My mind-set is still the same. I still

> want to eat like the big girl before the op. I look in the mirror and
> still see a fat girl.

Gastric bands can be highly effective in treating morbidly obese patients who risk serious illness or even death because of the strain their weight is placing on their health. However, they are not a 'quick fix' and should ideally be embarked upon alongside some form of psychological treatment, such as counselling, to combat the underlying emotional issues fuelling the patient's desire to over-eat.

Medication

According to the NICE guidelines, medication should not be used as a stand-alone treatment for eating disorders. Antidepressants, such as fluoxetine (Prozac), may be recommended and prescribed in combination with psychological therapy, to help sufferers manage the anxiety or depression which may run alongside or overlap with an eating disorder. However, these are rarely prescribed to those under the age of 18.

Lucy, a former sufferer of an eating disorder co-morbid with anxiety and depression, explains how medication helped her to think more clearly:

> I have had medication for anxiety and depression which has definitely helped me get over the toughest stages and free up my head, so I can see difficult situations more clearly with a more positive mind. It doesn't help completely but it does stop smaller issues turning into big ones, like they have done before; it also allows me more headspace to do everyday activities and feel more comfortable in social situations.

Doctors are advised to bear in mind a number of things if they do prescribe medication for someone with an eating disorder. They need to take into account how the effectiveness and side effects of certain drugs may be altered if they are taken by someone with malnutrition. They also need to consider how likely it is that someone with an eating disorder will stick to a prescribed course of medication, particularly if, for example, weight gain may be a side effect of taking that drug.

Doctors may advise people with eating disorders to take vitamin and mineral supplements to increase the chances of their body getting the nutrients it needs. They may also prescribe medication to treat brittle bones (osteoporosis) as this can be a side effect of someone depriving their body of certain nutrients over a prolonged period of time.

Most medications can have a variety of side effects, so it is always advisable, before starting, to read the information leaflet provided. This will help the sufferer and their carers understand the possible changes that may be experienced as the drug begins to get into their system, and hopefully starts to work beneficially.

Medication should always be monitored by a doctor or GP, and the risks and benefits explained. Do not be afraid to ask any questions about anything you are unsure of with regards to a medication. Should you notice any drastic changes in the sufferer's behaviour, or severe side effects, you should recommend that they consult their doctor immediately.

To conclude

There is no 'correct' or 'right' path to recovery. You may find either a single treatment or a combination works best. The important thing to remember is that there is, without doubt, a form of treatment available that can help your loved one overcome their eating disorder. If one treatment is not working, do not be afraid to change track, and try another. It is quite common for sufferers to try various therapies before they find the right treatment for them as an individual.

Your loved one showing a willingness to get better is a huge step forward, and sometimes it can be frustrating and challenging for carers and sufferers when there is a delay in finding an effective treatment. I hope this chapter has assisted you in making sense of some of the terms, buzz-words and theories and will help you in making an informed decision about what to try next, always remembering that recovery is possible.

At the back of this book (page 315) you will find a list of resources and practitioners, all of whom I have personally worked with, researched and/or spoken to at great length about the treatments and methods they offer. I do urge you to get going as soon as possible before the eating disorder becomes completely habitual and, if you can afford to, start a treatment that seems right in your case rather than waiting for state-funded help as this can, sometimes, take a long time to be available.

Chapter 6

Eating disorders and wellbeing

In addition to treatments, which may be effective singly or in combination, it is essential that sufferers – and their carers – also make positive efforts to improve their wellbeing. In today's pressured world this is important for everybody, but at no time more so than when combating a mental health issue. In this chapter I look at a range of elements that can improve wellbeing and, in combination with the treatments you may decide to choose, give the best chance of working.

We live in an age where what was once considered alternative treatment is now becoming much more mainstream and widely accepted. I would encourage you, the reader, to be open-minded towards all the avenues potentially leading to recovery, both conventional and so-called 'alternative' treatments that are available to you. The approaches described below are not mutually exclusive to conventional treatment, but can work successfully hand in hand with it, thereby aiding healing for the sufferer and, in some cases, the carer as well. It goes without saying that basic self-care is of paramount importance, including getting the right amount of sleep, exercise and relaxation. This has been borne out by my own experience, both personally and professionally.

I have asked specialists within each field, all of whom I know personally, to help give you an understanding of how their individual discipline can help eating disorders and general mental wellbeing for both carers and sufferers alike.

Sleep

Sleep plays a vital part in good health and wellbeing throughout a person's life. Getting enough quality sleep at the right times can help to protect their mental and physical health, quality of life and overall safety. According to the National Sleep Foundation, for a person's overall health and wellbeing, school-age children (6-13 years) need approximately 9 to 11 hours sleep per night, teens (14-17 years) need approximately 8 to 10, and adults (18-64 years) need approximately seven to nine hours.

There is a close relationship between mental health and sleep. Many people who experience mental health issues also experience disturbed sleep patterns or insomnia. Over a long period of time, disturbed sleep can actually lead to a mental health condition or make an existing mental illness worse. With lack of sleep, the person may:

- Experience lowered self-esteem through inability to cope.
- Experience social isolation.
- Struggle to deal with everyday life.
- Experience low mood.
- Experience low energy levels.
- Develop depression and/or anxiety.
- Experience an inability to carry out usual social activities.
- Have feelings of loneliness.

Most importantly, being constantly tired can affect a person's ability to rationalise anxieties and banish irrational thoughts. It could feed into negative thinking patterns which are often associated with eating disorders and other mental health issues. This can also work the other way around, with the anxiety and over-thinking that is typical of eating disorders leading to restlessness at night that can make sleep so much harder to achieve.

Tara says of how important sleep is for her:

> Getting an adequate amount of sleep each night is paramount for mood stabilisation.

The night-time hours can be especially daunting for those with eating disorders. There can be a vulnerability associated with sleeping: a dread of the terrors that sleep may leave them more open to, as well as the fear that slumber will undermine the resolve and single-minded focus that they cultivate during their waking hours.

The sufferer may therefore fight against sleep, facing the next day exhausted and even more vulnerable to the dark and irrational thoughts that fuel the illness. So the cycle of physical exhaustion, mental distortion and disordered eating continues, and serves as a huge hurdle to sustained recovery.

While some experts recommend that an adult should have between seven and nine hours of sleep a night (see above), others say that the quality of sleep is far more important than the quantity. For example, if a person has six hours of high-quality, uninterrupted sleep they will receive more benefit than having eight hours of restless, interrupted sleep. Sleep is not just time out from people's busy routines; everyone needs sleep to help both their mind and body recover from the stresses of everyday life. Sleep is a healing process, one I cannot champion enough for people suffering from eating disorders and, indeed, any other mental illnesses. Sleep has played a vital part in my daughter, Samantha's, recovery, as she says:

> Although sometimes I found it hard to get to sleep as my head was full up and I could not think straight, I would listen to relaxation music which would help me to drown out the

thoughts, making it easier to get to sleep. I found that having slept I would wake up feeling more refreshed. Sometimes if I was able I would have a nap during the day which I found really helped me to think more clearly too. Without sleep I did not have the energy and headspace to cope with and move past the thoughts. Sleep has been a major part in my recovery.

Samantha's experience makes so much logical sense, but sleep is often a forgotten ingredient in the recovery process from an eating disorder. Like many people in the general population, those with eating disorders easily fall into poor bedtime routines, checking social media late at night or watching TV as the hours tick by, forming habits that undermine good mental health and lead to physical and mental exhaustion in its place.

Getting a good night's sleep is crucial for both the sufferer and their carers alike. There are things that we can all do to help us achieve this:

- If possible get into a routine of going to sleep and waking up at the same time, although this is always not realistic for everyone, I know.
- Develop a pre-bed routine, which may include having a bath, or reading or listening to relaxation music, getting the mind into a relaxed state; this should help one to drift off more easily.
- Allow no iPads, smart phones, television or electronic games in the bedroom. Some people experience disturbed sleep due to the use of technology in the bedroom and blue light from many devices can enhance wakefulness. Going to bed and then spending time on these devices can stimulate the brain, making it more likely to wake up in the night and then have trouble getting back to sleep, due to feeling the need to check for messages, social media etc.
- Make sure the bedroom is dark and as quiet as possible,

and the temperature is comfortably cool (but not cold).
- Alcohol and caffeine can also disturb sleep, as does rich food eaten late at night, so avoid these.

The benefits of adopting positive sleep habits are huge. For people with eating disorders, having the energy to do things that they love, to connect with others and build a meaningful life away from the illness, are the cornerstones of recovery. But these foundations are so much harder to build if they are exhausted.

Having seen at first hand how regular, good-quality sleep has benefited Samantha, giving her the energy and strength she needed to be able to challenge and overcome the negative thoughts in her head, I cannot reiterate enough the power and importance of sleep.

Yoga

Yoga is fast becoming a part of many people's everyday routine, with many feeling the benefits of it both mentally and physically. Speaking from experience, both the carer and the sufferer can potentially benefit greatly.

Yoga and massage specialist, Debbie Pennington, tells us more about yoga and how it can benefit eating disorder sufferers and general mental health and wellbeing:

There have been several studies over the years in relation to the possible benefits of yoga to sufferers of eating disorders and the results are very positive. Yoga is often used as a complement to eating disorder treatment; the combination of the two have been shown to enhance self-esteem whilst also decreasing body dissatisfaction, anxiety, depression and disordered eating behaviours, without negatively impacting weight.

Yoga is not just an exercise class, it's a lifestyle, working on the whole with the body, Asanas (postures), breathing techniques and meditation.

Maybe even resulting in a different way of looking at life and life around you. The aim is to lead a Holistic life. As you may know Holistic means a balance of mind, body and spirit. These three components of each of us are inter-connected and when one is impaired it has an effect on the whole. Practising yoga helps us to re-align and helps to bring a sense of calm, balance and self-worth back to us, among many other benefits. The process of meditation helps us to focus on something such as our breath to start to eliminate the busy constant chatter of our minds. It's perfectly normal to have a never-ending stream of thought in our heads but it's a fact that a lot of it is worry and non-positive thought. With many people, their eating disorder symptoms can worsen when in a state of anxiety and yoga meditation embarks us on a journey to start to look at our thoughts from a different perspective and then try to eliminate and calm the mind, creating space and a sense of peace, even if just for a minute. These skills can then be taken through daily life by practising mindfulness in our daily activities. If suffering from mental health issues such as an eating disorder, these skills can be invaluable. There are different types of yoga out there and it can be difficult or even daunting to know which to choose. Vanda Scaravelli-inspired yoga highlights the importance of being kind to yourself; this seems to be the obvious way forward to many of us. To make changes you need to listen to your body, going with it and not against it, to take the time to know yourself. It may be that no changes are to be made and we learn acceptance. It is not about pushing your body into that perfect textbook-shape but thinking about what needs to be released to move in a certain way and what needs to be engaged and Tadah! You have found yourself there, and found out something about the real you along the way.

The philosophy and theory of yoga were written down thousands of years ago and they have stood the test of time. GPs and medical organisations are recognising its benefits more and more, which is fantastic. Being yogic does not mean we are ignoring the pathological facts when we have problems like mental health but that we are also recognising what cannot be seen and does not show on an X-ray. Alongside our human knowledge of Anatomy, it all fits together and makes good sense. Let's try to address the root of a problem and not just treat the symptom or subdue it with pharmaceutical drugs.

When asked if there was anything else she would like to add, Debbie concluded:

There's so many benefits that result from the practice of yoga it's difficult to summarise and so better that they are experienced. Quite often on completion of an hour yoga class that incorporates relaxation, posture work, breathing and meditation, you will feel fulfilled, renewed, calm, happy and feel a sense of self-worth. Try it for yourself, and don't worry – no need to feel self-conscious, nobody's judging you in yoga and all are welcome no matter your age or weight or ability. The more you do the benefits and results will be more apparent. One predominant word in yoga philosophy is Ahimsa – I will try to explain this important term. Ahimsa means maintain compassion towards yourself and others. It means being kind and treating all things with care. Embedded in the Vanda Scaravelli-inspired yoga, the principle of Ahimsa is first and foremost related to ourselves. Ahimsa teaches that our yoga practice becomes our way of being in the world.

Mindfulness

Life at times can be hectic, therefore it can be easy to rush through each day without stopping to appreciate the here and now. Paying more attention to the present moment – to your own thoughts and feelings, and to the world around you – can improve your mental wellbeing. Some may call this awareness 'mindfulness'.

Catherine Kell, a therapist and parenting coach, explains what Mindfulness is:

Mindfulness is a way of training the mind to be present. It is a secular meditative practice, which involves being aware of your own moment-to-moment experience and doing so with an attitude of kindness, acceptance, compassion and non-judgement. When we learn to observe our thoughts and feelings, and not engage with them or try to change them, we can create space to respond rather than react. It is in this space that we can break the cycle of our habitual reactions and patterns of thinking, and this has huge significance for maintaining mental health.

When asked how Mindfulness can benefit mental health, Catherine says:

Mindfulness can have a very positive effect on mental health and general wellbeing, and more and more studies are now being conducted to gain longer-term evidence of the mental health benefits of mindfulness. For example, for people suffering with recurrent depression, studies have shown that following their participation in a full Mindfulness-based Cognitive Therapy (MBCT) programme they are less likely to experience future depressive relapses. Details of studies and ongoing clinical, peer-reviewed research in various mindfulness-based interventions can be found easily online and specifically at the Oxford Mindfulness Centre at www.oxfordmindfulness.org. I know from my own work with children and adolescents that the teaching of mindfulness has been beneficial to their mental health in a wide range of areas such as strengthening awareness, attention, focus, emotion-regulation, appreciation, resilience and also alleviating stress, nerves, worry, ruminative thoughts and anxiety. Mindfulness can also benefit sleep. For some, mindfulness is completely transformative in terms of ending painful cycles of depression or compulsive behaviours. Not only can mindfulness improve mental health but, importantly, the learning of mindfulness techniques also provides a person with tools and practices to enable themselves to maintain good mental health, to stay well. Skills such as learning to unlock the mind from negative over-thinking, over-analysing and rumination as well as recognising the patterns of thinking that cause unhappiness, can last a lifetime.

Chapter 6

Reflexology

Reflexology is a complementary therapy that is based on the theory that different areas on the feet correspond with different areas of the body. Working these areas can help aid relaxation and allow us to cope better with the stresses that life can bring.

Alison Fuller, hypnotherapist and reflexologist, explains how reflexology can benefit mental health and wellbeing:

Many who experience some form of mental illness usually suffer from high levels of stress, anxiety, depression and unwanted thoughts which leave them feeling overwhelmed, exhausted and unable to cope with day-to-day life. They frequently find themselves in a state of fight, flight and freeze, unable to break the cycle. Reflexology can have a wonderfully relaxing effect, encouraging the mind and body to return to a calmer state. In a calmer state, levels of the stress hormones adrenalin and cortisol reduce and the body begins to rebalance. This can then help with anxiety and depression by lifting mood and raising endorphin levels that induce feelings of wellbeing and aid sleep.

It is a deeply relaxing treatment and many express benefits of restored sleep, an increased feeling of wellbeing and a sense of calmness returning, thus helping to break the fight/flight/fear pattern. Reflexology can aid digestive related conditions, migraines and hormonal imbalances that often accompany mental health issues. These are usually signs in the physical body that all is not well.

In theory, all the systems of the body are mapped out on the feet and known as 'reflexes'. By working each reflex, the body is encouraged to rebalance and restore naturally. As an example, the spine is located on the inside edge of the foot. When worked thoroughly, the nervous system switches into a calmer state and patients usually experience a sense of deep relaxation.

Acupuncture

Traditional acupuncture is based on ancient principles which go back nearly two thousand years; over this time it has been found to have great benefits on mental and physical health and function. The focus is on the individual and not the illness, therefore two people with the same diagnosis could receive different acupuncture treatment. It is believed, by traditional acupuncturists, that illness and pain arise when the body's qi, or vital energy, is unable to flow freely – therefore, the overall objective of acupuncture treatment, is to restore the body's balance.

Angela, TCM acupuncturist and sports therapist, tells us more about these benefits:

Little research has been conducted into the use of acupuncture treatment for sufferers of anorexia and/or other eating disorders. There have been a couple of studies where acupuncture showed promise as an add-on treatment in improving co-existing problems such as depression and anxiety levels which are very high in this group of sufferers.

There is some literature about how acupuncture, chinese medicine, Qi Gong and acupressure can help with mental-emotional wellbeing and despite the relatively little research on acupuncture for general anxiety disorders, what is out there seems to be leading to positive outcomes in the use of acupuncture for mental health. It has in fact been shown that acupuncture can promote relaxation by activating the parasympathetic nervous system and it can lead to positive mood changes by regulating the body's neurotransmitters and hormones (such as GABA (gamma-aminobutyric acid), serotonin and dopamine).

Traditional Chinese Medicine (TCM) has been used for thousands of years as a main medicine to treat a variety of conditions. It works by restoring balance to the body's energy system, or Qi. It is based on the belief that Qi flows along meridians, or energy channels, all over the body, linked to our internal organs, and when there is imbalance, such as arises from Qi or blood stagnation, Qi or blood deficiency, or an imbalance of the yin and yang energies of the body, it gives rise to various pathologies. However, unlike the Western medicine approach which is more of a 'one size fits all', TCM takes a more holistic approach. The body and mind are very much interconnected. Emotions when out of balance can affect our internal organs, but also an imbalance of the energy in our internal organs can influence our emotions and general wellbeing. More specifically, TCM believes that each organ is influenced by specific emotions: Anger affects the Liver, Joy affects the Heart, Sadness affects the Lungs and Heart, Worry affects the Lungs and Spleen, Fear affects the Kidneys, Shock affects the Heart. Examples of the physical effects of an emotional conflict are: Fear, which affects the kidneys and when out of control may cause symptoms such as diarrhoea, incontinence, palpitations, insomnia and night sweating; Pensiveness, or constant thinking and brooding, which affects the spleen and can cause the Qi to knot with symptoms such as poor appetite, tiredness, and abdominal bloating.

A TCM practitioner, during a treatment, besides using acupuncture, may also use other techniques such as cupping, moxa or herbal medicine and most importantly will give dietary and lifestyle recommendations, together possibly with bodywork and/or breathing exercises (such as meditation techniques and Qi Gong), all tailored to the patient's individual needs.

From personal experience, patients overall report an enhanced feeling of wellbeing and relaxation following an acupuncture treatment. This, per se, leads to reduced stress and anxiety and an increase in positive thinking. In the specific case of anorexia sufferers, and by working alongside a complex network of other health professionals, it can help them come back to full health.

Reiki

Reiki is a Japanese technique used for stress reduction and relaxation that also encourages physical and mental healing. It can also help to support mental clarity and spiritual wellbeing.

Janine Lowe, Reiki practitioner, Feng Shui consultant, NLP and life coach, explains more about how Reiki works:

Reiki is a hands-on and hands-off therapy facilitating deep levels of relaxation, stress relief, energy renewal and healing. Reiki can be used for distance healing using the Reiki symbols. The Japanese word 'Rei' means universal and 'Ki' means life force. Reiki is the universal energy used for restoring balance to mind, body and spirit.

Reiki restores balance to the body's vital energy, allowing the recipient to absorb what they need. Healing is not necessarily curing, but instead is about restoring balance which can include change, which takes place on the physical, mental, emotional and spiritual levels. When giving Reiki, the therapist sometimes places their hands on the clothed client or may hover their hands over the body, moving around different areas of the body where energy flow is most needed, allowing the client to relax; sometimes clients are so relaxed they fall asleep.

The benefits may occur in different areas of our lives, including diet, sleep habits, exercise, spiritual practice, improving mental and emotional health, and attitude and intentions, nurturing ourselves and others.

The ultimate aim of Reiki is to bring about a calm and meditative state and a sense of emotional and spiritual wellbeing. Ultimately, Reiki enhances the body's self-healing process, and its beneficial effects in conditions related to stress and mood, therefore, benefit both the sufferer and the carer alike.

Massage

Massage therapy is a common treatment for the relief of sports injuries, strains and physical rehabilitation. However, its benefits are more than just physical; it can also be an effective way to relieve anxiety, depression and other mental health issues as well as help to improve sleep quality. Although life stresses are unavoidable, negative feelings and insomnia can be helped with the positive benefits that massage therapy can offer.

Chapter 6

Debbie Pennington, yoga and massage specialist, confirms this:

Touch has extraordinary healing power and it is something massage therapists learn about in training. Caring and compassionate touch is something that over thousands of years has largely declined between humans, especially in the UK. Massage is a valuable therapy that is often misunderstood and considered to be more of an indulgent treat than an aid to wellbeing. You only need to look at the animal world to see physical interactions that are instinctive and natural, that which may be missing from the lives of many people.

Several research projects have shown that touch in general, and massage therapy in particular, are effective in reducing many patients' dissatisfaction with their bodies and it also helped to improve the perception of self. Some people with issues or phobias around touch may specifically seek out massage as a way to experience positive touch in their lives. The benefits of massage in respect of eating disorders, as long as the client is accepting of the touch, can be great, including deep relaxation, regulation of breathing and heart rate, improving sleep, reducing muscle tension arising from nervous tension, calming of the mind through the release of emotional stress, and helping to stem panic attacks and heart-pounding discomfort.

Most eating disorder sufferers experience a chronic state of anxiety which can build and build, and massage has the capacity to bring those levels down to base again and re-balance the emotions, helping reinforce a parasympathetic state of wellbeing. This is not a cure but regular massage and breathing techniques can prove to be a lifeline when living with an eating disorder.

Drama

I have seen at first hand how participating in drama has enhanced the sense of self and mental wellbeing of my own daughter. Samantha began doing drama workshops at our local theatre when she was well into the recovery process, but still felt there was 'something missing'. Being a naturally shy person, drama gave Samantha the safe place she needed to explore emotions. It has completely transformed the way she sees herself and her communication skills and has given her the confidence she so desperately needed. In some ways, I would say that it is drama and finally finding herself through it that has helped strengthen her recovery from mental illness. Actor and coach, Dave Spinx, kick-started Samantha's renewed love of drama. He says:

When I first met Sam, I quickly realised that I was dealing with someone who was uncertain and unclear about who she really was. There was a lack of confidence and direction and I felt that it would take something special to get her on the right road. I was only there to teach drama, but in our one-to-one sessions it clearly became drama therapy as well. That special something came from Sam herself. From learning how to listen, questioning her decisions and reaching inside for the right answers, she soon became a different person from the isolated young lady whom I first met. Who would have thought that just a few years down the road she would be completing a full-time drama degree with a whole new future in front of her? I now see a confident and healthy, beautiful young woman – someone who showed the willingness and had the courage to step outside of who she was, to become someone she wanted to be.

Samantha would like to add:

Drama has given a home to my imagination and a place for my mind to run free; it's where I have always belonged but had never found; this is a feeling that makes it worth overcoming any mental illness to me.

In drama, we learn how to inhabit another character. If people can channel this skill and use it to create a confident version of themselves, they can practise walking, talking and behaving in positive ways until these become second nature. Those who suffer from low self-esteem can often go on to develop a mental illness. If people do not understand what motivates other people to behave the way that they do, they can end up believing that everything that happens around them is a reflection of them. People with low self-esteem and mental health issues can often feel guilty for no reason at all. Drama helps them to think about why characters might act the way that they do and understand that human beings are complex and not everything centres around them. Charlie Brooks, actress and drama teacher, says:

> Drama can help with mental illness by themes of inclusion, memory and escapism, and by taking on another character. Self-esteem can be promoted by being part of a team, relying on others, progression, and reward from rehearsals to the finished show.

For shy people, drama is one of the few times in their lives where they can step out of the label of being a shy person. They are given permission to scream, and shout, and laugh without fear of judgement. Drama pushes people's boundaries, helping them to realise that they do not have to conform to the label they have been given. It can help them to realise what they are capable of and what they can be. Most of the plays and television shows that are written are about consequences too. Looking at a human story from the outside, people can identify the ways that the characters might have made different decisions to bring about a more positive outcome. They can then apply this to their own lives, realising that they do have the power to influence what happens around them and, more importantly, to themselves. On a final note, at the time of writing this, my Samantha has just finished her Stage and Media degree at Kingston College of Further Education, something that three years ago, I would not have thought possible. She has pushed herself in every which way outside of her comfort zone, continually challenging herself – never letting her mental health issues define or stop her from pursuing her passion. All of which could not have been achieved without the unconditional first-class teaching, constant care and support from all of Samantha's wonderful tutors – to them I will always be grateful. Some of Samantha's tutors would like to add to this. Laura McCormack, the course leader, says:

Over the last two years the course team have all watched Samantha grow in confidence and self-belief. She has lovely comic qualities and her eccentricity is charming and watchable; she shows a natural flare for communicating a story to an audience. Sam has been embraced by her year group, in part due to her own warmth and openness, and through this supportive environment she has really come into her own. It is going to be an exciting next few months watching her grow to her fullest.

Blair Kelly, one of Samantha's lecturers, says:

I have worked with Sam since 2015 when she undertook the HNC Performing Arts, and she is now in her final year of the BA Acting for Stage and Media. Sam has continually challenged herself, and there is a marked difference between her confidence in my singing classes on the HNC, to the singing class in BA Year 2, and now again in Professional Practice in BA Year 3 where she is making active contributions to class discussions and challenging other students' statements with authority. Sam has transitioned from the fear of getting everything wrong in her first singing classes with me, to being an empowered actor with confidence and flair.

Carlos Santos, lecturer and course leader, concludes with:

Sam is now defined by her successes, not her challenges; they have become invisible to the naked eye and all we see now is her beauty.

Music and art

Some people find it really difficult to express how they are feeling with words. They might even feel that what they are going through cannot ever be expressed adequately by words alone. For these people, a creative outlet might help them to explore and exorcise negative feelings and embrace new and positive ones.

My Samantha tells us of why she enjoys writing her poems (some of which are in this book):

> I write poems mainly as a creative outlet for all my thoughts, but I also feel I have an important message to share with the world that could possibly help others understand and overcome mental illness. The thoughts often come to me in the night; perhaps it is my subconscious pulling out the scars it has wanted to get rid of for so long in a way that can possibly prevent others having the same pain.

Art and music therapy have long been shown to increase effectiveness when used alongside traditional therapies like counselling and CBT. These activities often have a cathartic quality in themselves, without needing to be analysed.

Charlie, who is now recovered from anorexia nervosa, says:

> I have realised that the only way to get my emotions out in a healthy way is art. Now literally everything I feel comes out in my art. Usually I don't realise until I've finished and suddenly feel better. I look back at my work and see something very familiar!

Jan, a carer and former eating disorder sufferer, adds:

> I find crafting helps me to relax and put things into perspective.

In just the same way as drama, art and music are reflections of the human condition. They allow us to explore how we feel and behave and why, in a safe and healthy way. They can also evoke emotions. Some people are often frightened of expressing feelings like sadness and so keep them cooped up. Music and art can connect them to their inner voice. They can be a way of unravelling complex or frightening situations and emotions.

Neil Long, radio presenter and voice and confidence coach, says:

Music can evoke strong feelings and memories. This process can, with the latest psychological techniques, be nurtured and created deliberately. This process could be used to create strong associations between self-esteem and a well-loved music track.

If a person is particularly 'into' an artist or band, this also helps them form a sense of identity and connect with others who think in similar ways, decreasing any sense of isolation.

Performance coaching for carers

Supporting others can be mentally and physically exhausting. As a parent or carer, you probably spend a lot of your time focusing on everybody else, always putting everyone else's needs before your own. However, looking after your own wellbeing is just as important for you, your loved one and the whole family, as they can only be as strong as you are. Leanne Poyner, life and performance coach, echoes my thoughts:

As a carer for someone with any mental illness, there is a huge amount of physical and emotional pressure on you, and you will most likely be living your life through the person you are caring for. By this I mean your thoughts will be consumed by them, how they are feeling, what their day is about and physically this may involve you carrying out many additional tasks in your day to minimise the burden on the individual you are caring for and make their day that bit easier to cope with.

Therefore, it is essential to ensure that you, the carer, are equally looking after your own mental and physical wellbeing to enable you to be that tower of strength for the individual you are caring for. To enable this to happen, you need to take time for you, to continue to have dreams and make short- and long-term plans to enable these dreams to become a reality. Performance coaching is key to this process.

A good analogy of how your life may feel at the moment is that it is like a tumble dryer. All your thoughts and feelings are whirling around, with no structure, pattern or control. Performance coaching helps you to stop the tumble dryer, unpack the clothes and fold them into nice organised piles. Working together with your coach, you can then start to identify things that are important to you, what motivates you and what you want to achieve. It could be big or small; the main aim is that it gives you a sense of achievement and it is something that you have control of. The key focus of coaching is that you are setting goals that are dependent on you, not reliant on other people, and that you are in control of. For example, it could be making time to go to the gym three times a week, setting up a small business, seeing your parents more often, or taking time to read for 20 minutes before bed each night.

A performance coach will not tell you what to do, will not judge, will not give you solutions or tell you what your dreams should be. By asking the right questions of you, the coach will enable you to recognise what you really want, in line with your values, and help you to create your own plan of action, that you will work towards in a realistic timeframe set by yourself. The priority of performance coaching is you, and you need to be living your life as fully as you can, to enable you to have the inner strength and drive to help support others.

To conclude

The willingness of a sufferer to engage with alternative therapies shows that they are seeking positivity and a way to combat and conquer their illness. This is one of the most crucial and valuable steps towards recovery.

For the carer, alternative treatments can provide respite in the form of 'time-out' to help renew their strength, emotionally and physically, and to enable them to face the challenges that they deal with in their role as a carer for someone suffering from an eating disorder.

I cannot reiterate enough that everyone is different, and if one therapy does not work for you or the sufferer, be open minded and do not be afraid to try another. This chapter has provided only a brief description of each therapy. Full details of the therapists mentioned above are provided in the Resource section at the back of the book (page 320).

Chapter 7

Eating disorders and other mental illnesses

Astonishingly and sadly, around one in four people in Britain will experience some form of mental illness in their lifetime, ranging from the more common and well-known issues, such as depression, anxiety, OCD, eating disorders and self-harm, to rarer, lesser known ones, such as schizophrenia and personality disorders. It is important to remember that this figure is only based on the registered sufferers actively seeking medical help; I am sure there must be countless others who are suffering in silence, both in the UK and internationally, adding to these ever-increasing numbers.

My personal and professional findings, more recently confirmed by a survey I prepared in which numerous people kindly participated via my social media channels, support the suggestion that eating disorders may also be directly interconnected with other mental illnesses, such as anxiety, depression, self-harm and/or OCD. A staggering 87 per cent of sufferers surveyed had at least one other mental health issue in addition to their eating disorder. The results of this survey highlight how anorexia nervosa, bulimia nervosa, over-eating and other eating disorders frequently co-exist alongside other mental illnesses.

In an ideal world, someone suffering from multiple mental illnesses would be treated as an individual, so allowing the multiple illnesses to be treated at once; this would be a different and possibly more effective approach than treating each mental illness separately. However, sadly, due to an over-stretched and under-funded health system, this is not always possible.

Aimee shares her frustrations from her own experience:

> Mental illnesses cannot be separated into neat little boxes and treated separately – often they entwine and feed off each other. My local NHS funding body only allows one referral for mental illness at a time – you cannot be treated for more than one simultaneously. This is a very dated and simplistic approach. It is mainly dictated by money and rules of funding, rather than by the benefit of what the patient needs.

Sue, mother of Lucy, says of her daughter's experience:

> From the start of her illness, the psychiatrists were wondering what had come first, the depression or the anorexia, and therefore what should they treat. In many cases, treating anorexia and re-feeding the brain lifts the depression and people start to make a recovery. However, in Lucy's case, after two years of treatment for an eating disorder, the NHS services decided that transferring focus to the depression would facilitate recovery of the eating disorder. Unfortunately, transferring focus enabled the eating disorder to gain strength again and eating became more of a problem at a faster speed than the depression counselling and medication could help her.

To help you understand the possible links and connections between eating disorders and other mental illnesses, I will endeavour to outline the more common mental health issues in greater detail in this chapter, together with the possible indicators when interlinked with eating disorders.

Like eating disorders, all mental health issues can affect anyone irrespective of their age, gender, sexuality, ethnicity or social background. The effect on each individual can vary, as can the length of time a person suffers from them. These disorders can be defined as health conditions that influence a person's way of thinking, feeling and/or behaving. Individuals who have milder symptoms of mental illness may not appear visibly ill in a physical sense to the outside world, but the distress, and difficulty in mental functioning, on the inside can cause great fear and anxiety. These vivid thoughts and internal feelings can become stronger and much worse if left undetected and untreated, and the sufferer will be ill equipped to tackle this alone. If the symptoms are more severe, there may be more obvious external signs. Either way, mental illness is just as serious as any other physical condition and deserves the same level of attention, respect and intervention. Yet, sadly, it is often misunderstood and dismissed because of the lack of visible evidence. It is important to remember that it is the most natural thing in the world to feel happy and uplifted when something positive happens in our lives, as it is to feel sad, anxious, fearful or angry when something negative or worrying occurs. My mum once pointed out to me that bad days are essential in life if we are to recognise and appreciate the good days. Part of ensuring good mental health and wellbeing is the ability to recognise the difference between natural emotions and prolonged unnatural ones, possibly indicating a potential issue.

As with eating disorders, other mental illnesses can be kept secret by the sufferer, who will at times feel embarrassed, ashamed and lonely, but because of this elusive nature it is difficult to quantify and measure the actual extent of the problem. Personally, I would be inclined to measure the severity by looking at the impact on the life of the person experiencing the illness and those of the people around them.

Questions you could ask yourself are:

- Is the person able to concentrate in school?
- Are they able to hold down a job?
- Are they able to socialise?

- Are they able to maintain friendships or romantic relationships?
- Are they able to sleep at night?
- Are they looking after their body and physical health?
- Is their unusual behaviour causing disruption within the family or home environment?

All of these factors can be negatively affected by mental illness on quite a significant scale.

Before I begin to describe some of the signs and symptoms, I would like to reiterate that this is only a general and fairly basic guide. Everyone experiences mental illness in different and diverse ways, making it impossible to encompass each and every sufferer's experience. Parents, friends, partners and carers who regularly spend time with their loved ones will know them better than anyone else, but hopefully the information below will help to determine when the line has been crossed between common-or-garden angst and something deeper and potentially more sinister. At risk of repeating myself too much, there is no substitute for intuition, so if you feel that something is amiss then there's probably good reason for further exploration.

In my experience, there are five main types of common mental illness, eating disorders (as a general term covering many different types of disordered eating) being one of them, so I have described the remaining four – anxiety, depression, OCD and self-harm – and how they may present themselves below. I have also given brief descriptions of body dysmorphic disorder, bipolar disorder, borderline personality disorder, substance abuse and post-traumatic stress disorder, which may also cross over with eating disorders. Although each has its own and varied characteristic symptoms, they are often intertwined and tend to mimic symptoms from one another.

Anxiety

Anxiety can stand alone in the form of 'generalised anxiety disorder' and can be the starting point of many other mental illnesses. It is the most common form of mental illness in the Western world and can be the glue that holds all others together, perpetuating the cycle: it is both the cause *and* the effect.

Anxiety is a general term for a variety of disorders that cause nervousness, fear, apprehension, paranoia and/or worry. Life can be full of stressful situations and most of us live with a heightened sense of unease accompanied by a moderate level of anxiety, due to the unsettling world we live in today; it is our nervous system's normal response to a perceived threat or danger. However, when it gathers momentum and the sufferer finds it impossible to control, it can become a mental illness and can be physically and emotionally debilitating.

When it comes to the link with eating disorders, there is thought to be a very strong association with anxiety, with one recent study suggesting that six in 10 women with anorexia or bulimia nervosa also had an anxiety disorder.[13]

Mental and physical symptoms of anxiety vary widely, but can include experiencing:

- feelings of panic, fear, paranoia, insanity and uneasiness
- repeated thoughts or flashbacks of traumatic experiences
- disrupted sleep, nightmares and/or an inability to get to sleep altogether
- cold, sweaty, numbness or tingling in the hands and/or feet
- shortness of breath, rapid or irregular breathing or palpitations
- bouts of dizziness, nausea and possibly a dry mouth
- feelings of avoidance of certain places or items.

Anxiety can be specifically an issue for the younger generation as they are not always able to verbalise or convey how they are feeling, let alone understand it. Children are growing up faster than ever before, and as parents or carers it can be hard for us to appreciate just how difficult they may be finding it, coping with the pressure of school and friendships as well as their feelings and ever-changing hormone levels as they grow up. Their interaction with social media and the internet is often an attempt to understand the world, and can cause its own problems.

Listening to many of my clients, from age eight upwards, I often hear that their anxiety is heightened after spending time on social media sites or reading magazines, watching internet channels or reality TV shows, to the point that some even have to remove themselves to avoid the constant barrage of mixed messages and confusion. All of these can give a false perception of how they think their life should be, and media influences such as these can make the sufferer feel inadequate, insignificant, excluded and invisible.

Anxiety is by no means exclusive to children; it equally can affect adults in their everyday life. It is estimated that approximately 25 per cent of adults suffer from anxiety at some point in their life. These figures do not come as a surprise, bearing in mind the ever-increasing pace of life, combined with the pressures of everyday living.

Anxiety and eating disorders

A highly anxious person may develop some form of coping mechanism to help combat the overbearing anxiety, which then leads into another form of mental illness, such as an eating disorder, stealthily linking them together.

Generalised anxiety disorder (GAD) or another form of anxiety disorder tend to be relatively common in people with eating disorders, as these two conditions can feed off and fuel each other.

Someone with an eating disorder may experience high levels

of debilitating anxiety due to worry and fear surrounding food and the inner workings of their eating disorder. At the same time, for someone suffering from anxiety, being able to control what they eat or how much they exercise can relieve them of one of the symptoms of their anxiety though, of course, from an objective perspective, in this case they are simply swapping one set of troubling symptoms for another, placing the eating disorder in control rather than themselves.

Alice talks about how her anxiety fuels her eating disorder:

> When I feel my anxiety is high, I do notice my eating disorder becomes worse and more difficult to try and deal with. I think this is due to me using the eating disorder as a coping strategy rather than dealing with the situation in front of me in a better way.

Depression

Depression is a common condition that can cause lengthy periods of low mood, a lack of interest in the things that the sufferer used to find enjoyable, feelings of guilt and low self-worth, disturbance in sleep patterns, loss of appetite, loss of energy or compromised concentration. Depression is very different from just feeling fed up, a bit sad or down in the dumps, which we all feel from time to time, usually due to something specific that affects us on a personal level. A person suffering from depression will experience these feelings too but in addition to this they suffer from the permanent weight of extreme anxiety, negativity, hopelessness and despair. These feelings do not subside but stay with the sufferer every hour of every day like the darkest of clouds, overshadowing everything they try to do.

There are two types of depression: reactive depression and organic depression. The difference between the two is that the onset of organic depression comes from within the sufferer for no apparent or specific reason, completely unrelated to the external features and circumstances of their life. Reactive depression is the complete opposite and can actually be a very rational response to events such as the death of a loved one or the breakdown of a relationship, redundancy or the diagnosis of a terminal illness. Reactive depression can pass when the person becomes acclimatised and adjusts to the emotional trigger.

As for eating disorders, successive studies do seem to show that depression can be a factor in both the onset and continuation of the illness, with a high proportion of people with eating disorders also having a history of depression.

People who suffer from depression are often unaware that they are in the grip of it unless it is pointed out to them by someone who knows them well enough to recognise the symptoms. Similar to some other mental illnesses, this condition can distort their perceptions of what is and is not normal for them. It is often borne out of low self-esteem, anxiety and/or another mental illness, or in reverse it can be their root cause.

By its very nature, depression is not a logical response to the things a sufferer has in their life: it does not take into account their luxuries, their possessions, their circle of friends, their social life, their income. It can strike anyone indiscriminately at any time. Many successful, popular, wealthy professionals who appear to have 'everything', with the world at their feet, can be battling inwardly with depression.

My dear friend, Bobby Davro, talks of his struggles:

> To the outside world, I am a successful, confident, funny entertainer. However, what would surprise many people is that at some of the highest points of my career, I have suffered from dark times, depression, low self-esteem and a feeling of worthlessness. It is in my experience that antidepressant medication and the like are prescribed too easily, leaving the patient unaware of an alternative therapy that in the long term can be a much better alternative to improve their mental health.

Chapter 7

Roughly 50 per cent of depression sufferers, once recovered, never experience it again in their lifetime, but sadly for the remainder, there can be unpredictable recurrences throughout the years which can make things incredibly difficult for them and their families.

Typical psychological symptoms of depression include:

- sleeping a lot or experiencing insomnia
- feeling very sluggish or being overly fidgety
- having trouble focusing for any amount of time and experiencing a lack of motivation
- experiencing a continuous low mood or sadness and feeling irritable and intolerant of others
- experiencing a lack of enjoyment in previously enjoyable activities
- starting to feel anxious or worried and experiencing low self-esteem
- experiencing feelings of worthlessness and hopelessness
- having difficulty making decisions
- experiencing suicidal thoughts or thoughts of harming others
- experiencing feelings of guilt and suffering from tearfulness
- having thoughts of death.

Typical physical symptoms of depression include:

- a change in appetite, and weight loss or weight gain
- a lack of energy and/or slowed movement or speech
- changes to the menstrual cycle (in women)
- unexplained aches and pains.

Typical social symptoms of depression include:

- reduced contact with friends
- reduced interest in hobbies and activities
- decreased performance at school or work

- difficulties in home and family life
- taking part in fewer social activities.

Again, personally, I will say the most important thing to look for is a change in a person's demeanour. If, for example, a teenager continually says, 'I hate the world' but then regularly goes out to meet with their friends at the park or goes to play a ball game, or takes part in other fun activities in contrast to the words they mutter, then the chances are, they are probably not depressed. If a loved one or a friend constantly complains about how much they hate their job or asks, 'What is the point?' yet goes to play golf, or socialises regularly, having fun and living in the moment without being constantly preoccupied, then the chances are they are probably not suffering from depression either. However, please remember, prolonged apathy and constant negativity are the building blocks of depression. If the sufferer is constantly feeling that everyone else's life is somehow better than theirs, and what is the point of their life, and what are they doing with it, then there could be a need for help and medical intervention.

Depression and eating disorders

There is evidence that a significant number of those diagnosed with eating disorders also have a history of depression, with persistent low mood contributing to the onset of an eating disorder. However, that connection can also work in the other direction, with the malnourished brain and body of an eating disorder sufferer having a negative and debilitating effect on their mood and outlook. Furthermore, the restraints and control that the continuous cycle of their eating disorder brings can impact on a sufferer's life, contributing to the onset of depression. To say it is a 'chicken and egg' situation is not to make light of it, as sometimes it can be truly difficult to see which – if either – illness came first.

Antalia shares her experiences with suffering from both depression and bulimia simultaneously:

> I think the mix of my depression and bulimia was a concoction of disaster. These dark thoughts of self-hate and unworthiness constantly filled my mind and I think the only way I could try and release this heavy weight was to purge (throw up). It was an act that I thought I had under control and would help me deal with these feelings, but it turned out that my bulimia was in fact fuelling them; I didn't feel good, so I didn't eat well and I didn't treat my body respectfully. I cannot say for sure that if I didn't have depression that I wouldn't have developed bulimia, but I do feel there is a strong link between them. They both infect the mind like parasites and they are both really hard to just 'get over'. I live with them both still now, eight years later, and I do not know if they will ever leave. All I can do is try to be strong and to not let them shadow any more of my mind.

Like all mental illnesses, there is no simple or straightforward journey to recovery with depression and an eating disorder, but a willingness on the part of the sufferer to get better, coupled with the support, persistence and knowledge of an understanding carer, will increase the chances of success.

Obsessive compulsive disorder (OCD)

As the name suggests, this disorder is formed of two distinct parts – obsession and compulsion. Intrusive thoughts form the mental aspect of the condition and these thoughts often give way to compulsive (or repetitive) behaviours.

Most of us have worries, doubts and superstitious beliefs of some kind. It is only when your thoughts and actions make no sense to others, become excessive or begin to impact your ability to live a normal life and to affect people around you that it is officially recognised as a condition. Many people have described themselves as 'a little bit OCD' when what they really mean is that they like to keep their house clean and tidy or have a very organised filing system, for example. Neither of these are characteristics of the illness if they are in a manageable form. It's important to recognise the distinction between 'OCD' as a generalised slang term and the medical condition, which can be totally debilitating.

Some people experience intrusive thoughts, but do not have the desire to carry out compulsive actions. However, much of the time the two components will go hand in hand.

Obsessions are involuntary, seemingly uncontrollable thoughts, images or impulses which occur over and over in the mind. A person experiencing intrusive thoughts will not invite these thoughts or enjoy having them, but cannot seem to stop them from invading their mind. Some people describe these thoughts as being 'like a stuck record' and just as irritating, yet actively trying to stop them can, perversely, make them worse.

Compulsions are behaviours or rituals that must be acted out again and again. Usually, compulsions are performed in an attempt to make obsession go away. For example, if you are afraid of germs and cannot seem to think about anything else, you might develop elaborate cleaning rituals. However, the relief is short lived. In fact, the obsessive thoughts will usually come back stronger.

In its simplest form, OCD occurs in a four-step pattern:

1. Obsession – The mind is overwhelmed with a constant obsessive fear or concern, such as one's house being burgled.
2. Anxiety – The obsession provokes a feeling of intense anxiety and distress, often causing the 'worst case scenario' to be envisaged or imagined, sometimes repeatedly.
3. Compulsions – A pattern of compulsive behaviour is adopted in an attempt to reduce the anxiety and distress, such as checking all windows and doors are locked three

times before leaving the house or going to bed.

4. Temporary relief – Compulsive behaviour brings transitory relief from anxiety.

Obsession or anxiety will almost always return after the above cycle has been completed, causing it to start all over again. Compulsive behaviours in themselves can often result in anxiety, as they become more and time consuming. Anxiety can manifest itself in obsessive thoughts and so the condition spirals.

It's difficult to give a definitive list of signs and symptoms of OCD, since there are infinite things that can trigger an obsession and its related behaviour. Some of the commonest obsessions are:

*   Fear of being contaminated by germs or dirt, or of contaminating others.
*   Fear of causing harm to the self or others.
*   Intrusive sexual, explicit or violent thoughts or recurrent images.
*   Obsessive focus on religious or moral ideas.
*   Fear of losing or not having things that may be needed.
*   Order and symmetry – the idea that all physical objects must line up 'just so'.
*   Special attention to something considered lucky or unlucky ('superstitions').

The commonest forms of compulsive behaviour are:

*   Counting, tapping, repeating certain words or doing other seemingly senseless things in an attempt to reduce anxiety.
*   Spending a lot of time washing or cleaning, either the body or the environment.
*   Repeatedly checking on loved-ones to ensure that they are safe.
*   Excessive double-checking of locks, appliances and switches.
*   Ordering or arranging objects into specific patterns.

- Praying or engaging in rituals triggered by religious fear to an excessive extent.
- Accumulating junk such as old newspapers or empty food containers.

Without adequate coping mechanisms, OCD can eat into so much of a person's life that they find themselves unable to do anything else. This can result in extensive difficulties at home, school and work.

Obsessive compulsive disorder and eating disorders

The connection between OCD and eating disorders can be so close that often the parallels can become so blurred that it is hard to separate the two. Statistically, those with eating disorders have a higher rate of OCD, and vice versa, so diagnosis and separation of the two conditions often remains indistinct due to their striking similarities. The difficulty lies in recognising whether the condition is:

- Food-related OCD: A fear of food contamination/only magical numbers of mouthfuls of food allowed per mealtime/only certain coloured foods allowed/restricted food groups.
- All of which may bring about food limitations thus leading to weight loss.
  or
- An entirely separate eating disorder characterised by abnormal or disturbed thinking and eating patterns.

Harriet talks of her experience:

When I was young I developed a deep fear of being sick. This, over the years, caused me great anxiety around food and led me to restrict my food intake, purely because of my fear, not for any other reason. When my parents took me to the doctor after noticing I was losing weight, and refusing to eat most solid foods, I was diagnosed with an eating disorder. I was admitted to an inpatient unit where I was treated for my diagnosis. It was a very confusing time for me as I was being treated for something I did not have. One day I was able to explain my actions with someone listening and managed to get the right help. I am now free of my fear. It was never an eating disorder I had; it was OCD.

Whether dieting and exercising excessively with anorexia nervosa or binging and purging with bulimia nervosa, both behaviours characteristically stem from intrusive obsessive thoughts based on body image, perfectionism and social approval. In both cases, the incessant food and body fixations lead to anxiety levels spiking that can only be reduced by ritualistic compulsions, such as cutting and weighing food or compulsively purging to relieve the obsessive guilt and shame following binges, or in some cases just eating. The common denominator and unquestionable link between OCD and eating disorders is the engulfing presence of obsessions and compulsions and the feeling of never being 'just right'.

As OCD sufferers will repeatedly check locked doors and windows even though they know they are locked, a sufferer of anorexia nervosa, who knows they are thin, will continue to feel compelled to lose weight despite the image they see in the mirror, as they are just not thin enough, as will a sufferer of bulimia nervosa with their binge/purge cycle and a compulsive eater for whom the amount of food they consume will never be enough.

Aimee talks of how her OCD and eating disorder are interlinked:

For the past 10 years, OCD has been very closely linked with my eating disorder in many ways. I have many rules, routines and rituals regarding what I eat, how, why, when, and who with.

I developed these to minimise the chance of me over-eating or bingeing. My OCD now fuels the eating disorder itself. I am aware that these rules are self-imposed, but I cannot bring myself to stop them. They have become my safety mechanism to ensure nothing bad happens and therefore it feels counterintuitive to let them go.

Self-harm

Self-harm means exactly what it says – a person chooses to inflict physical harm on their body. It varies from person to person, but it is usually a way of indirectly dealing with difficult or complicated issues in a sufferer's life; it is often inflicted by means of cutting or burning the skin. It can also manifest as a sufferer putting their safety in jeopardy by voluntarily being in hazardous situations or exercising to the point of pain. The mental health charity Mind defines self-harm as 'a way of expressing very deep distress'. Often people do not know why they self-harm. It is a means of communication which cannot be put into words or even into thoughts, and has been described as an inner scream.

Eating disorders can also be described as a form of self-harm due to the physical damage endured by the body in order to block out what is happening in the mind. As with other mental illnesses, such as OCD, self-harm is inflicted to bring relief to the sufferer, albeit only temporarily, so the cycle repeats and repeats with the behaviours becoming both physically and mentally addictive and, in some cases, more severe.

According to the Mental Health Foundation, the UK has the highest incidence of any European country for self-harm. It affects 400 in every 100,000 of the population – males and females equally until recently. Last year, a report in the *British Medical Journal* found that self-harm among girls in the UK aged 13 to 16 had risen by 68 per cent in just three years.[14] Now a Children's Society survey of 11,000 14-year-olds has indicated that more than one in five girls in Britain are self-harming along with one in 10 boys.[15] These figures are more likely to be much higher, though, as many people who self-harm do so in secret and seldom tell anyone. Although anybody can be affected, the majority of people who self-harm are between the ages of 11 and 25 years old. Higher rates of self-harm are evident in people already suffering from borderline personality disorders (see page 189), depression and eating disorders.

Self-harming can include scratching, pinching, hitting or cutting different parts of the body, hair-pulling, burning, or anything which is done deliberately to cause pain, including less obvious forms such as risk-taking, drug overdose or simply not taking care of physical or emotional needs.

In children, harming animals, pets or younger siblings can also be a sign of internal anxiety which if left undiagnosed could then lead to other mental health issues, such as eating disorders, depression and OCD.

Many young people who self-harm say that it enables them to feel something, rather than the numbness which can be associated with depression or other mental illnesses. Whilst teenage girls often use self-harm as a physical expression of familiar yet painful emotions, teenage boys are likely to self-harm because they do not have the emotional vocabulary to express how they feel. Self-harm can be a way of attention seeking, 'physicalising' an internal pain for an outside world to see in a way that demands interaction. It can also be an indicator of suicidal thoughts, allowing the self-harmer to test the water without actually attempting the real thing. It is often described as a response to a pressure-cooker of emotions that build up on the inside; self-harming is a way of releasing that pressure. It can be linked to feelings of self-loathing, unworthiness and low self-esteem.

The symptoms of self-harm can be very hard to spot in young people, because they will very often conceal them from their parents, teachers and friends. Although, in contrast, self-harm has recently been noted to be 'contagious' in schools whereby students will emulate each other's inflictions. It is therefore a good idea to ensure that all friends connected to a self-harmer know that intervention is taking place, giving a strong and clear message that it is a very serious issue and not to be mimicked.

Self-harmers young and old will usually cut parts of their body – often arms or upper legs, which can be hidden under clothing. However, you know your loved one, and you will recognise any change in their behaviour which could indicate self-harm; this could include unexplained bruises, hair loss or bald patches, scars, wearing long sleeves or long trousers even in hot weather, and generally spending a lot of time alone. Some of the signs of self-harm are explained as 'accidental', with the harmer making excuses for the bruises or scars. This means the most important factor to consider here is the frequency with which these 'accidental' injuries appear and the persistence of the injury. Recognising the difference between a one-off or a recurring pattern is vital.

Some of the physical signs to look out for include:

- unexplained bruises on parts of the person's body
- cigarette burns on parts of their body
- cuts on parts of their body
- excessive hair loss/unexplained hairless patches on the scalp
- obsessive exercising (more than the daily recommended time per day)

    According to the NHS adults aged 19-64 should do 'at least 150 minutes of moderate aerobic activity such as cycling or brisk walking every week and strength exercises on 2 or more days a week that work all the major muscles (legs, hips, back, abdomen, chest, shoulders and arms).'

- covering the body with layers of clothing, especially long sleeves, particularly in hotter weather

- low mood / tearfulness / lack of motivation or interest
- changes in eating habits, or becoming secretive about eating – including rapid weight loss or gain
- alcohol or drug misuse.

Self-harming has reached a very dangerous era by way of the internet, where sufferers, once perceived to be secretive and ashamed of their self-inflictions, covering up to hide their scars or abrasions, are now joining online communities and sharing with other self-harmers their scars like 'badges of honour', their painful and misplaced pledge of allegiance to a very disturbing worldwide club.

Self-harming can be a visible indicator of a much deeper and more dangerous emotional issue that requires intervention.

Self-harm and eating disorders

There is certainly a strong link between self-harm and eating disorders, with the former occurring in around 30 to 40 per cent of people with a clinically diagnosed eating disorder.[16]

In some cases, self-harm and eating disorders exist together, with sufferers employing different behaviours from both illnesses in the pursuit of coping with, or blocking out, feelings of anger, shame, loneliness, guilt or other difficult emotions, and also as a way of punishing themselves and expressing hatred or revulsion for their bodies.

For others, one may follow the other. If someone tackles the physical effects of an eating disorder, reaching a healthy weight for example, but does not explore the emotional root of their problems, self-harm may step into the footprint of the eating disorder, developing as a way to replace it. To break free of that destructive cycle, sufferers of both self-harm and eating disorders should address the psychological foundations that their illness is built upon.

Charliee, who suffered from bulimia and OSFED for just

under 10 years, tells us of how her eating disorder co-existed with self-harming:

> When I was first referred to the community mental health team, I was also diagnosed with bipolar. I also self-harmed by cutting and am now left with many scars which will likely be there for the rest of my life. It became more than a coping mechanism; I couldn't go a day without self-harming. It was the only way I could make sense of my eating disorder and it became part of my 'routine'. I'd always feel light-headed after purging and hate myself for what I had just done. It made me feel 'abnormal' and self-harming was the only thing that grounded me.

Body dysmorphic disorder

Body dysmorphic disorder (BDD) is an anxiety disorder specifically linked to how people view their body. People with BDD see their physical appearance differently from how other people view them.

They might have obsessive worries for hours a day about one or more flaws in their appearance – flaws that are invisible or nearly invisible to others. BDD sufferers may also develop compulsive behaviours around their physical appearance, such as obsessively looking in mirrors, using heavy make-up, or seeking cosmetic surgery.

These fixations will interfere with their day-to-day life, affecting their work, social life and/or relationships. These obsessions and routines can also trigger a range of emotions, including shame, guilt and loneliness, and may overlap with other mental illnesses, such as depression and OCD.

BDD and eating disorders

BDD and eating disorder sufferers share a number of similar traits, such as having an overly poor body image, low self-esteem and worrying excessively about physical appearance. However, while eating disorder sufferers mainly focus on weight and shape, people with BDD may have concerns about a particular part of their body as well as, or instead of, concerns about their weight. While it is possible to have BDD without having an eating disorder, and vice versa, it is also possible for the two to overlap and co-exist.

Bipolar disorder

Bipolar disorder, formerly known as manic depression, is a condition that affects the person's moods, which can swing from one extreme to another. People with bipolar disorder have the low and lethargic spells characteristic of depression, but they also have manic episodes where they feel very high, restless and overactive. Recognising and enjoying the 'normal' spectrum of moods for any consistent period of time is something that often eludes bipolar sufferers.

During depressive episodes, people with bipolar disorder may feel worthless and directionless, taking them to such lows they consider, or even attempt, suicide. During the manic phases they may be bursting with energy and ambitious plans and ideas; however, this may lead to lack of sleep, irregular eating patterns and spending unnecessary amounts of money. It can also be accompanied by symptoms of psychosis, where they see or hear things that do not exist.

The high and low phases of bipolar disorder are often so extreme that they can interfere with everyday life.

Bipolar disorder and eating disorders

Bipolar disorder is thought to be present in around four to six per cent of eating disorder sufferers.[17] It is thought that it most frequently occurs with binge eating disorder, followed by bulimia nervosa and then anorexia nervosa.[18]

Having both present inevitably makes the treatment of the two illnesses more complicated. While there is effective medication for many sufferers of bipolar, those medications can be very hard for those with eating disorders to take correctly or stick to consistently. Furthermore, the antidepressants which may be prescribed for eating disorder patients may not be recommended for those with bipolar.

Borderline personality disorder

Borderline personality disorder (BPD) is a complex and serious mental illness, characterised by very unstable emotional and impulse regulation. People with BPD may have a contorted sense of self and may find themselves overly dependent on their relationships with others. Self-harming behaviour, such as hurting oneself, attempting suicide or abusing substances, is often also part of the illness.

Given these manifestations of BPD, it is perhaps not surprising that a significantly higher incidence of eating disorders has been found among those with borderline personality disorder compared with the general population.

According to the *Diagnostic and Statistical Manual of Mental Disorders-IV (DSM-IV)* there are nine different criteria that can manifest within someone with borderline personality disorder:

1. frantic efforts to avoid real or imagined abandonment
2. a pattern of unstable and intense interpersonal relationships characterised by the person alternating between extremes of putting the loved one 'on a pedestal' and devaluing them
3. identity disturbance – that is, strongly and persistently having an unstable self-image or sense of self
4. impulsivity in at least two areas that are potentially self-damaging (e.g. spending, sex, substance abuse, reckless driving, binge eating).

5. recurrent suicidal behaviour, gestures or threats, or self-mutilating behaviour

6. emotional instability due to highly reactive mood (e.g. intense episodes of unease/dissatisfaction, irritability or anxiety, usually lasting a few hours and only rarely more than a few days)

7. chronic feelings of emptiness

8. inappropriate, intense anger or difficulty controlling anger (e.g. frequent displays of temper, constant anger, recurrent physical fights)

9. transient, stress-related paranoid thinking or severe dissociative symptoms (breakdown of memory, perception, awareness or identity).

At least five must be present for someone to be diagnosed with the condition. In some ways it is possible to draw very clear parallels between these BPD criteria – including self-mutilating behaviour, self-damaging impulsivity and an unstable sense of self – and the key characteristics of an eating disorder.

Borderline personality disorder and eating disorders

Some experts have proposed that it could be the indicators of BPD which put someone at risk for developing an eating disorder. For example, the chronic impulsivity and desire to self-harm could then lead someone to develop some problematic eating behaviours, which might, over time, escalate to an eating disorder. Similarly, engaging in eating disorder behaviour could trigger BPD in someone with a susceptibility.

However, despite these parallels, BPD and eating disorders are two separate mental illnesses and, as such, treatment is likely to be needed for both. As with other illnesses that intertwine, it is just as important to recognise and treat the individual symptoms as it is to recognise those that overlap. Both are highly complex illnesses and can be very difficult for loved ones to fully understand and navigate.

Evelyn, says of how her BPD and eating disorder fuel each other:

> My BPD and eating disorder are definitely linked together. BPD is often triggered by interpersonal relationships, as are eating disorder symptoms. Any instability in my life will trigger thoughts of wanting to be perfect, fear of failure and abandonment, which in turn leads to a need to regain control. A way to regain control is restricting what I eat (for example). Sometimes paranoia from the BPD will cause perceived instability (rather than actual instability) and this can again trigger the eating disorder symptoms.

Substance abuse

Substance abuse occurs when taking a mind-altering substance begins to have an impact on someone's physical and mental health. It may affect how they deal with the world around them and how they handle the responsibilities of day-to-day life.

Alcohol dependence is the most common form of substance misuse, and reliance on other drugs, including cannabis, crack, cocaine, heroin, amphetamines, and also laxatives and diuretics, also falls into this category.

Substance abuse is a mental illness in its own right. Its mind-altering effects can also exacerbate other mental health conditions, or it can become more entrenched as it becomes wrapped up in another illness, such as an eating disorder.

Substance abuse and eating disorders

The link between substance abuse and eating disorders is stark. It is believed that up to half of those with eating disorders abuse alcohol or illicit drugs, a rate five times higher than in the general population. Furthermore, eating disorders and substance abuse share a number of common risk factors, including family history, low self-esteem, depression, anxiety, and social pressures.[19]

There is even a slang term which explicitly links alcohol abuse and eating disorders: 'drunkorexia'. This is often used by younger people and refers to starving all day so that the calories usually consumed through food, can instead be 'saved' for a drinking binge later in the day. The perceived advantages are both lack of weight gain and faster inebriation. However, the consequences can, of course, be serious, leading to risk-taking behaviour and possible black-outs in the short term and to longer-term effects that include liver damage and malnutrition.

Post-traumatic stress disorder

Post-traumatic stress disorder, often shortened to PTSD, is an anxiety disorder that is triggered by stressful, shocking or frightening events. When someone has PTSD, they often experience flashbacks and nightmares. They may have problems sleeping and find it a real challenge to concentrate on other areas of their life as they battle complex and disruptive feelings, including anger and guilt.

The disorder was first recognised in war veterans (you may have heard the term 'shell shock') but it is now recognised that it can be caused by a wide range of events and experiences, from witnessing a terrorist attack to suffering a bereavement.

Of course, it is normal to feel a range of emotions after a traumatic experience, but for people with PTSD, these feelings persist, having a significant impact on their day-to-day life. PTSD is thought to occur in around a third of those who have been through a traumatic experience, although it is not clear why some people have it and others do not.[20]

PTSD and eating disorders

PTSD is thought to be more likely to be present in people with eating disorders than in the general population. This may be because eating disorder behaviours, such as not eating, bingeing, purging or exercising excessively, may be used as a way of coping with the difficult emotions of PTSD. People with the disorder may use destructive eating habits as a way of distancing themselves from the pain of the traumatic experience they endured.[21]

To conclude

I hope that reading this chapter has given you an insight and better understanding of the more well-known and talked about mental illnesses, in turn demonstrating the inter-connective and complex nature of mental illness as a whole. Very rarely do symptoms fall into one neat, generic category, so for the majority it is hard to distinguish one condition from another. However, again I cannot stress enough the importance of following your instincts and arming yourself with as much applicable knowledge as possible to help you and your loved one find the right recovery path together, remembering always that recovery is possible and sustainable, provided the sufferer really wants it.

Chapter 8

Eating disorders in men

By Dr Russell Delderfield, University of Bradford, UK

A lot has changed in the last decade, and when it comes to male eating disorders that can only be a good thing. When Lynn originally wrote about men in the first edition of *Hope with Eating Disorders*, campaigning by, or on behalf of, men was in its early days. She pointed out that male eating disorders had existed as long as their female counterparts, which is true, of course. She also wrote that there was 'a greater conspiracy of silence' when it came to men. This is something that has begun to change.

More recently, men's experiences have the hit the press. More men, and their loved ones, are willing to talk openly about what they live with, and their experiences of recovery and treatment. Male eating disorders have even been debated by government. It would be easy to believe that a focus on men may no longer be relevant, that there is now enough awareness that most young men will realise that they are not alone. Or that you, as their families and loved ones, won't be shocked by a man with an eating disorder because you thought that eating problems were a woman's issue.

I wish it were that simple. I follow plenty of men on Twitter who are open about their battles with body image, food and exercise. I've seen celebrities discuss their disordered eating candidly in interviews. But we still need this chapter because myths and misunderstandings are everywhere, even though we know more now than ever before. What I hope to give you here is enough information so that, if a man you care about has problems with eating, or receives an eating disorder diagnosis, you will feel that you know enough to begin supporting them in their journey out of disordered eating.

As you read through, you'll see extracts about particular men; all of these are from my research. They have been anonymised and have given their permission to having their experiences used in publication, in accordance with the ethical practices at my university.

What do we know?

Earlier in this book, information was provided about what the main eating disorders are, how they are diagnosed, and what to look out for (see Chapters 1 to 3). More so than ever before, overall, the diagnosis and 'symptoms' of anorexia, bulimia and binge-eating disorder in men are similar to those in women.

Two decades ago, a leading expert, Arnold Andersen,[22] was clear that eating disorders in men should not just be treated as a biological or medical problem. He claimed we should be looking at the culture of the society in which they develop. Despite the last 20 years, our understanding is still dominated by a relatively narrow clinical point of view. Whilst important, it limits our understanding to what can be identified through medical assessment... and what has been identified through medical assessment has usually come from the largest patient group: women, with a few men who have been treated. So, when I say that 'overall' things are similar, I should add: 'as far as we know, to date'.

This is not to say that we know nothing at all. I gathered over 280 male-focused scientific studies in my research – that is a lot of information once you bring it together. This number continues to increase steadily and each year we learn something new.

Chapter 8

Beyond the immediate shared symptoms of anorexia nervosa (AN), bulimia nervosa (BN) and binge eating disorder (BED), there are various things we think are similar between men and women:

- We know that issues around control (or relinquishing it) feature in both men and women's eating disorders.
- Being bullied tends to feature in the past of those who develop a damaging relationship with food and eating, even men. Especially if bullying was related to appearance.[23]
- Perfectionism has been found to be a trait in both, when it comes to AN or BN.[24]
- Men with anorexia are at similar risk of osteoporosis.[25, 26]
- The levels of unhappiness found in men with AN or BN match those in women patients.[27]
- Even when adults are diagnosed with a 'relatively new' disorder – binge eating – there are few differences between men and women in terms of its development and diagnosis.[28]
- Websites and online chat-rooms that supported people in maintaining their disorder, rather than seeking help and recovery, were once thought to be the preserve of women. These 'pro-ana' and 'pro-mia' spaces are now known to be used by men, too.[29] These spaces are heavily contested ground, with clinicians warning of their dangers, but men reporting that they help to feel understood and belong to a community without being made to feel 'weird'.

Peter

Having dealt with weight that plummeted, only to soar again, taking him back to his schooldays when he was bullied for being obese, Peter began using website communities:

I've recently got onto a blogging website where people talk about their ED; ana, mia, and pro-ana groups. I genuinely [do] not condone pro-ana in anyone... but still I do it to myself...

He had fleetingly felt the elation of control and the power of having redesigned his body through weight-loss. Then he was thwarted when a period of depression and having to withdraw from university led to his weight gradually increasing again. Feeling out of control, Peter's seeking out of a 'like-minded' community is perhaps not surprising. And community is key here – it's about not being alone with the effects of the disorder. This can be a difficult set of relationships to break.

Discovering the differences

I can't cover all of these differences, so I will share the main ones. Bear in mind that these continue to be hotly debated by researchers and medical professionals, and are liable to change.

- One of the most profound differences between men and women, is that men are simply less likely to end up presenting with an eating disorder.[30] So, whilst there have been some startling headlines of late, claiming huge rises in male disordered eating, these continue to be significantly outnumbered by female cases.
- It has been suggested that despite ending up with an eating disorder, men are less anxious about their body image.[24] This contradicts some of the things we will see below.
- Osteoporosis, which occurs in anorexia, was found to be worse in males. In fact, even if their illness had a shorter duration, men still ended up with lower bone mass.[31]
- In men, a history of physical abuse through domestic violence (as opposed to sexual abuse) was found in those who went on to have eating problems.[32]

Joe
What Joe endured illustrates this issue about physical violence. Joe was already struggling having lost his elder brother to suicide. He began to try to lose weight, having felt he was overweight previously. He resorted to all sorts of methods to try to bring his

weight down and describes how much he couldn't abide himself. Then things deteriorated:

The next two years saw my problems with eating and depression worsen. After being intensely beaten by a family member, I found myself homeless again, leaving my house in fear of further violence... I had continued experimenting with laxatives and anything else I could obtain to try and purge myself of food.

For Joe, laxatives were the antidote to bingeing on bland, stodgy, cheap food. He was not to discover until much later that this did not really undo the binge, it only damaged him. The violence he experienced may not have been at the beginning of his disordered eating, but it certainly marked a low point, from which things began to get worse, and from which he felt he had no escape. He was alone, without a home and living in fear should he try to return. It is little wonder that he would try to find a way to cope, and to soothe himself during all of this. Not surprisingly, what was meant to be a comfort swiftly became something that was ruining him and making him more ill, until he finally sought help and ended up being referred to an eating disorder service.

- Despite claiming that symptoms are similar, we know that men are more likely to use excessive exercise as a weight control or 'purge' response in disorders like bulimia.[33]
- Young men also appear to be harder to diagnose[34] as they may not have an easily recognisable 'drive for thinness'.[35] This drive is usually found to some degree even in non-anorexia disorders. We know, for instance, that clinicians sometimes fail to diagnose eating disorders because, apart from with anorexia, men may not appear greatly underweight or overweight.[36]
- Rather than 'media images' (see Chapter 12), there is some evidence that men's behaviours are more influenced by their friendship groups' comments. This can result in experimenting with the use of strategies that become damaging, such as purging or fasting.[37]

- More men leave treatment having reached medical thresholds for 'health', but they continue to experience a poor quality of life, when compared with recovered women.[38]
- And, related to this, the death rate amongst men, after being discharged from treatment for anorexia, remains higher than that for women.[39]

Better diagnosis

Getting a diagnosis was listed above as one of the ways men can differ from women. It is also hampered because so few men fit in the AN, BN or BED categories. They tend to be diagnosed with OSFED. This means the disorder is deemed to be atypical (compared with the diagnostic criteria, at least). 'Other specified feeding or eating disorder' (see page 59) means that there is no clear outline of what the disorder is. Worse, it means that there is often no standard pathway through treatment that a professional can plan or prescribe. Many men fall foul of this.

As I have said, these unspecified eating disorders account for the majority of male diagnoses.[40] As such, diagnostic criteria that men have to meet to access treatment have been criticised as being fundamentally flawed.[41] After all, GPs and nurses may be familiar with the symptoms of anorexia, bulimia and now BED but what about an 'and everything else' classification that incorporates all other atypical symptoms?

The obvious consequences of this are twofold. First of all, this could account for the lack of men in treatment if a less-obvious eating disorder simply cannot be identified. Secondly, it can result in a lack of a clear way forward for treatment, as most treatments are designed for the main diagnosable eating disorders.

Rick

As a teenager, Rick struggled to cope with his new reality when his parents' marriage broke apart and he ended up living with his dad full-time. He lost weight when he fended for himself while his dad was out exploring life as a newly single man. He would have friends over to play games, and while they would eat and drink, he would exist on meagre amounts, using the hangout as a distraction, as there were no structures or mealtime.

It was at this time, aged 16, that I was forced to go to the doctor's and was diagnosed with depression for the first time... I started to take up walking, and would often go on coastal walks for up to and over six hours a day.

Despite the weight loss, depression was the diagnosis; at the time, it is likely that Rick would not have met the required low weight to be found anorexic, as these weights were based on women's bodies. His walks ensured his weight stayed low, he escaped from his home situation, and he could lose himself for hours at a time. These things certainly suggest all was not well, but they do not feature as easily diagnosable symptoms for professionals to spot.

Almost all of the research that I have drawn on above uses statistical analyses to present data and interpret findings. These statistics are generated from results found through various tools – questionnaires, surveys and scales, used during clinical assessments, where the practitioner would use it (as a part of the process) to evaluate a patient's symptoms and their severity.

There is a misleading use of language here because I actually mean 'women' when I say 'patients'. In fact, when these same instruments have been used on men the results have proven far less reliable.[42, 43] This has not gone unnoticed by researchers and healthcare professionals: 'continuing to view EDs through the lens of female gender means we risk omitting important information about the male experience...'.[44]

This has led to the development of male-oriented assessments, such as the Eating Disorder Assessment for Men (EDAM), which is a self-report questionnaire,[33] but it will take time for this to be reliably tested before becoming more widely available.

Bodies, sexuality and gender

Even if we set aside the problem of getting diagnosed, what about men themselves? Earlier, I mentioned that it was thought that men had less of a drive to be skinny, and for years we thought that body ideals for males hadn't really changed.[45] It was assumed that men developed damaging behaviours with food and exercise regimens to try to avoid difficult or painful feelings or moods,[46] rather than because they were unhappy about their bodies. Indeed, we barely considered that their bodies played a part. Men were judged by their earning potential, ability to protect, ability to provide a stable home, or exercise boardroom power (they still are) – but not whether or not they had a 'muffin top' or a lithe frame.

We now realise that men are just as dissatisfied with their bodies as women, although it has been suggested that this is less to do with wanting to be thin.[47] Instead, they were preoccupied with whether they were gaining a much-prized muscular body.[48] It was suggested that men weren't worried about 'weight' as far as the scales were concerned but they were worried about becoming a 'man', in the bodily sense. Rather than a 'drive for thinness', there is a 'drive for muscularity'.

This is the so-called 'buff agenda', where bodybuilding is no longer just for (semi-) professional bodybuilders. Recreational body-building means that more men are investing time in changing and re-shaping their bodies in an attempt to grow more muscle. This has led to an increase in supplements and substance use, such as anabolic steroids – food alone is no longer enough to gain the amount of acceptable muscle. Failing to achieve this has been linked to feelings of inadequacy and failure in young men.[49]

A gym-goer named Kevin, interviewed about his gym and diet obsession that was destroying his life, called the condition he experienced 'bigorexia',[50] a term that seems to have been in use in the gym community for a while, and which reflects the fact that big was never big enough, when it came to bicep circumference and thigh-size.[51]

Bigorexia, or to give it its formal name, muscle dysmorphia, may appear to be a detour in a book about eating disorders. After all, it sounds much closer to body dysmorphic issues, which can exist with or without any distressing relationship with food. I cannot miss including it, however, because it is so uniquely linked with male experience. The people who interviewed Kevin studied 108 bodybuilders and made a comparison between traditional anorexia and something they referred to as 'reverse anorexia nervosa'.[52]

The similarities between anorexia and muscle dysmorphia are difficult to ignore. The women with anorexia and the men with bigorexia had similar psychological traits, including experiencing obsessive compulsions, perfectionism, an inability to gain pleasure from pleasurable pursuits not related to their obsession, narcissistic tendencies and a consuming drive to exist as an ideal version of themselves.[53, 54]

Genuine muscle dysmorphia results in sustained, toxic relationships with food, diet, supplements and all associated behaviours. Men may follow rigid and uncompromising diets. Indeed, some of the disruption to social and family life is often due not only to training regimes but also to having to prepare and consume highly specific meal plans. This is not to suggest that all people who go to the gym and lift weights are automatically bigorexic. And, of course, not all men want a gym-worked body. Let's return to Peter.

Peter

In recent years, I've looked to pictures of women and the like I find attractive... I think they would never like me or want to be with a guy like me, fat. I never wanted to be muscular and macho and large.

Here, Peter bucks many of the trends we've just explored. He doesn't want to be big and muscly; he just wants a body that women, who he finds attractive, will want. He wants to be wanted. And to be wanted or found to be appealing, this means he can't be what he is – a fat man. This is Peter's experience of where a man's body meets a man's self-esteem: his sexuality.

The first work around sexuality was not any old sex; it was about homosexuality or bisexuality. Not that long ago, being gay or bi was said to be a risk factor for eating disorders in men[55] because these men are more likely to feel acutely aware of what makes a man look masculine and, therefore, desirable. Recently, that has been debunked and we now think that more gay or bisexual men appeared in health services, because they were more likely to be in touch with social, health or community services working on a range of issues they faced.

Instead, what's been discovered is that men of any sexuality can end up with an eating disorder and that sexuality itself (of any kind) is a potential factor.[56] Also, creating an idea that eating disorders don't really affect heterosexual men is damaging; it could make men less likely to seek help, because they may believe they have failed at being 'real men'[57] when this is simply not the case.

In the last decade, it has been suggested that we are experiencing the effects of 'hyper-sexuality', where society has become overly concerned with sex and sexual attraction. Not only young women, but now young men, are internalising messages that sex appeal equates with self-worth. This makes us vigilant, and many men have succumbed to 'persistent body surveillance'.[58] This means constantly assessing and judging one's body to ensure that one can be confident in one's ability to attract others.

And what binds all of this together, both muscularity and sexuality? Well, muscles are 'good'. I should explain that further. Disturbingly we have found that even children, young boys and girls, opt for more muscular toy action figures. The more muscles, the better. When they are asked to explain their choice, heroes are equated with strength, and muscles are evidence of strength...and 'muscles are good.'[59]

What about strength that cannot be evidenced by pumping iron, I wonder? Being supportive, being caring and attentive, being loving, just being there for others. I know lots of men who achieve these things. They may go to the gym as well, but that is not the sum total of who they are and what they offer. More so than ever before, our outward presentation, our appearance, is there to be made over, reinvented, sculpted and displayed on the streets and on social media. Men are not immune to this.

I want to add a final word here, given we are looking at men's bodies and their relationships with masculinity and sexuality. It's something that's often missed, and whilst I can't do it full justice, I can at least raise your awareness of it. What about those men or women whose gender isn't a simple question of biological sex? Those people for whom their body at birth is not the experience they actually live or want? When it comes to transgender and eating disorders, most of our understanding comes from case reports,[60] where biological males have undergone gender re-assignment procedures to be women.

Male-to-female trans people reportedly struggle with a drive for thinness and may be more prone to anorexia- or bulimia-related disorders. Another observation is that the disordered eating was definitely bound up in body perception issues, and even body dysmorphias. A recent scientific study has not proved that eating disorders are more prevalent in trans people, but it did suggest that the likelihood of having issues with food and eating was increased.[61]

There is less known about females who transition to men,[60] I'm sorry to say. Where people occupy a less 'binary' space on a spectrum of gender identity – for example, those who start out life as male but do not have complete reassignment to a female body – we know even less.

What we do know is that, where eating disorders are concerned, transgender people can end up with a range of damaging or difficult behaviours around food that fluctuate as they experience the highs and lows of being on their journey through bodily change and expressions of femininity or masculinity. A trans person may have symptoms of acute anorexia, which over time may evolve into bulimia, or even binge-eating disorder. A holistic approach may work best, one that does not try to treat their eating disorder whilst ignoring their own relationship with their gender identification.

My advice would be to contact the Gender Trust for support and information, or another transgender charity. They will have experience of dealing with the issues and prejudices that trans people routinely face as they strive to become themselves. Whatever you do, if you are supporting a trans person through an eating disorder (and if it's appropriate to be disclosed), try to help ensure that any healthcare professionals involved use the person's preferred pronouns. This small gesture can go a long way to helping the man or woman know that they are working with someone who respects their gender identity.

Getting help

Getting support can be hard, unfortunately. It has been suggested that this is even harder for men. Denial, shame and stigma, due to a fear of being perceived as 'less of a man' function as obstacles to accessing help and support.[62] The man in your life may not see their all-consuming calorie control and excessive commitment to fitness to be problem behaviours, for example.[63]

Eating disorders are already felt to be shameful and involve a great deal of secrecy,[64, 65] but this is 'amplified' in men because 'men are reluctant to admit to having a problem, let alone a "women's problem"'.[66, 67]

When people without eating disorders were surveyed, researchers did report that respondents thought that having anorexia was 'less masculine'.[68,69] This is a lot for a man to battle against. There is also more self-stigma; when asked about bulimic people, male respondents from another survey said that they believed that the sufferer was personally responsible for their bulimia.[70] This flies in the face of the messages in this book, but sadly, it does suggest that men are exposed to and fear these attitudes.

George

In some cases, the stigma is just too much to tackle and it can actually lead to a man deciding that he simply cannot disclose that he is struggling with something. This is George's experience.

My problem revolves around compulsive exercise and many of the traits of anorexia. I am attempting to recover without any formal professional help (so far successfully). This decision not to get professional help was down to the stigma involved with having an eating disorder.

He felt that, as he might have to notify work about treatment (a part of his life he had worked hard to maintain despite the severity of his illness), he could not risk anyone finding out that all was not well. He decided he would use self-help methods to try to recover, and enlisted the support of his friends in helping him to do this in a way that was meaningful to him.

To be as courageous as possible, even in the face of a poor diagnosis or looks of disbelief from others, men need just as much support as anyone else.

When a man gets access to help, as I said earlier, there are no treatments that are proven to be better for men. Instead, there are some treatments currently thought to be effective for men and women. You will now be aware of CBT (page 112), for instance, which was tested with both male and female patients.[71] It was found that both could benefit from it. There is evidence for other treatments, of course; see Chapter 5 of this book for plenty of ideas.

For young men, family therapy (see the New Maudsley Model on page 118 and Counselling on page 132), which is also used with women, may be available. This can be tough but ultimately worth it, as recovery of an individual in a family is often a family effort. Everyone can help, and the sufferer can learn that his disorder not only affects him but others around him, and that they are invested in his recovery.

We need more evidence that support and treatment may be better if they are adapted with men in mind.[72] Male-only self-help groups can be useful in proving to men that they are not alone in their condition, whilst allowing privacy. As observed about a male-only group: '…offering men a space to talk about emotions can feel a bit like trying to get a cat to swim; technically it can do it, but it is not the done thing for a cat.'[73]

The question as to whether tailored all-male treatment models are truly effective in helping men recover is unanswered at the moment; there are so few services, it is currently impossible to tell. Ultimately, any of the treatments that are suggested in this book are well worth exploring for a man who wants to recover – leave no stone unturned.

Advice to carers

We prize fitness in society, so disorders such as anorexia, at least at first sight, are often missed because the boy or man may just be really committed to fitness, sports and training goals. As previously said, we also have a time-honoured tendency to overfeed men – the 'he's a growing boy' problem – so disorders that involve consuming (lots) of food can easily be confused with having the hale and hearty appetite we foster in males.

There are some things to consider:

1. Men are good at keeping things to themselves – we still raise them that way. Don't blame yourself that you didn't spot something or that he didn't talk to you sooner. Just focus on the fact that he feels he can talk now. If you need access to more information, the charity *Men Get Eating Disorders Too* (see page 316) is a good place to start.

2. 'It takes a village to raise a child.' Negative influences aren't automatically something you have or haven't done at home. There are stories from boys' families that show clear evidence that trouble comes from beyond the family.[74, 75] We've rapidly discovered that men are not immune to the pressures they face from society about how they look, what their bodies should be like and what they should (or shouldn't) do to cope.

3. Try not to assume that having disordered eating means there must be an issue with sexuality; whilst this can sometimes be the case, even leading clinicians now think that much of the research linking eating disorders with being gay or bisexual is flawed.

4. Less likely, but you still see this appearing: having anorexia or bulimia doesn't mean the man is 'in touch with his feminine side'. I've heard men say they've been told that they're 'sensitive'. Firstly, what's wrong with that? Secondly, it's a twentieth-century nonsense that to be sensitive is to be 'feminine' – anyone who knows any man intimately will know that we all have our sensitivities – things we can cope with and things that we can't, where we need help.

5. If health services focus on a broader diagnosis, such as 'depression', don't be surprised. It's more common that

men present with more than one key illness or condition, and it's common that another of these is diagnosed sooner or more readily than the eating disorder. Do be persistent if you and the man himself feel that there's more to the eating-related problems.

6. Men are notably less likely to use vomiting to get rid of food. That doesn't mean they're not bulimic. The information on this is more detailed. Men tend to favour laxatives or 'compensatory behaviours' in order to counteract their binges.

7. Remember that there is a compulsive, needs-driven element to a man's eating disorder or exercise practices. Just because they might be receiving treatment, doesn't mean they won't carry on their behaviours or secrecy around food or related issues.

8. Inpatient and outpatient treatment is tough for anybody, but often for men they may be surrounded by female patients, rather than a balanced mix of genders. This can sometimes (not always) make them feel even more isolated. Even if the boy or man won't talk about their disorder, or say that things are going okay, they still need you there at every opportunity for visits or to take part in any family-based treatments (see Chapter 9).

To conclude

We have come a long way in our understanding of male eating disorders. Researchers and clinicians are right to a degree: many of the behaviours and some of the treatments aren't any different just because someone is male. This doesn't mean that men don't feel 'different'. We're so keen on making sure that men and women know that they are definitely different from one another these days, how could men not feel different when they end up with a disorder that is so firmly connected to their body and what they do with it?

It is still the case that men are, generally, not really encouraged to communicate when they are struggling. A wry quote from Steve Blacknell continues to capture this well:

> *Men by definition are a tarty breed, not given to opening up… more likely to talk about West Ham than one's waist measurement. So, on the basis that it's tough enough for this wretched species to communicate on touchy topics such as this, imagine a shy man with a problem.*
>
> *I am a born communicator. Some are, some aren't. Luckily I have the talent to impart feelings, emotions fears and tears*
>
> *Others are not so blessed.*

What I have learnt is that the more men who talk about what they've been through, the more likely we are to teach younger men that it's okay to voice this difficult stuff. The more we voice the difficult stuff, the more likely we are to get care, support and services when we most need them. I don't study male eating disorders because I believe them to be radically different from female eating disorders; I study them because we've not got enough of those voices.

Men still need to know that what Steve says is true: 'It's a people disease, not a woman's disease.' Once our attitudes and services reflect this, then we'll have finally made a difference. Perhaps in another decade's time, this is what I might be telling you in a future version of these pages. I certainly hope so.

Chapter 9

Eating disorders in relationships and the home

Relationships

Modern everyday life can be incredibly stressful. Every generation that has ever existed and evolved has probably said the same thing; however, that does not make it any less true. Today, the expectations of how family and personal life should be have been completely transformed from how they were even 30 or 40 years ago.

The planet is forever changing, technology advancing, and the population is expanding at quite a pace. In the West, we undoubtedly have more freedom of choice and are less confined to the traditional gender roles than in previous generations. Whilst these advances are inevitable and largely to be embraced, within relationships, some of the realities of contemporary culture, such as technology, diet, acquisitions and global issues, have proved to be inadvertently damaging.

As with every single one of these elements, we cannot control the challenges and misfortunes that come our way, but we can control how we deal with them and how we allow them to affect our relationships with those around us. Everything is okay in moderation. We do not have to allow ourselves to be glued to our devices 24/7; we do not have to allow ourselves to make the wrong dietary choices for our brain's wellbeing and balance; we do not have to allow ourselves to be made to feel inadequate by the riches of others; and whilst we would like a better future for our planet, we need to try to understand that it is a global effort, not the weight of the world on one person's shoulders.

How we navigate our lives significantly affects how we manage our relationships with others; within a family/ partnership, it is quite normal to have fraught and challenging times, as individuals – all with different personalities and needs – jostle to find their own voice and be heard, all together, all under one roof, even without having someone with an eating disorder or, indeed, any mental illness thrown into the mix.

When living and coping with the dreadful effects of a loved one who has an eating disorder, it can put an enormous strain on personal and professional relationships and the toll it can take on all concerned can be devastating.

Every day within my work I see the shattering effects that mental illness can have on the sufferer and their loved ones, and every day I am continually confronted by the pain and trauma that mental illness can bring to the home environment. I have seen and experienced at first hand how it can rip families apart and drive a wedge through once solid relationships, bringing them crashing to their knees.

I will never forget when Samantha was in the throes of her eating disorder and OCD, my husband, Kevin, described our everyday family life as being as if someone had picked our house up each morning and given it a good shake, bringing mindboggling chaos and turmoil for the rest of the day, until bedtime once again restored the peace and calm – until the next day and the whole cycle would begin again! Equally, I can speak at first hand that with the right support, understanding, patience and unconditional love, the damage can, in time, be repaired and family dynamics restored, bringing them closer together, more united and stronger than they have ever been. My family is a real example of this.

The effect on family and friends

Parent/carer

A mother's love
by Samantha Crilly

It watches over when I sleep
Catches the bad dreams before they land
Strengthens me as it holds my hand
A feeling so spiritual, so unique
Surrounding me with love and hope
Putting faith inside me when I can't cope
By my side for when my demons appear
Be my shield for when they come near
To die before me with no fear
Some say it's an angel looking down from above
But I know it's down here… it's my Mother's love

Your intrinsic instinct as a parent or carer will be to protect the person you love from suffering and to take away their pain and confusion, but when faced with the demons that are mental illness this is probably one of the hardest fights you will ever be faced with… I know it was for me.

You will probably know your loved one inside-out, so witnessing their bizarre behaviours or hearing their irrational thoughts, totally out of character to the person you once knew, will undoubtedly be quite difficult and painful.

The sufferer could potentially be afraid and possibly even embarrassed by what they are experiencing, as they may not understand what is happening to them themselves. Often, they will be worrying what people would think of them if they knew what horrible and disturbing thoughts were really going through their minds.

Chapter 9

I have already talked about how one of the first signs of an eating disorder can be a change in a loved one's personality. Those changes are likely to deepen over time as the person's brain is taken over by the mental illness. They may become deceitful and cunning, lying to you to cover their tracks, and inevitably over time this is likely to weaken the trust that you, their parent or carer, has in them. Of course, this is understandable; however, try to remember it is the eating disorder that is changing them, and therefore it is the eating disorder you need to fight – not your child. As hard as it is, try not to be afraid of what you cannot see, remembering that behind the eating disorder, your loved one is still there, and they, not the eating disorder, would want you to fight on their behalf.

As a parent or carer, if your life is anything like mine was, compromises, challenges and sacrifices are now quite possibly a part of your everyday life and relationship with the sufferer.

Sue, whose daughter, Lucy, is in recovery from anorexia, orthorexia and binge eating disorder, tells us of the effect the eating disorders had on everyday life and the relationships around her:

> It caused a lot of pressure on my marriage as well through exhaustion, lack of time, fear, changed priorities, financial (I had to give up work) and we could no longer just 'go out' or 'go away'. (It felt worse than having a toddler again.)
>
> Simple things we once enjoyed as a family, like picnics, going out for dinner on special occasions, fish and chip night, popcorn and a film etc – in fact anything around food or family time – became a thing of the past as food was such a massive issue and Lucy became more reclusive into her own space/room.

Debbie talks of how her daughter's illness affected her own relationship with her partner at that time:

As she was fading she wanted and needed me. She was like a puppy following me around. She cried a lot. My heart broke at how sad and fragile she had become. My partner of four years never understood how she needed me and I had to be there for her. The relationship ended.

As you try to make sense of things that seem nonsensical, you will no doubt be finding it very difficult to know the right thing to say or do, overwhelmed by the enormity of an illness that you may not always physically see. You will probably be feeling like you are walking on eggshells most of the time, worried that you may say or do the wrong thing, or concerned that you are somehow to blame, that something you did or said triggered this illness, and that, if you do or say the wrong thing now, you may make it worse.

Blaming yourself will only hinder you in that fight. From what I have learnt, both personally and professionally, I can honestly say that most of the time parents, siblings or loved ones are not to blame – despite how others, sometimes, may make you feel. It is just one of those things that sadly seem to affect some people and not others. So please, before you read any further, as hard as it is, try to stop blaming yourself; it will only be a waste of your precious time and energy which can be put to better and more positive use.

I found, in my own experience, that learning as much as I could about the illness and the way that it was affecting Samantha, helped me to be better equipped to handle and understand some of what she was experiencing without being manipulated and divided by it. Researching and gaining as much knowledge as I could, helped me to strengthen my armour against the eating disorder finding its way through. Doing this will help you see that every individual's battle with an eating disorder is different and unique to them. It will help you fight to find the treatment that works for your loved one. And it will help you support and encourage them through the darkest times, keeping your loving relationship with them alive, even as the eating disorder does all it can to come between you and the rest of the family.

Be prepared, as sometimes things can get worse before they start to get better; it can often be a 'one step forward, two steps back' scenario. Try not to compare someone else's recovery with your loved one's, as there can be a wide variation in a person's response to treatment; changes can be slow and gradual and unique to that person, but all are of equal importance. When small improvements take place, be sure to acknowledge them and voice your encouragement – it is one of your strongest tools in keeping your relationship with your loved one as tight as possible. I know it was for me.

As a parent or carer, you should never lose sight of the person who is still there, masked by their eating disorder. Vow to be stronger and more powerful than the illness that is ravaging them and waging war on family life. Never lose hope that they will get better, while also reminding yourself to have a life outside the eating disorder.

The healing process is unique to every individual so there are no time constraints on how long the recovery time will be; therefore, it is really important to try to continue doing the fun things you previously did as a family, such as the cinema, museums, shopping, watching a TV programme, anything to keep the natural momentum going. Try and make sure these times are as free from the eating disorder as possible, where the subject is neither acknowledged nor discussed, to enable both the sufferer and their loved ones to enjoy just being together in some shape or form of 'normality'.

Siblings

It is important to remember that siblings struggle just as much as the sufferer, if not more at times, as they not only witness the pain their loved sibling is going through but feel pain themselves

as they can often become unintentionally side-lined as a result of the sufferer becoming the main focus of concern for those around them, as the eating disorder disrupts the home and family life.

Chris, the father of Kate, who is now recovered from anorexia says:

> Everything revolved around Kate, leaving Kate's sister Lizzy to 'get on with it'. Even during the day away at work, it was very stressful waiting for the phone call about what Kate had or hadn't done at any time.

Melissa, Kate and Lizzy's mother, adds:

> The stress levels in the family were very high, and Kate's younger sister [Lizzy] really had to put up with a lot of difficult behaviour from her sister. She had to be incredibly patient and forgiving. She is naturally empathetic, kind and patient, which made life much, much easier for us but meant we neglected some of her needs at the time.

Some of the feelings that siblings experience may be similar to how their parents or carers feel. Like other family members, they may feel guilty or worry that something they said or did caused the eating disorder. They might feel angry that this illness has come uninvited into their lives, throwing everything they once knew upside down. And they may constantly ruminate on the causes and possible solutions.

Fiona talks of how her son felt when his sister, Katie, was suffering from her eating disorder:

> My son, who is two years younger than Katie, was very angry about the situation but not to her. We had had some behaviour issues with her when she was at high school and at the time he was embarrassed to be her brother. He felt this was another time of her demanding our attention.

There are also feelings that are unique to siblings. It is understandable that they may feel left out, forgotten about and left to cope alone when all the focus seems to be on the person suffering. Witnessing the tears and arguments, the tense family meals and perhaps the stress on their parents' relationship and others around them, they may also feel very anxious about what terrible effect the eating disorder may have on their own life.

Siblings may have different thoughts, questions and concerns that will need acknowledging and talking about openly. They may be scared or frightened for their brother or sister who is struggling with a mental illness; they probably will be worried about their parents and how they are coping, whilst also being concerned for their own future and that of their siblings, fearful of the unknown and uncertain of what it will bring for everyone involved. They may feel anger, resentment, frustration and a little embarrassed at the prospect of what others may think and say.

It is important that siblings can be allowed to participate to a certain degree in the recovery process to help them remain hopeful about the future, but only if they want to be, as their thoughts and decisions need to be respected at all times. Helping their sibling will also give them a sense of achievement and inclusion and increase their own self-worth. If they can find time to carry on doing the things with their sibling that they always did, this can really help. They may also find that their brother or sister with the eating disorder feels more comfortable opening up to them than they do to their parents. If they are able to create that safe and supportive place for their sibling to come to, siblings can play a very special role in a person's recovery.

A lot of the time, what siblings of sufferers require is simply an acknowledgement that the situation is difficult for them, too. My husband and I were careful to spend time alone with Charlotte and to give her as much attention as we were able to. In retrospect, it was also important that Charlotte felt part of the team giving support and care to Samantha. To exclude her (perhaps misguidedly, believing we were protecting her) would have exacerbated the situation.

My Charlotte says:

> I was always very included in Sam's recovery. Mum and Dad brought me along to every appointment; it was my choice to be there for her, and it really made me feel part of the process in making her better. I also think it helped me to understand her better and what she was going through, and in turn made us closer in the long run.

However, that is not to minimise the toll it can take. Siblings too need someone to talk to. They need time when they can be with their parents, sometimes to discuss the eating disorder and the impact it is having on them, the sibling, but at other times to enjoy some space to talk with their mum or dad away from the illness. If they struggle to talk to parents, siblings may find a listening ear with someone else – another member of the family, a teacher, friend or therapist.

It is not that unusual for siblings to question their own eating habits or weight, especially as there is so much focus on food within the family and the home. It is important that they find a channel or outlet to talk about this.

My girls are now 27 years old and the love they share remains as strong as ever due in part to Charlotte's involvement in Samantha's recovery. I feel incredibly blessed that it has strengthened their bond, not weakened it.

Samantha speaks of her love for her sister:

> Charlie (Charlotte) and I have always been unconditionally close but when I started to really get into my recovery that was when we really started to get our relationship back. It was all about me opening up about it and Charlie wanting to listen and understand. She never judged me; she just wanted to help and took on board everything I said. This made it a lot

easier to go out in social situations and to be able to do stuff together as she knew what I was able to do and what I wasn't and what I would find hard. Thus, she put me at ease so I was able to be myself rather than have a voice in the back of my head telling me something was wrong. Charlie and I often laugh about it and joke as well, which always takes the edge off it a bit!

Charlotte powerfully concludes:

For my sister and I, in the end, it has made us closer than ever; she is my best friend. I don't know where we would be or what we would be doing today if it wasn't for the mental illnesses and what we have gone through, but I do know, now it has almost come to an end, I wouldn't want to be anywhere else.

Extended family members and friends

It can be difficult for those closest to someone suffering from an eating disorder to understand the change in their loved one. For extended family and friends, who do not see how much of life is affected by the illness, it is probably even harder to come to terms with. This often causes parents and carers to struggle to ask for help, fearful that others will not understand, which is why it is important that the wider family and friends make parents/carers/close family aware that they are willing to help without question or judgement.

Fiona, mother of Katie who is now recovered, says:

One uncle who Katie was very close to could not understand any of it and on being told she was about to be admitted to a hospital replied to her, 'Why can't you just eat a Mars Bar?' Another uncle, who Katie was not as close to previously but who had in the past suffered from depression himself, was fantastic with her; he was not frightened of asking her questions about how she felt.

It may take those outside the immediate family a while to accept and understand that an eating disorder is not simply 'attention seeking' or a 'fad diet'. They may not fully understand the deep psychological roots that underpin an eating disorder, nor grasp that for a mental illness like anorexia nervosa or bulimia nervosa, there is no quick fix or cure. Coming to terms with the fact that an eating disorder is an illness, in the same way that people might suffer from asthma or diabetes, for example, can also be difficult to fully comprehend. It is important to acknowledge at this point that older carers may struggle to understand eating disorders within their family. My mum describes her feelings when my daughter Samantha became poorly:

> I was frightened of the illness because I realised I knew nothing about it and, worse, I couldn't get my head around it to try to begin to understand. In my childhood, what little food we had was there to nourish the body. Surely this eating disorder couldn't have been around then? But yes, I suppose it could after all, because an eating disorder (I now understand) is a mental illness. In our generation we didn't talk about what we couldn't see or didn't understand.

I can remember when it became apparent that my daughter, Samantha, had an eating disorder, my own parents initially found it very difficult to make sense of her distorted way of thinking and why this was having such a devastating effect on her health. Coming from a generation where mental illness was unspoken of and family matters were kept very private, it was difficult and confusing for them both, but despite their uncertainty, they listened without judgement, offering nothing but love, encouragement and support, which has been priceless to Samantha and the family as a whole. My mum in particular went above and beyond and, as hard as she found it sometimes, she never lost hope that Samantha would make a recovery.

Samantha says of how the mental illness has brought her closer to her grandma:

> Grandma always wanted to understand and listened to every bit; she never judged and just wanted to get it. She always tried to put herself in my shoes and relate to my problems herself and what she has been through in life. Grandma never asked for what I couldn't give her; we would talk about so much random stuff as well, like when she was growing up, so it would take my mind off things that were going on in my head.

My mum concludes:

> We have become closer during this long journey, the reason being we can talk as equals and listen and accept. She tells me her thoughts, I tell her mine. We laugh when we say or hear something funny and we hug when it is sad.

Romantic relationships

Some people with eating disorders say it is like having a person inside their head telling them what to do, or what not to do. When it comes to romantic relationships then, it is perhaps not surprising that it might feel that there is a third person in that relationship – the eating disorder. That can leave partners sometimes feeling that they come second, after the illness, and, if their partner's symptoms become more entrenched, a distance may develop between the couple which may prove hard to accept.

Lizzie, who is now fully recovered from bulimia (see page 42), tells of her relationship challenges in the past:

> I have experienced break ups due to the illness. One ex was so disgusted by it, he asked his parents to give me a lecture on it.

Will speaks of his experience:

> I have generally done a good job at hiding the eating disorder apart from two ex-girlfriends (one who was diagnosed with an eating disorder years ago), who I let in on my secret, so to speak. The constant obsession with food, its calories, how much I needed to take and a massive avoidance of sugar proved too much for the one ex-girlfriend who didn't have an eating disorder.

The implications can be more practical, too. People with disordered eating may avoid invitations to eat out, or social situations where what they eat is taken out of their control. Even just enjoying the simple pleasure of sitting down to a meal with the person you love can be a challenge when one of you has an eating disorder. Because of the body image issues and hormonal imbalances that can go with eating disorders, sexual intimacy may also be affected, creating an even greater distance between those with eating disorders and their partners.

However, despite all the obstacles, the person behind the eating disorder is still the person their partner fell in love with. If they can keep believing this, supportive partners can play a crucial part in recovery. By showing their loved one the joy that can exist outside their mental illness, they can give sufferers the strength they need to eventually get better.

Dan and Paige tell us of how they strengthened their relationship. Dan says:

> It was very hard on both of us since when the disorder first appeared we were at universities at other ends of the country. It took us a long time to get our bearings because our relationship changed drastically overnight.

Paige follows with:

> It affected my relationship with my boyfriend. It caused a bit of strain when I was first diagnosed, but just like with my mum and dad, our relationship has become stronger. He was supportive with any problems I had and made me feel better when I was feeling down. Despite the problems my eating disorder caused to my relationships, they have all become stronger to help me through.

The key is for partners to learn as much as possible about eating disorders, so they understand the behaviours that can be so difficult and frustrating to witness. They need to allow their partner to talk when they feel able. Getting support, either through counselling or group therapy, may also be valuable. The more you learn about them and their eating disorder, the more the mutual trust and understanding will grow and strengthen.

I have seen at first hand how toxic and destructive relationships can be when you have two people suffering from mental illness, and although never intentional, the illnesses can feed off each other in a negative way, so bringing both people down with it. However, in some cases, it can work the opposite way, and if the foundations are strong enough, two people can work together to make it a success.

So, with this in mind, I believe that the right relationship with the right person can add positivity, confidence and assurance to the recovery process, in ways that family members cannot. If the circumstances present themselves, and the sufferer feels ready both emotionally and mentally, then I think they should welcome the possibility of letting a new kind of love into their hearts, as this is just one of life's natural progressions.

Friendships

Much has been written about sufferers of eating disorders and their immediate family, but much less has been written about the close friends who have to watch the sufferer struggle through the effects of their condition.

Rachel says of how she has lost friendships, but her husband has stayed by her side:

My eating disorder has definitely affected my relationships over the years. I have lost friends through it and even partners. I am lucky enough now to have an amazing husband who tries to support me the best he can. Yet over the years due to my state of mind and neglecting relationships to exercise etc, people have walked away, called me selfish etc, as they don't understand what it is like to live in my head with an eating disorder.

The knock-on effects of an eating disorder can extend far beyond the inner circle of the sufferer. If you are a friend to someone with an eating disorder, I would advise you to research and learn all you can about what your friend may be feeling, so that you can get a better understanding, which will enable you to offer friendship and support to them in the best way possible and at a level they feel comfortable with.

Patience, a willingness to listen without judgement, and love, can go a long way. On some occasions, the sufferer may not wish to discuss their illness with friends; they may just want you to be their piece of normality – their one connection to a life they once recognised, a life before their mental illness. This connection will give them hope, so try to engage in everyday conversations, things that you share a common interest in, or even just everyday mundane things that they will listen to, to escape the confines of their disordered thoughts. Do not expect too much from them though in return. There will be a long road travelled, but as long as they know you have their back and are there for them it will bring comfort to them in their dark times. Above all, positivity is the key: in fact, it is the most valuable thing you can offer your friend. They will respond far better and quicker without negativity and pessimism.

It can be hard to know how to offer practical help, but there are things that can be done to ease their load. Simply involving them in the same things you would have done before they were ill can show them the life there is outside the eating disorder. You can also offer to go with them to appointments or help them out with day-to-day tasks, and when you do go out together, choose your activities wisely, avoiding doing things that centre around food.

Remember, your friend does not want this eating disorder that occupies their every waking thought, just as much as you do not want them to have it. Keep reassuring, praising and encouraging them that recovery is possible; they need to be aware that they have a team supporting them, willing them to get better. In this case it really does take a village, not an individual. Communicate positively, directly and clearly; be kind and patient; accept and do not judge; be a sign of strength, not weakness.

Samantha's best friend, Zoe, who has walked by her side throughout her journey, sums friendship up beautifully:

In truth, Sam suffering from mental illness does add a complication to our friendship. It is a subject that I try to, but often can't, fully comprehend. There's almost an unspoken agreement between us, I won't always understand what she's going through, and she won't always be able to commit to doing things. We don't have to talk about it, but we can when she wants to. The end result is a best friend who is great in so many other ways and her challenges are an accepted part of that friendship. It's similar to a friend in a foreign country or a friend with a new baby; it can be difficult to maintain a connection sometimes. But stand by a friend with mental illness, because when they are ready, they will be one of the most tenacious, courageous people you will get the honour of being friends with.

Relationships – in conclusion

I would like to add, whether you are a parent or sibling, a partner or carer, a friend or work colleague, the road to recovery can be a long one, it takes time to travel it, and the experience cannot be sugar-coated; but having someone walk those miles with you, however rocky, can make all the difference.

Samantha summarises with:

> Although I have had my fair share of mental health issues and challenges, I have also been incredibly blessed to have such wonderful family and friends around me; I am not sure where I would be without them.
>
> My mum in particular, no matter how bad it got, has always been by my side, with her unconditional, non-judgemental love, never giving up, always supporting and encouraging, which over time, gave me the strength, determination and courage to push forward, believe in myself and the spirit within me to recover and get my life back. Although not an easy journey, it has been one worth taking and I can honestly say it was a fight I am glad I took on and won!

Eating disorders in the home

When a family member or loved one has an eating disorder, the strain on the home can be enormous. No one is left unaffected as this unwanted stranger storms into family life, turning everything on its head. Somehow, amid this turmoil, a carer has to find the strength to support the sufferer through the chaos, even when sometimes it can be tempting just to scream and shout at the unfairness of it all.

I know how difficult it can be, how angry, frustrated, worried, and scared you are probably feeling. I know that you probably feel lost, with no map or guide telling you where this journey is going to take you and which way you should turn for the best. However, there are some markers along the way which will help: unconditional love, patience, lack of judgement and understanding from everyone in the family home may help you all through.

I do, though, recognise that, when an eating disorder comes into your lives, trying to live in a united household can seem very much easier said than done. It is true that family life will be disrupted, and everybody within it may have to make some changes and sacrifices to accommodate the ongoing recovery of the person with the eating disorder. In turn, this may destabilise the happy family life you once knew and have worked so hard to create.

It is not an easy task, but establishing and maintaining a positive emotional balance – one of acceptance, understanding and cooperation – in the home is crucial for the person suffering and the family as a whole, something I know again is easier said than done. I have listed below a variety of suggestions and ideas to provide you with some tools for family members to help cope with some of the challenges of living with a person with an eating disorder.

Recognise the warning signs

Eating disorders are a mental illness and, while you may think the physical signs may be obvious, that is not always the case, and particularly not in the early stages. Being alert to early problems is important, as the sooner your loved one receives help, the more positive the outcome is likely to be.

First and foremost, be aware of any changes in their character. You know your loved one best and if you notice behaviour that is out of the ordinary for them, stay alert to any other changes that may be happening. With hindsight, many carers see that their loved one became angry, withdrawn, forgetful and/or pre-occupied. This is important because it is the outward sign of the turmoil they are fighting in their own head. It is important to remember that these changes can develop slowly, but with time they could advance into something bigger and more sinister.

Also look out for the following:

- There may be some sort of secretive behaviour around food.
- They may have rituals either before, during or after eating, such as taking an extra interest in how food is prepared, or always going to the bathroom after a meal.
- They may make excuses to avoid family mealtimes.
- Hobbies they once enjoyed may be pushed aside, and friends and social occasions avoided.
- They can often seem tired, stressed and/or preoccupied.

Charlotte looks back at the warning signs she saw in Samantha:

Looking back, the biggest sign for me was that Sam started to throw away her packed lunch every lunchtime at school and only drink a bottle of water; this was very out of Sam's character as she used to love lunchtime. When we would get home, she would then make excuses as to why she would not want dinner as well; then, I knew something was wrong.

Avoid making personal criticism

The way in which you react to your loved one's distorted thinking and disordered eating can have a big impact on them and how they feel. Often, sufferers of eating disorders are already harbouring a lot of self-blame and judgement, so, when criticised or blamed for their behaviour, their symptoms can get worse. I know myself how frustrating, difficult and hard it can be for all the family members; however, do try to detach yourself from the behaviours, and view them as the eating disorder and not the personality of your loved one, always remembering that that person is still inside. By doing this, you will hopefully be able to stay connected with the person you love, rather than allowing the eating disorder to alienate you from them. Remember, it is the eating disorder you are fighting, not each other.

Sue, the mother of a former eating disorder sufferer, tells us of the difficulty she faced:

> We have always been close and still are – but she/the illness will be very aggressive towards me, physically, emotionally and verbally, and has pushed me to the limits; at times like this, it is difficult to 'like' the person she has become and what it is doing/has done to the family.

Acknowledge small steps forward

This is where being tuned in to the person with the eating disorder is really helpful. Sometimes tiny steps forward can be barely noticeable, but it is important to remember they are still steps forward nevertheless; recognising and praising them as such is crucial to recovery. While these improvements may seem insignificant and small to the family members, they will have taken immense effort and an iron will and may have been very painful to accomplish. Giving your loved one the recognition they deserve for this incredible effort will spur them on to take more of these small steps forward.

Acknowledgments of these seemingly small accomplishments can be a powerful tool that encourages them to keep trying and to not give up. This also can let them know that their hard work and efforts to recover are being recognised whilst also being a powerful motivator.

Angela, mother of Sophie, shares what she found worked:

> To give Sophie encouragement through her recovery we put into place a star chart system; we would ask Sophie one thing she would like to do or to have and she would then work towards that. This gave Sophie the drive and strength she needed to push herself just that little bit more. After a while she was then able to motivate herself; she just needed that little push and acknowledgement in the beginning.

Refrain from reinforcing disordered eating behaviour

Family and friends can inadvertently become involved in the behaviours of an eating disorder sufferer. It may seem, at the time, the only way to help reduce the anguish that the sufferer is experiencing. By giving into their requests not to join family meals, for example, the carer is unintentionally reinforcing and strengthening the illness as opposed to challenging and overcoming it. If possible, talk together as a family, with the sufferer, about how to tackle their illness and make sure that everyone in the home and wider circle is working to the same goal. Involving the person suffering enables you to find ways around their thinking and behaviour, so encouraging very small changes that they may feel able to manage. Follow this up with heaps of praise for the efforts they are making.

Be as kind and patient as possible

Irrespective of their age, or position in the family, allowing the sufferer the time, space and security they need on their recovery path will also enable them to open up and relax a little more around those closest to them. Help them by vocalising and acknowledging that you accept and understand how difficult things are for them, empathising and reassuring them that there is nothing they could say or do to make you stop loving or caring for them. This will give them the courage and confidence they need to continue in the right direction. By keeping the boundary walls down between you and the sufferer, you are reinforcing the recovery cycle and creating an open, non-judgemental environment for them, which is exactly what they need to keep challenging themselves and to move forward.

That feeling of working together can be immensely valuable to someone battling an eating disorder. It helps them to feel understood and trusted, giving a gentle boost to their self-esteem which is so important for recovery.

Benjamin says of the kindness of his girlfriend that helped him through:

> Lily, my wonderful girlfriend, was the cornerstone to my recovery, not just by being there for me when I needed her, but also by giving me the space I needed and not smothering me when she realised I just needed my own company. She really empathised with me, which I do think at times was hard for her to do, but she always did her best to support me in whichever way I needed.

Find the humour

Finding the humour in an eating disorder can be pretty hard and sometimes may feel impossible; however, where there are opportunities to lighten up, grab them with both hands. If you are able to find the lighter side of situations, it will help you get through them together. Just make sure the sufferer feels respected and is not left out of the laughter.

Try and seek out the humour in other aspects of life too. Allow yourself to laugh with your loved one, just as you used to. Enjoy a funny film together or tell them an amusing story about someone or something else. I would encourage you to actively seek out ways to laugh and smile together, and each moment of happiness will help loosen the grip of the illness on their mind.

Harry, whose sister suffered from bulimia nervosa, says of how he and his sister found common ground:

> It took a while, but my sister and I can now share a laugh when she does something I don't understand. She knows I find it difficult, but instead of making it awkward, we just laugh, even when it doesn't seem like it would be funny...I think it's the only way we can get through it.

Keep your family routine 'normal'

Do not give up on your own everyday life or your life together with your family. Make time every week to do something you or your family particularly enjoy, together or by yourself. It could be listening to music, reading a book, going to the cinema, or going for a walk. Setting aside time to do your favourite activities can help relieve family tensions, whilst reinforcing the bond.

My Charlotte echoes the above:

> Going for a walk on the beach in our favourite part of the country was the best medicine for all of us; it gave us time to all breathe and be out of the everyday rut.

Remember, there is life outside of the eating disorder for everyone in the family.

Keep communication open and positive

Communication is paramount, to enable a balance to be found, between supporting your loved one and standing up to the eating disorder. When an eating disorder is present, you should expect and be prepared for communications to require extra effort, time and patience.

When talking to your loved one who has an eating disorder, try to put yourself in their shoes, however difficult that may seem. Just showing that you are trying to understand how they may feel will be comforting to them and will help them build the trust that will allow them to open up and talk to you more. That makes it more likely that you will be able to work together to find the right path forward and hopefully on to recovery.

It is also important to communicate with the other members of your family and wider circle, showing that you care about each other and appreciate each other's efforts. Good everyday communication can also make it easier to bring up issues, make requests when needed, and resolve conflict if and when it arises.

Whether you are talking to the person with the eating disorder or another member of the family, try not to be judgemental or impose your own view. It is important that everyone knows that they can be open with what they say and will be given a fair hearing.

My Samantha says of how finding the courage to open up to me has helped her:

> Talking to my mum about the thoughts in my head was at first extremely hard, until I realised she had no judgement, just unconditional love. I began to open up to help her understand the thoughts in my head and what they used to say and the reasoning behind them and my actions. She was able to really understand what I was going through and start to help me move forward in my recovery.

Do whatever you can to promote self-esteem

I think that self-esteem is one of the greatest gifts you can bestow on someone you love. Encourage them to talk to you, to share their views and praise them for doing so. By gaining self-assurance, they will understand that everyone is unique, and help them to say no to the pressure to conform to some of the skewed expectations that society and peers may place on them. Boys and girls, men and women alike, need this same encouragement.

Set a positive example

The pressure from society affects most of us, and for our own self-esteem, as well as our loved ones', we also need to critically challenge the negative narrative around body image, weight and food that it is all too easy to fall into. Avoid criticising yourself or others, especially making comments about appearance, and focus instead on the inner qualities that really matter.

Try to maintain family mealtimes. Even if your loved one will not eat, encourage them to sit with you. Try and make that time together a fun, positive experience, rather than turning it into another battleground about food.

Say the right thing

It can be really hard to know what to say to someone with an eating disorder. You do not want to ignore the illness, but sometimes you just do not know if you are saying the right thing.

As my mum explains:

> Once I knew of the illness and then understood it was a mental illness I became very careful and wary – should I say – not to say the wrong thing, frightened of hindering the healing process that was, hopefully, taking place.

With help from my past and present clients and others with eating disorders, I have put together a list of some words that are helpful for those with eating disorders, and others that are best avoided.

What to say

- You might ask questions such as: 'Can you tell me what is happening?' or 'Do you feel you would rather talk to someone else about this?'
- Give them space and time to express themselves, asking: 'Would you like my advice or would you rather I just listened?'
- Encourage your loved one by saying something like: 'There is nothing you can say that will stop me loving you.'
- Praise them for every small step forward by saying: "This must be hard for you, but you are going to get through it,' or 'I am so proud of you.'

- Help take away their fear by telling them: 'You are not alone and I want to help you in any way I can.'

What not to say

- Try not to apportion blame or anger by saying things like: 'Why are you doing this to us?' or 'Look at the effect this is having on the rest of family.'
- Try not to minimise the problem by saying 'What do you have to worry about?' or 'This is all in your head.'
- Try not to ask someone to 'snap out of it' or 'pull yourself together'. Eating disorders are complex, deep-rooted problems and cannot be switched off like this.
- Try not to comment on the person's body or weight or say things like 'You look great now you have put on some weight.'
- Try not to judge them, whatever they confess to you. Tell them: 'I respect your viewpoint' even if you do not agree with what they are saying.
- Try not to say 'I do not know how to help' as they are looking to you as someone to help take their pain away.

A lot of the time, simply just listening can be helpful. It is important to talk to the sufferer in the same way you have always done – remembering they are the same person that they were before.

Zuzanna, now recovered from anorexia and bulimia, shares an insight into her mind at the time she was suffering:

> Whenever someone would make a comment about my thinning body and looking unwell, I would take it as praise. Whenever someone would say I looked 'better' or 'healthier', I was secretly upset.

Look after yourself

Supporting others can be mentally and physically exhausting. As a parent or carer, you probably spend a lot of your time focusing on everybody else, always putting everyone else's needs before your own. However, looking after your own wellbeing is just as important for you, your loved one and the whole family, as they can only be as strong as you are. You may not be able to take a break every time you need one, but it is important to have some time that is yours, whether it be, going for a walk, meeting a friend, doing a relaxation class, or simply reading a book or a magazine. By doing this, it will enable you to recharge your batteries, so when you re-enter the eating disorders battlefield, you do so with renewed energy and focus.

Jeff Brazier, life coach, supports self-care, whilst caring for others:

> Sometimes in life we become so busy looking after everyone else that we forget to adequately care for ourselves. Regardless of how noble the cause, the problem with this is that if all is not balanced within us as a result, our ability to tend to the needs of others is diminished. We must first give to ourselves if we are going to give openly to others.

To conclude

There is no definitive, right or wrong way to work together as a unit in the home; every situation, every sufferer, every family unit and every home environment is different, but by everyone sticking to the basic fundamentals and working closely together, for the benefit of everyone involved, you will be on the right path.

Chapter 10

Eating disorders in education and the workplace

Education

Eating disorders can affect anyone regardless of age, gender, sexuality, social background and / or ethnicity; however, the most common time for them to take root is during adolescence. For this reason, it is crucial for us to understand how the school years can have an impact on the development of an eating disorder, and also how head teachers, teachers and support staff are in a pivotal position to recognise the signs and symptoms and, in turn, the potential onset of an eating disorder. This then can enable them to trigger the early intervention which is so key to tackling this mental illness successfully.

If we look at it in realistic terms, the secondary school years in particular are a perfect breeding ground for eating disorders: adolescence itself is a time of great change, physically, mentally and emotionally. The physical changes in the body can be difficult to handle in themselves and can make young people feel incredibly self-conscious. They inevitably measure themselves against their peers, which can lead to feelings of inadequacy and self-consciousness and push their self-esteem into freefall.

At the same time, huge hormonal and brain changes are underway, often throwing logical reasoning off-kilter and opening the door to confusing and sometimes irrational thought processes. Add in the emotional upheaval of moving to a much larger school setting, making new friends and understanding their sexuality, and really, we have to wonder how any teenager emerges from these difficult and challenging times unscathed by mental illness.

Of course, most do manage to survive this period of their lives without major difficulties, but for a sizeable minority, the onslaught is just too powerful. For those, an eating disorder may present a coping mechanism, a way of gaining control when they feel so much of their life is out of their hands. Ironically, letting an eating disorder in can ultimately result in these vulnerable teenagers losing control completely.

As well as the unavoidable changes that occur during adolescence, other factors can also influence whether someone changes their behaviour around and attitude towards food. Bullying, peer pressure, moving schools or colleges, and exam pressures can also play a part. These are all things that schools should, if possible, be aware of.

Bullying has been shown to be a particular risk factor for eating disorders. Statistics from the US suggest that as many as 65 per cent of people with eating disorders say bullying contributed to their condition.[76]

Eve reflects back on how being bullied led her to a destructive path:

I suffered years of bullying throughout high school and so when I started skipping snacks and lunch in favour of hanging out in the library alone to read and study, I didn't recognise what was happening until I was deep into the depths of my anorexia.

While bullying can occur for many reasons, weight is one of them. Those who have a higher weight are six times more likely than their more slender peers to be teased,[77] and we know that even a throwaway comment about someone's size or shape can have a huge impact on them if they are vulnerable to developing an eating disorder. That said, any kind of bullying (not necessarily just about what someone looks like) can lead to plummeting self-esteem, which, as we know, is often one of the root causes of an eating disorder.

Peer pressure – the desire to 'keep up' with one's friends – can also play a part. There is no doubt that during the school years, from an increasingly young age, there is pressure to look a certain way. When young people compare their own body to their friends' (or to a celebrity) they are naturally more vulnerable to body dissatisfaction and self-doubt if they feel they do not measure up.

Hannah Arbuckle, a year 6 primary school teacher, says:

> We haven't had any children who have been suffering with an eating disorder; however, their self-awareness, body consciousness is much more prominent now than ever before. I put it down to social media and the internet.

Furthermore, how their friends behave can have a huge impact. There is some evidence that eating behaviours can influence and spread within a friendship group and while for some extreme weight loss or binge eating may be a passing phase, they can quickly become deep-seated in those who are more vulnerable. Dieting is a major risk factor for developing an eating disorder and is rife in schools where adolescents may be fixated on achieving a certain body shape, mistakenly believing that this will make them happier, more successful or more popular.

Hannah, who is in recovery from anorexia nervosa, talks of her experiences in school and her friendship group:

> Food is such a big topic that people talk about at school, whether it is an issue for them or not. Often if there is a party

> or gathering coming up, girls can spend days 'slimming', e.g. eating very little. Being in recovery from an eating disorder I can find that very hard to be around.

Melissa Helliwell, secondary school teacher, shares her thoughts:

> Currently in our area (Bournemouth), we have a significant number of situations where students have adopted a 'pack mentality' or, as they see it, regarding eating disorders, as a 'support group mechanism'. This links to misunderstanding information as in many cases they are putting their own spin on an already diagnosed and well-known condition.

A recent survey revealed that 27 per cent of teenagers care more about their appearance than their physical health, and that a third of boys surveyed feel pressured to attain a muscular figure, while 55 per cent of girls feel the pressures of being 'skinny'. Nearly half of the girls in the survey (47 per cent) said they had gone on a diet.[78]

That pressure to conform to a certain ideal is felt particularly strongly during adolescence, not least because young people can feel that success has to be achieved, no matter what the personal cost. There can be pressure to get good exam results, to achieve on the sporting field, to get into a certain school set or to move onto a particular college or university. Not achieving these things can leave a young person feeling that they are somehow lacking and that they must be to blame. That is when the desire to 'gain control' can come to the forefront once again.

Those with perfectionist tendencies may be particularly vulnerable. They can set themselves extremely high, often impossible, standards, possibly because they believe that if they meet these lofty benchmarks they will be worthwhile and successful. They may be seeking perfection in their school results, their sporting achievements or their body shape or weight. If they cannot achieve the impossibly high standards they set for themselves, they may then feel a failure.

Angela, mother of Sophie who is in recovery from an eating disorder, says of her experience:

> As parents we have never put any undue pressure on Sophie. All the pressure seemed to come from herself. She continually strived for more and was never satisfied with her achievements. The eating disorder started to appear when she was in year 9 and was practising for some exams; it spiralled pretty quickly as she used it as something she thought she could be the best at.

Particularly stressful times, such as exams, can be another trigger point for those at risk of eating disorders, while those already experiencing disordered eating may find their illness gets worse at these times of increased pressure. It is not unusual for people to react to stress by eating less or more, skipping meals or forgetting to eat. However, for people at risk of eating disorders, this can be particularly serious, especially as it is likely to be coupled with a time when they are setting themselves very high standards, are unsure about what the future holds, and when they may also be isolating and distancing themselves from those who care about them the most.

Teachers are well placed to spot the early signs

Teachers are in school to teach and, with increasingly stretched budgets and the pressure for their students to perform, we cannot deny that their jobs are harder than ever. However, they are also human beings and if faced with a student who they worry may have an eating disorder, few would I am sure turn their backs. However, they are not experts – and no one expects them to be.

Melissa, mother of a recovered anorexia sufferer, explains how her daughter's teacher was the first person to bring to light concerns about a change in Kate's behaviour:

In the previous October parents' evening, Kate's teacher remarked that she had noticed a big change in Kate's behaviour – that she was withdrawn and distracted and seemed unhappy. We put it down to a difficult friendship and a 'phase'. Even over the next few months, I didn't recognise she had an eating disorder, just continued to put her difficult behaviour (morose, moody, not getting along with her sister) down to her being pre-teen, tired and fed up with her friend. It wasn't until the following March that I could see that she might have a psychological problem, when she completely stopped eating her packed lunch and when asking her to eat something made her panicky!

It may therefore be helpful to note the signs of an eating disorder that may become particularly noticeable in the school environment.

It is also important to remember that these symptoms can also be present in boys as well as girls. Causes for concern may include the following – the teenager may:

- start to isolate themselves
- start to avoid eating around others
- display unusual behaviour around food
- struggle to concentrate in class
- show signs of tiredness and irritability
- display rigid behaviour patterns
- display weight changes up, down or fluctuating between the two
- show signs of low confidence and self-esteem
- set themselves unreasonably high standards
- wear baggy clothes or several layers of clothing
- start excessively exercising
- visit the bathroom more, especially after meals
- regularly skip lunch/throw their lunch away.

Hannah Rushbrooke, who is now fully recovered from OSFED, says of how her teacher at school had noticed something was amiss, and consequently approached the subject with her, leading to the first steps of early intervention:

> My teacher asked me to stay behind class and she sat me down and asked me if I was OK. She sensed something was very wrong, I hadn't been my normal bubbly self and I had grown gaunt. I remember the words 'I have a problem with food' fell out of my mouth. It felt immediately terrifying that I'd told someone, and it was no longer my little secret, but I also felt slightly relieved. It was a rocky road to recovery from that point, but that was the turning point... I had finally acknowledged I needed help.

How teachers can help

School staff not only play an important part in noticing the signs of an eating disorder, hopefully leading to early intervention, but they can also support the friends and family of someone suffering from or recovering from an eating disorder. A trusted teacher may also be the person that a student confides in if they are worried about their own mental health.

Richard Styles, head of year 10, discusses how he would support a student:

> The majority of young people who suffer with an eating disorder worry about having a lack of control – with eating, yes, but also with the knock-on effects of this. Having a meal with friends becomes problematic; having a much-needed snack in lesson time can lead to self-consciousness. The first step towards recovery is to ensure that the young person has a robust structure in place, which they feel complements their dietary requirements. As with the majority of mental health disorders, the ability to vocalise how you are feeling and be listened to and guided is paramount.

In an ideal world, it would be even better if schools could have a specific eating disorders policy, explaining the key risk factors and most likely symptoms they may see in their pupils, all laid out in language that is easy to understand. The policy would also lay down exactly what teaching staff should do if they suspect one of their pupils is at risk of developing an eating disorder, and who they should talk to in the first instance. Without clear leadership like this, it can be easy to approach things in the wrong way, or simply adopt a 'wait and see' approach that we know can be detrimental to a good outcome.

Melissa Helliwell, secondary school teacher, shares her thoughts on how the education sector can support young people:

> I believe that from a 'teacher' point of view, the education sector is not equipping schools, who have an increased and increasing responsibility to care for the 'whole student', with the tools to be effective in helping to 'prevent' problems and also 'support' young people. Obviously, there are a myriad of differing reasons for such a situation; however, information about issues such as 'eating disorders' are expanding all the time and we have an obligation to keep up. Time is a huge factor against making progress in this area as there are so many situations we could find ourselves in with the young people of today. It would be beneficial to have overview sessions and then designated teams across the school departments to ensure that areas of concern are not missed/do not go unidentified or unsupported. With more and more schools being in Academy Trusts (established to undertake strategic collaborations to improve and maintain high educational standards across a number of schools), this would be an ideal scenario to ensure we are meeting the needs of the complex and individual young people in our care.

Schools also have a part to play in looking after the siblings of someone with an eating disorder. When my Samantha was ill, we worked very closely with her form tutor, who was keen to support not only Samantha but also her sister Charlotte. We were acutely aware that Samantha's illness would affect Charlotte, and that she would at times feel neglected, concerned, resentful and stressed. The school kept an eye on Charlotte and was always sympathetic towards her situation, not just Samantha's.

Charlotte, as a protective older sibling (if only by an hour and 20 minutes), felt a huge pressure to look after her sister and had difficulty in dealing with the stress and worry associated with this responsibility. She became angry and frustrated for a time. She says:

> I felt quite alone and never talked about any of this to anyone. I felt like I had to be the strong one for everyone, especially at school. I had to protect Sammie as we were not at home for Mum or Dad to look out for her. I felt like I was the one who had to be watching all the time. The teachers supported Samantha a lot, and I am so grateful for this. We had a good group of friends around us that were always so patient with us and understanding. However, school years were very difficult, and I became someone, looking back on it now, that was totally not me.

Lessons in prevention

A school's role is not just to act when it is worried about a pupil. It is also to educate, inform and support pupils throughout their education, helping them understand about how to eat healthily and helping nurture their confidence so that they grow up with a strong sense of self. Good self-esteem and a confidence in one's own body is a powerful defence against a mental illness such as an eating disorder, and schools have an important – and wonderful – part to play in strengthening that armour that will protect their pupils throughout their life.

There are many opportunities throughout the curriculum to help young people grow a knowledgeable, confident and resilient attitude towards themselves and their bodies. From PSHE lessons through to PE, there are opportunities to discuss health and well-being. Home economics is another area where a healthy attitude to food can be nurtured. Even history lessons can shine a light on the fickle attitudes to body shape over the centuries, providing a point of discussion about unrealistic ideals.

Tea Gray, secondary school teacher, says:

In my 14 years of teaching I have never had training on eating disorders – only how to spot certain signs as part of safeguarding training. Students often hide eating disorders – I would really like training on how to encourage students to discuss their feelings with staff and be able to show them where to get help.

Through involving pupils in discussions about eating disorders, schools can help all young people to be aware of them, to provide a network of support for current sufferers and to look out for the signs and symptoms among their peers. Young people need to be aware of the dangers and consequences to their health and happiness, in a climate in which eating disorders are often glamorised or glossed over. It is, however, important that this is done in the right way, with an appropriate degree of sensitivity and within a wider context which all students can relate to.

In Chapter 3 we briefly touched upon 'wannarexia', which, while not technically an identifiable eating disorder in the medical sense, is a dangerous condition increasingly affecting teenagers. Many young women are surviving on very little food for days on end in a quest to emulate a super-slender beauty ideal, and young men are being tempted into making dangerous forays into steroids and creatine (a 'nutrition' shake laden with chemicals) to achieve the elusive 'six pack'. It would be futile to quibble about where the line is drawn between an eating disorder and a confused attitude towards food, when the salient fact is that a large proportion of the under-25s are taking dangerous risks with their diet and exercise regimes which could have a severely negative impact on their long-term health.

This is precisely why the common thread of low self-esteem which unites all of these behaviours needs to be emphasised and addressed, in the school environment as much as anywhere else. Samantha, of course, is in a position to comment on this from the perspective of having been a student with an eating disorder:

> I feel not all the focus should solely be on food and what you can't do; it should be on what you can achieve and what else you can live for, i.e. friends, hobbies and talents. This I feel will help sufferer see outside their illness and encourage them to see what they can get better for ... it certainly worked for me!

As a parent, this is something worth knowing. Often parents try to counteract extreme diets or a sudden gym obsession by telling their children that they are 'fine' or 'gorgeous' just the way they are. Having had an insight into many teenagers' motivations for embarking on extreme dietary and exercise regimes, it appears that this well-meaning gesture might not always be the correct tactic.

Debbie, the mother of a former anorexia sufferer, tells us of how her daughter's dieting and exercise spiralled out of control:

> My daughter left junior school obese. Aged 13 she dieted and exercised and looked amazing. I was so proud of her. Everyone complimented her. But she couldn't stop. I walked in on her in her underwear and was shocked at how skeletal she'd become. We needed help.

In reality, sadly, there is no shortcut to combating the low-self-worth epidemic in young people. Insecurity is, to a certain degree, a normal part of growing up. The answer lies in allowing teenagers to understand their value and recognise their talents, and in so doing allowing them to see that they can be successful without becoming a carbon copy of someone else.

To go to school or not?

When Samantha became very poorly, my first instinct, as a mother, was to take her out of school completely. Her frail state, both mentally and physically, meant that, logically, she was not fit for much besides lying on the sofa at home.

There are probably many medical professionals who would argue that this instinct was correct. Physically, certainly, Samantha should have been pretty much sedentary and conserving calories. However, as we now know, eating disorders are a mental illness, and I could not help but be concerned as to what keeping Samantha away from the routine of a normal life would do for her mind-set.

As much as I wanted to keep my baby at home and wrap her in cotton wool, I also recognised that this would not be the best way to help her towards recovery. At home she would have more time to obsess and to focus on food, to navel-gaze and to be gripped further by her demons. Doing nothing day after day would have made her forget who she was. She would have become her eating disorder; it would have defined her and that is an almost insurmountable obstacle to overcome. Once a sufferer allows themselves to believe that their eating disorder is an integral part of them, they will find it even harder to relinquish it completely.

Looking back, Samantha recognises that our decision to keep her in school was the right one. She also, having learnt about the experiences of other ex-sufferers, believes that being placed in full-time medical care might have taught her habits that would have made it even harder for her to get better. Remembering her time in school, she says:

> Although my exercise and food intake was monitored to an extent whilst I was at school, I still felt a lot freer than I would have done if I hadn't been there. I also now realise how much

Chapter 10

> the teachers supported me and how much extra help they gave me. This helped me to keep up with my studies, which led to me doing really well in my GCSEs – something I never thought I would have been capable of!

A key part of recovery is allowing a sufferer to see who they are and what their life could be like outside their illness. And so we took the decision that Samantha should remain in school and maintain as normal a routine as was possible. This was no easy feat. The decision involved my attending regular, intense and lengthy meetings two or three times a week at the school, and her teachers monitoring her closely, yet in a way which did not make her feel stifled. I was lucky to have the unequivocal support of the staff at Hinchley Wood Secondary School, Surrey, which allowed us to present a united and consistent front, enabling us to bring Samantha back to health.

One particular tricky issue was to negotiate Samantha's love of sport. While, as her disorder developed, she had become increasingly obsessed with exercise, attending after-school and evening clubs almost every night, sport had been something she enjoyed before she became ill. Sport was a part of her personality, something which she had to learn to enjoy in a healthy way again during her journey to rediscovering herself.

Luckily, her PE teachers, Leanne and Caroline, recognised this. Caroline says:

> As a PE teacher you are in a position where you are one of the most likely people in school to spot [an eating disorder]. I think exercise was part of Sam's anorexia, which was why it was so important to keep the fun and social element of it, too, so it didn't just become a bad thing.

Leanne continues:

> I kept a close eye on Sam. I let her join in [games] as usual,
> having made sure she had eaten prior to the lesson (or after-
> school clubs) because I wanted her to continue to do the things
> she enjoyed, but not overdo it.

As she recovered, Samantha also had to eat regularly during the day, and her teachers, supporting this, allowed her to eat in class rather than disrupting her routine and embarrassing her by making her leave the lessons to eat at the appointed times.

Our decision to keep Samantha in school was a personal one that felt right for our family and which ultimately, we believe, helped Samantha to recover. Other families will take a different view, possibly through discussion with health professionals. I respect that others will decide to keep their child out of school, and I hope, through the reasons given above, that others will understand why we chose a different path.

Melissa Helliwell ends this section, giving us her thoughts on how to support a student:

> This requires care, patience and time. …Knowing they have a
> safe place or sounding board is a good start.
>
> Keeping lines of communication open as much as possible
> between all stakeholders ensures support without being
> 'smothered'. Being consistent but flexible. Routine is a major
> part of the condition, therefore you need to adapt to the needs
> of the student and others involved in their care. Everyone
> should be aware of stress points within the student's life – not
> to take them over, but to ensure support is there should it be
> needed.

Eating disorders at university

The move from school to university can be a difficult one to make, involving leaving home for the first time, meeting new people, facing unknown experiences, and having to take control of your own finances – and own life – for the first time. It is no wonder that it can be a particularly challenging time for those with an eating disorder or those vulnerable to developing one.

While some students adjust with apparent ease to the transition, others may feel overwhelmed by the new responsibilities they face. Most expect university to be the best days of their life, and if it feels very differently, they may turn to individual coping mechanisms, such as controlling what they eat, to handle the enormous tide of change.

All this can be made worse by the move away from home. Without the support circle of family and established friendships, it is easy to feel very isolated. It is also very hard, in that new and unfamiliar environment, to find someone to trust and confide in. That means that those battling a mental illness can find themselves often suffering in silence, their eating disorder or anxiety steadily gaining control often without anyone really noticing.

Hannah Rushbrooke shares her experience:

> I relapsed at university pretty much straight away. The transition from the safety net of your family home to all of a sudden being independent and having total freedom was absolutely terrifying and the emotions that came with the change presented themselves in eating disorder behaviours once again. Beyond the element of my new-found freedom in terms of living arrangements, I faced the pressures a lot of students find themselves with, which were keeping up with the social side of student life, balancing that with my degree itself and working at a part-time job...it was all overwhelming and looking back I don't know how I did it, especially when in utter turmoil with my eating disorder.

The situation can spiral out of control with terrifying ease. With no one cooking the student meals or watching what they eat, it is worryingly easy for them to adopt a very strict diet or an obsessive attitude towards food and exercise.

Universities have increasing awareness of their res-ponsibilities towards students with mental illness, but the nature of college life, where individuals can so easily slip under the radar, makes providing a safety net for the most vulnerable more challenging. I would urge parents or carers who have a niggling concern about their loved one not to ignore it, even – or maybe especially – if they no longer live at home. Make regular visits to your child, talk to them often, encourage them to share their worries or concerns, and follow your instinct if you feel that something is amiss.

The workplace

Those who struggle with eating disorders at school or university may continue to battle this mental illness when they are in the world of work. Others may find that an eating disorder actually develops when they are older, possibly as a direct or indirect consequence of their working life. Furthermore, there are many thousands of people at work today who will be desperately juggling the demands of their employment with the stress of caring for a loved one with an eating disorder. All of these people's health and productivity could be compromised because of this mental illness, making it essential that employers play their part in creating a working environment which is both knowledgeable about eating disorders and supportive to those who are affected by them.

Mental health in general is currently a hot topic and employers are starting to recognise their responsibility for supporting employees with a mental health issue as much as they would someone with a physical illness. However, it is questionable whether eating disorders are being properly recognised as part of this discussion.

In a survey I carried out through my social media channels into sufferers' experiences of having an eating disorder while they were working, just over half of respondents said their colleagues and bosses were aware of their eating disorder, yet a similar proportion felt that their employers were not as supportive as they could have been.

This suggests that there is some way to go to educate employers, managers and human resource teams about eating disorders. Having a vague working knowledge gleaned from articles in the press or anecdotes from friends is rarely enough. There are so many myths that pervade society about eating disorders that it is not unreasonable to ask companies to have a policy around them and provide regular training for those who oversee teams of employees. After all, eating disorders do have the highest mortality rate of any mental illness.

Promoting a respectful and understanding environment at work is also important. Feeling able to open up about a mental illness such as an eating disorder, and believing you will be supported for doing so, could be absolutely critical in helping someone you work with get the help they need.

One of the participants of the survey says the following about their new job, which is refreshing and encouraging to hear:

> I am starting a new support work job, where the employer is very keen to look after the wellbeing of the workers, e.g. open-door office policy, no pressure to work more hours than I can manage.

Spotting an eating disorder at work

As we know, early recognition of an eating disorder can lead to early intervention, and that places someone in the best possible environment for recovery. This is where everyone, from families and friends to schools and workplaces, can play such a key part.

Many people spend eight hours a day at work, five days a week. That is more time than some of them spend with their families. It means that the opportunities for spotting the signs that a colleague is struggling with disordered eating are frequent. However, even if someone suspects that a colleague may be at risk, they often do not know what to do about it.

I have already covered in earlier chapters the signs and symptoms of an eating disorder. These all still apply. At work, however, there are a few other things that colleagues can also look out for. These can include:

- Skipping meals or only taking small portions
- Eating very rigid and ritualistic meals. This may include taking the same foods to work every day which may be perceived as very 'healthy'.
- Poor job performance or increased absenteeism.
- Difficulty concentrating at work.
- Taking frequent, prolonged toilet breaks.
- Frequent mood swings, self-esteem issues, compulsive behaviours or signs of depression.
- Exercising in an obsessive or compulsive way, despite poor weather, extreme tiredness or injury.
- Dramatic weight loss or gain.
- A marked preoccupation with food.
- Evidence of binge eating, such as finding wrappers or containers that suggest someone is regularly over-eating.
- Withdrawing from social activities, such as not joining colleagues for lunch or after-work get-togethers.

In the survey I carried out, the eating disorder sufferers who responded told me the effect their illness had on their working life. Time and again they talked of the deep fatigue that engulfed them during the working day. Many of them mentioned how hard it was for them to concentrate on their work. Others raised the issue of eating in front of colleagues and how uncomfortable or self-conscious that made them feel. There were, in other words, many signs that they were suffering. However, for some, having a routine, and being in a different environment from their home, could work in a positive way towards aiding recovery, as Lucy explains:

> Getting a more permanent job and more hours has helped hugely because I eat at the correct times and it helps me stay busy throughout the day instead of thinking about food or getting bored and bingeing; it also allows me to have money to buy foods I would like to eat, which helps me stay satisfied and stops me wanting to binge.

It is also important to remember that eating disorders can affect anyone. They do not discriminate on the basis of gender, race, sexual orientation, ethnicity or age. Being aware of the signs and acting on them if you are concerned, no matter whether they are male, female, young or older, could make a real difference to the outcome of a colleague's illness.

How colleagues and employers can help

It is one thing being concerned about someone at work, but quite another knowing what to do about it. Remember that anyone at work has the right to privacy and, regardless of your relationship with them, sharing your concerns with others may breach this confidentiality. If your company has a human resources department, this may well be the best place to take your concerns.

If you are close to them and consider yourselves friends as well as colleagues, then you may feel able to broach the subject with them directly. If that is the case, it is best not to accuse them of having an eating disorder. Instead tell them how you are concerned and are there for them if they would like to talk or get further help. Encourage them to speak with a professional.

Ethan tells us of how he approached a work colleague about his concerns:

I had noticed that a colleague of mine was becoming more and more absent from work and would often shy away at lunch time. He seemed to have lost his sense of humour and was becoming quite withdrawn and introverted, which was completely out of character for him. I arranged for us to go for a drink after work; in this time he seemed quite eager to open up after I broached the subject gently. I think for him this was a stepping stone towards him getting some help.

Whether or not someone in their team shows any sign of an eating disorder, or indeed any other mental illness, employers should feel a responsibility to make their workplace as open and supportive as possible – and that means doing the right thing as well as saying the right thing. Employers, line managers and human resources teams should, if possible, send out a strong signal that their staff's mental health is valued, and that people can feel confident that raising issues about an eating disorder will be supported and not discriminated against.

There are many ways that employers can demonstrate this. Simply by encouraging an environment where people are listened to will help to build trust. Allowing employees to speak up, to voice ideas, to play a part in the direction of the company will reassure them that what they say matters. If and when in the future they need the support of their employer, they will feel more confident that they are likely to get it.

Being a considerate employer, creating opportunities and learning, and encouraging regular one-to-one meetings and mentoring, will also help build trust and give employees somewhere to turn and raise concerns if they need to.

If an employer or manager finds out or suspects that an employee has an eating disorder, the crucial first step is to give them the chance to talk honestly and openly, and this should continue if they take time off sick. They should ask what their employee needs, such as an extra break or time off for counselling or medical appointments, and make reasonable adjustments to help. It is also important to remember that everyone's experience of mental health issues is different, and the support provided to employees should – as much as possible – be tailored to that individual's needs.

It is not an employer's job to be a therapist to someone in their team. Instead, they should provide the individual concerned with access to information which they can use to get the support they need. This may include details of a confidential telephone service or of one-to-one counselling sessions with a qualified therapist.

Promoting wellbeing at work

In addition to providing an open and supportive environment at work, employees – and businesses themselves – will also reap the rewards of a workplace that actively promotes and encourages wellbeing. From providing strong managerial support to introducing wellbeing activities, such as yoga or meditation, a responsible and caring employee can have a truly positive impact on its team's mental health and happiness.

As well as looking at the messages that their attitude gives out, employers should also consider how the physical environment of the office may have an impact on those struggling with disordered eating. Are there suggestions or posters that put an undue focus on weight or body image, for example? It is also helpful to think of the culture around eating and lunchtimes. Are colleagues encouraged to eat together or is there an unspoken expectation of eating at desks or not taking a break at all?

Finally, creating a working environment that promotes a good work/life balance is absolutely vital for good mental health. Recognising when someone feels overworked, under-valued, lonely or disrespected reflects an employer who cares about their workforce. Promoting discussions about wellbeing and mental health is also important. It shows that these are not taboo subjects and means employees will feel more able to raise their own issues or concerns more quickly.

Supporting those caring for someone with an eating disorder

It is not just those who are suffering from an eating disorder who need a supportive employee. People who are caring for or are affected by someone else who is struggling also need understanding at work. Supporting a loved one with an eating disorder can be emotionally and mentally demanding, and it can also take up a lot of time. Employers who can recognise this and who can make the adjustments that an employee in this position may need will be rewarded in thanks and loyalty by their workforce.

Carers and loved ones of those with eating disorders should be treated with the same care and respect as an employee who actually has the illness themselves. They should be afforded privacy and confidentiality, and be asked what adjustments would help them balance the demands of their work and home life. Pointing them towards professional help and support can also be valuable.

Melissa, mother of Kate who is now recovered from anorexia nervosa, tells of how her work supported her unconditionally:

I work at the school my daughter was at when she was ill. As soon as she was diagnosed, I told my head teacher, and explained that we were looking for help for her, but that I had no idea what it would entail. My head teacher knew of my concerns previously, as I had talked to her and Kate's class teacher regularly leading up to the point where we had a diagnosis of what was wrong with her. Once we had met Lynn, we agreed Kate needed intensive counselling fast to halt progression of the illness and start recovery. I was relieved and so thankful that my head teacher straightaway offered me her, and her senior leadership team's, full support. I was released to take Kate out of school for her hour's counselling sessions three times a week, and not only that, then to take her home to have lunch, which at first could take over two hours to finish. Sometimes I would only make it back for the last half hour of the school day.

Kate could have the frequency of counselling she needed without me having to stress about work. Lunchtimes could take as long as they needed to take; tears, rantings and painfully slow mouthfuls were very difficult, but we consistently made it to the other side, i.e. a clean plate, because the pressure of time didn't exist. As a consequence of this intensive intervention, Kate's progress was incredibly quick, and after one school term like this, we could return in the September to a normal timetable. Without this caring, understanding and generous support, I don't know how things might have turned out. In the midst of a crisis like this, nerves are so overwrought and emotions so utterly exhausted, the freedom to focus on your child to this degree is priceless. The reward was a child well into recovery, and her mother back doing her full week's work, within a school term.

To conclude

It is essential that everyone involved in the life of an eating disorder sufferer employs compassion, understanding and patience. In this way, schools, universities and workplaces can become an effective part of the caring network for people struggling with eating disorders.

Throughout this book I have been careful to emphasise that eating disorders do not affect just the young. However, sometimes the underlying issues can begin to develop and form at this crucial age. Schools, colleges and universities are all environments where eating disorders can take root. Where schools can, they should incorporate self-esteem into their programme – and preferably from an outside speaker. I say this not because I believe teachers are ill-equipped to deal with the issues, but because I know that young people will often open up to a stranger, safe in the knowledge that they will never see that person again.

One charity local to me that believes passionately in the importance of making schools more aware of mental illness is the Grace Dear Trust. Sadly, Grace Dear took her own life in 2017 aged 27. She had been ill since her early teens but barely recognised her own demons, let alone felt able to open up to her family, friends or teachers.

Her younger sister, Hope, who helps run the charity her family set up in Grace's name, wants to give schools more help – both financial and practical – in breaking the silence on mental illness.

At the Grace Dear Trust we believe that the earlier people start talking about their feelings and start getting the help they need, the better the outcome will be for them. That's why we go into schools to tell them Grace's story as well as talking about mental health in general. We also provide funding to local secondary schools to train teachers and pay for counsellors, who can support students when they first ask for help rather than them having to go on waiting lists while their illness gets worse.

Schools have a really important role to play. The teaching and support staff see students almost as much as parents do. Furthermore, young people may sometimes find it easier to approach teachers, for themselves or on behalf of a friend, than they would a family member.

Mental illness is like a cancer. The sooner you catch it, the more likely you are to come through it.

Workplaces also have a part to play. A good employer will do all it can to promote a happy, healthy and respectful working environment, and should feel a sense of duty to understand mental illnesses, including eating disorders, and the effect they can have on the lives of their employees.

Chapter 10

One initiative that could help to support those with eating disorders in schools, universities and at work is the Mental Health First Aid movement (mhfaengland.org), a community interest company that aims to train one in 10 people in Britain to recognise the signs of mental illness and to support those who suffer from it. If MHFA's vision becomes a reality, there will be much more backing in future to support people to stay well, recover or manage their symptoms, no matter what stage in life they are at.

There is much more work being done to break the taboo around mental illness. My Samantha, a recent drama graduate, has joined with friends to develop a funny and thought-provoking sketch show challenging and breaking that stigma. Through her work with 'My Mental Life', she is turning the illness that once tormented her on its head, using humour to educate others.

I applaud her and all others working to support those tortured by mental illness, including eating disorders, and hope that many more people will take the opportunity to understand how sufferers feel, and find out more about what they can do to help.

Chapter 11

Eating disorders in exercise and sport

Exercise

Exercise is good for the mind, body and spirit.

Those who exercise regularly tend to do so because it gives them a greater sense of overall wellbeing. They tend to have more energy throughout the day, sleep better at night, have sharper memories and feel more relaxed and positive about themselves and their lives.

Activity and exercise are especially important for people living with, and coping with, mental health issues, not least because people who have mental illness can often have a higher risk of physical illness. Similarly, people with physical illnesses can be at a higher risk of developing mental illness, such as depression, anxiety, disordered eating and/or OCD. The body and mind exist in balance, directly affecting one another. Therefore, the challenge for someone suffering from an eating disorder is to strike a healthy balance of exercise within their lifestyle, without allowing it to become an obsession. Equally, learning to enjoy exercise can play a fundamental part within recovery from an eating disorder.

Scientists and research studies have discovered that exercise causes the brain to release chemicals (for example, serotonin) which can make you feel good;[79] these are the same components which are enhanced by antidepressants – but without the side effects!

Lucy, a former sufferer of anorexia, orthorexia and binge eating disorder, says:

> I go to the gym in moderation to help clear my head of anxiety and get endorphins, so that helps with my low mood.

Regular exercise can promote all kinds of positive changes in the brain, including neural growth, reduced inflammation, and new activity patterns that aid feelings of calm and wellbeing. It can also release endorphins, as Lucy mentioned, which are powerful chemicals in the brain that leave the person feeling energised and positive. Exercise can also serve as a distraction, allowing the person to find some 'time out' to enable them to break out of the cycle of their possible negative thoughts that feed their mental illness.

Mental and emotional benefits of exercise

- **More energy:** Increasing the heart rate several times a week will help the person to have more energy.
- **Stronger resilience:** When faced with mental or emotional challenges in life, exercise can help a person cope in a healthy way, instead of turning to alcohol, drugs or other negative behaviours that will ultimately make the person feel worse. Regular exercise can also help boost the immune system and reduce the impact of stress.
- **Sleep better:** Even small amounts of exercise at regular intervals can help to regulate sleep patterns.
- **Self-esteem:** Regular activity can benefit the mind, body and soul. When it becomes part of everyday life, it can foster a sense of self-worth and make the person feel

strong and powerful. They will feel better about how they look and by meeting personal goals will gain a sense of achievement.

- **Sharper memory and thinking:** The same endorphins that make a person feel positive can also help with concentration and improve the sharpness of the person's thinking for the tasks at hand. Exercise also stimulates the growth of new brain cells and helps prevent age-related decline.

Exercise can also have a beneficial social component. Being part of a team or club can help a person to feel they have a sense of identity and belong to a network of people, united by their passion for a particular activity. Working as a team through sport can help to build self-confidence and self-belief as well. All of which has to be a much healthier way to socialise than via the internet!

Tom, a long-distance runner, shares his experience of being part of a running community during his recovery:

> Whilst a desire to improve my performances was one of the contributing factors to my eating, the support of friends and other runners has been immense and invaluable.
>
> I became very guarded and reclusive during my illness, so feeling part of a community has helped increase my self-worth, my social skills and my wellbeing.
>
> It made me realise that I am worthy of fun, friendships and the support of others, and has also allowed me to track my physical recovery.

A person does not need to devote hours and hours of their day to exercise, or train at a gym, sweat buckets, or run mile after mile after mile to reap the benefits of it. They can obtain all the physical and mental health benefits of exercise with 30 minutes of moderate exercise five times a week or even two 15-minute exercise sessions five times a week will work equally as well.

Wendy Martin, a lecturer in sports and sports therapy, confirms the above:

> Exercise is essential if we are to lead a healthy and fulfilling life. The physical benefits have been widely reported for many years ... Psychological benefits should not be neglected and can play an extremely powerful role in the road to recovery for many individuals who have experienced disorders of the mind. Chemical activity triggered by exercise can reduce anxiety, stress and depression and can also play a role in improving immune function.

Tan Quddus, an experienced personal trainer, adds:

> There is such a strong link between physical activity and mental wellbeing that it simply cannot be ignored. Taking part in regular exercise reduces anxiety and depression whilst improving self-esteem, confidence and overall quality of life. Whether it's going to the gym or being outdoors, with friends and family or a personal trainer, exercise can play a vital role in maintaining health in both body and mind.

The message, here, is that sport and exercise are not the enemy, contrary to the beliefs of many.

Hope Virgo, author and mental health advocate, says of how she turned her obsession into a healthy relationship with exercise, so aiding her recovery:

> When I relapsed, I began to exercise too much again. Instead of letting it dominate my life I got a personal trainer who helped me get back on top of it, teaching me the benefits of other types of exercise and of weights. From varying my workouts it helped me see them as fun again. Something I had to learn to manage was my change in body shape and increase in weight due to muscle. I had to learn to love my body the way it was now and accept that I had changed shape.

In order to gain some clarity with regard to how to navigate the precarious line between beneficial exercise and compulsive exercise, I commissioned a survey of more than 500 past and present eating disorder sufferers, with a view to finding out what approach they took to exercise.

All participants in the survey were over the age of 16. Around 75 per cent were female. Of those surveyed, 38.1 per cent said they participated in strenuous exercise more than three times per week (for example, going to the gym). It is important to note that this is not recommended by medical professionals, who state that three times a week is the optimum number of times to perform strenuous exercise for people who are not training for a specific event. The most popular reason cited for undertaking this exercise was to maintain a desired body shape/look good. Having said that, almost half of those surveyed said they wanted to maintain a 'healthy body and mind', although 30.3 per cent also said they wanted to lose weight. From these statistics it is clear that some unhealthy attitudes and behaviours have lingered within the participants' minds.

At the conclusion of the survey, participants were asked if they had anything to add which they felt was important. Bearing in mind that we do not know the nature of the participants' past or present body or eating issues, below are some of the more interesting and positive replies, which demonstrate how to achieve a healthy balance:

- I do a yoga class once a week and yoga at home three times per week. I walk 40 minutes daily, quite fast, and walk on escalators. I go out dancing about once a month. Basically, I move for fun and/or to get me somewhere!

- I do not do as much intense exercise as I would like, but I have previously been in a place where I became obsessive, so the gym is not a good environment for me. I have found a balance by walking everywhere, up to five miles every day, which allows me to stay toned and really clears my head.

- I exercise because I enjoy it. I enjoy training for an outcome, whether to relieve stress or make the squad. I need to have some motivation, whether it is someone running by my side or something to aim for.

- It is important to relax properly after exercise so I meditate and/or pause and that gives me a more balanced perspective on life.

- I find exercise extremely empowering. Many believe that it is negative for people who are recovering from an eating disorder to take part in exercise; however, I have found weight training and sports supplements vital in my weight gain and recovery.

What we learn from these comments is that it is possible to find an exercise regime that complements recovery and a healthy, balanced lifestyle; however, it is also important to examine the motivations behind exercise in order to do so. The most important factors are:

1. The sufferer, or past sufferer, should choose a form of exercise they enjoy. Exercise should never seem like a punishment.

2. The sufferer or past sufferer should steer clear of any environments in which they once exercised compulsively, or used exercise to purge, prior to their decision to recover.

3. The motivation for exercise should always be to maintain a healthy mind and body – that might mean losing weight for compulsive or binge eaters, but that is a side-effect rather than the main goal.

It is also crucial for eating disorder sufferers to acknowledge that if they are exercising more, they will need to increase their calorie intake to allow their body to cope with the demands of physical activity. The following testament, from one of the participants of my survey, along with my own more positive experiences with my daughter Samantha, mean that I do not believe banning exercise altogether is effective:

> I have been on an exercise ban for 1.5 years and it still kills me every day. Everyone is so obsessed with exercise and calories, even people without eating disorders. My recovery has been so slow – I exercise in secret to stop from gain[ing] weight and to make me feel less guilty for going against the grain and having to eat more.

In this instance, the sufferer has been told, metaphorically, 'not to think of a pink elephant'. If she were allowed to exercise publicly in moderation and to enjoy it, then rather than see it as necessary in order to burn calories, it might very well do wonders for her mind-set.

My Samantha found exercise extremely beneficial, mentally and physically, throughout her recovery process. She worked with a highly experienced personal trainer, Jess, on a regular basis, who had a great understanding of mental illness, which meant that she was able to closely monitor Samantha's mental and physical progress throughout.

Jess Bonstein, a qualified personal trainer, speaks of their journey together:

My first impression of Sam when she first began training with me was of a quiet and unsure young girl. She was trying to be positive and bravely showed me a picture of what she wanted to achieve – a healthy, shapely body – but I could tell she was hesitant in believing that she could manage it. Watching her progress and improve was not just a physical journey. As her body grew stronger she grew stronger mentally, more positive and confident, not only in the gym but also outside of it. She regained her appetite, both for food and for life.

Samantha adds:

> Training has helped me build a strong, fit, healthy body that I am mentally in love with and physically know it is the foundation that will help me conquer the world!

Paige dittos Samantha's thoughts on how exercise has played a big part in her recovery:

> Exercise has really helped me. I have a personal trainer who tailors my sessions to suit me and ensures that I build muscle and become stronger instead of burning fat and losing weight. I think it is just as important as the therapy that I received.

For people who struggle with over-eating or have binge eating disorder, exercise – or simple gentle physical activity – can have many benefits over and above simply burning calories.

Jay Hurley, a highly experienced personal trainer, says:

People suffering from binge eating disorder tend to feel a loss of control when they binge. Exercise allows a little bit of control back to the sufferer; improving themselves and feeling better through exercise is extremely powerful. A release of 'feel good' endorphins like dopamine, norepinephrine and serotonin during and after exercise can help gain a better control over a binge eating condition. Whether the sufferer is overweight, or a healthy weight, exercise has been shown to improve self-esteem, quality of life and confidence.

However, for these people in particular, just the thought of exercise can provoke some difficult and sometimes shameful emotions. They may assume that gyms are not for 'people like me' and feel anxious that others will judge them if they do join an exercise class or take up a sport.

Supporting them to either overcome those feelings or find another route to physical activity is important. After all, exercise does not need to mean sweating in a gym or taking part in a team sport. Simply going for a walk, taking a swim, or joining an upbeat dance class are all ways of getting active and will have significant benefits, reducing the risk of illnesses associated with obesity, while releasing the feel-good hormone serotonin that can trigger a happier, more positive mind-set.

While exercise can be a really important part of someone's recovery toolkit, carers should be mindful of not pushing their loved one into something they do not want to do. In some cases, instead of buying them a gym membership or committing them to a particular goal, it could be more helpful to support them in gradually incorporating more physical activity into their daily life, such as walking instead of driving short distances and taking the stairs instead of the lift, or helping them find an exercise they enjoy.

Someone suffering from an eating disorder and/or other mental health issues may find it difficult to take the first step into healthy exercise. Here are some common barriers and some ways in which they can be overcome:

- **Feeling overwhelmed:** When a person feels stressed, anxious or low, the thought of adding another obligation can seem overwhelming and impossible. It is important to remember that physical activity helps us to do and cope with things better. So, try to think of exercise as a priority and find ways to fit small amounts into everyday life.

- **Feeling exhausted:** When a person is tired and lethargic, it can feel like working out will make things worse and is all too much effort. However, it is worth remembering that the truth is that physical activity is a powerful energiser. Studies have shown that regular exercise can dramatically reduce fatigue and increase energy levels.[80] The best place to start is at the beginning – for example, a person could go for a five-minute walk around the block or up and down the road, with the idea of increasing the time by a minute or two each time. As they start to feel the benefit from it, it will hopefully not be a chore but an enjoyment.

- **Feeling hopeless:** Even if a person is starting at rock bottom they can still work out. Exercise helps people to get into shape. If they have no experience of exercising, start slowly with a low-impact movement a few minutes each day and slowly building it up gently.

- **Feeling bad about yourself:** Most people are their own worst critic. No matter what your weight, age or fitness level, there are many others with the same goals of getting fit who feel the same. Being with people who are all in the same shoes helps. Perhaps take a class with people of a variety of fitness levels. Accomplishing even the smallest of fitness goals will help the person gain body confidence. Which can only lead to them feeling better about themselves.

Exercise can be enjoyed in many ways – throwing a frisbee with a dog or a friend, walking around a shopping centre, cycling to work or simply going for a walk. Activities such as gardening or even doing small improvements to the house can be good ways to start moving around more. As well as helping to become more active, these activities can also leave the person with a sense of purpose and accomplishment.

However, at this point I must emphasise, in some instances, that exercise can turn into an obsession and therefore have a negative impact on someone's recovery, particularly in those relating to eating disorders. Some people with mental health issues can use exercise to fuel their illness, as Hope, who is now in recovery from anorexia nervosa, explains:

Prior to getting unwell I had always been sporty. But as I got unwell exercise became one of my things I did. For me it became an obsession. A way to lose more weight and something to take my mind off things when I was struggling. I would exercise at all hours and push myself harder in all my training sessions.

Exercise should never become an obsession. A way to tell if someone is exercising excessively is firstly by monitoring how often they exercise. It is also important to monitor how the individual feels if their routine is changed. If they become anxious and panicked about missing a session of exercise, then their habit may have developed into an obsession and outside intervention may be needed.

Sport

Taking part in sport, from grassroots level right through to elite competition, is generally seen as a 'healthy' thing to do, and those who take part are seen to be living a healthy lifestyle. Those at the top of their game, competing at the highest level, are regarded as role models at the pinnacle of physical fitness.

It is hard then to square this with the uncomfortable truth that in fact eating disorders are more prevalent among athletes than they are in the general population. A recent study, quoted by UK Sport, has found an overall prevalence of eating disorders of 13.5 per cent, representing 20.1 per cent among female athletes and 7.7 per cent among males (although it could be said that men may be less likely to seek help or be recognised as having an eating or exercise disorder).

Within these statistics, it is now recognised that there are certain sports that represent a higher risk of eating disorders, with studies identifying that up to 35 per cent of those competing in certain disciplines may have some kind of disordered eating.

These studies paint a worrying picture at elite level; however, it is not only these top athletes that are affected. It is fair to assume that to a certain extent this will filter down to people competing at amateur and lower levels as well, and this is where parents, carers, siblings, coaches and club officials can help not only to identify where disordered eating could be present, but also helping to prevent an environment where such mental illnesses could develop.

This is particularly important for those involved in the types of sports where eating disorders are known to be more prevalent. The biggest risks occur in three areas, although there is of course some risk in all sports. The first are those sports where a certain body aesthetic has historically been seen as more desirable for success, which includes gymnastics and dancing. The second area of concern is those sports that are dependent on competitors being a certain weight, such as riding or judo. The third are sports where endurance is key, such as athletics and rowing.

In these sports, as well as all others, the people who surround competitors, from a grassroots dance teacher to an Olympic coach, are well placed to identify, or ideally lower, the risk of disordered eating. As we know, eating disorders are highly complex and have many different causes, but the right approach within the sporting arena has a very important and influential part to play. For example, making any comment about an athlete's looks or physique can be ill-advised as, no matter what the intention, they may interpret those words differently, perhaps as a criticism, or a reinforcement that their possible disordered eating is 'working'.

Tom, a long-distance runner who is now recovered, says of how one comment triggered his disordered eating:

> My eating disorder began after it was suggested I needed to lose weight to improve my sporting performances as a long-distance runner. As my eating disorder developed, it was closely linked to my levels of sport and exercise.

At all levels of competition, there are 'dos' and 'do nots' that the sporting community should, if possible, adopt as basic rules:

Do:
- respect the sensitivity of athletes and how they may respond to comments about their body.
- be very wary with body fat measurements and recognise that they could trigger or worsen unhealthy eating.

- remember the complexity of the relationship between weight and illness and a lower weight is not a guarantee of improved performance.
- supervise any weight-loss programme carefully by someone qualified to do so, such as a dietitian.
- promote a nutrition education programme within the squad or team.
- remember that young athletes can be especially influenced by the behaviour of role models.
- reinforce a positive mind-set in athletes, making them more resilient to disordered eating behaviour.

Do not:
- weigh athletes publicly or display weights in a public place.
- make derogatory comments about an individual's weight or body.
- recommend extreme or faddy diets.
- impose the same standards of weight or body fat on different athletes.

Teachers, coaches and support staff should ideally be familiar with the characteristics of eating disorders and should, if possible, know how to access the right help and support for any of their squad or class that they may be concerned about. Approaching anyone who may have an eating disorder is not always easy; however, it is vital not to ignore any concerns that any of the sporting team may have about an individual. Sport UK says that athletes who are a cause for concern should be approached early, directly and honestly, confidentially, and supportively, without apportioning criticism or blame.

Initially the athlete may deny there is a problem, but making them aware there are concerns will leave the door open for them to seek help when they are ready. If concerns increase and further attempts to address the problem are resisted, a decision may need to be made about whether to allow an athlete to carry on training.

Supporting an athlete through recovery is the next stage that requires patience, understanding and flexibility from the community that surrounds them. The uncomfortable truth is that recovery from an eating disorder is often a slow process, with two steps forward frequently followed by one backwards. Focusing on the process of recovery, rather than fixing on the desired end result, can feel more manageable for everyone involved.

As the sufferer themselves struggles to come to terms with having an eating disorder, it is important that those around them stay calm and show understanding. As they begin their journey to recovery, it is crucial to boost their self-esteem and confidence, listening to them and validating their feelings. A care plan, if possible, should lay out how teachers, coaches and support staff can assist the athlete in setting realistic goals and continuing to participate in their sport at an appropriate level, should they still wish to do so, and it be safe for them. As that journey continues, being informed about their recovery and helping them develop their goals and then tackle those challenges will be invaluable. As they begin to make real progress in overcoming their eating disorder, their sporting community can help and support them identify their limits and their potential triggers that could affect their recovery, and put strategies in place to avoid a relapse.

Managing all this in a sporting environment is not always easy, but patience, understanding and flexibility must override any desire to push an athlete back into the competitive, high pressure arena before they are ready.

Naomi Cavaday, former British tennis player, shares her experience and thoughts:

> I don't think I would have got help as early as I did if it was not for my career in tennis. I had got to the point where I couldn't even concentrate in matches as I was so consumed by the bulimia and I was devastated by this. Once I had significantly improved and had control of my eating disorder I knew that I needed to look after my mental health. I recognised that life as a tennis player makes this incredibly difficult – I was always jetlagged and exhausted, constantly travelling, by myself most of the time, and dealing with incredibly pressurised situations frequently. Stepping away from tennis was the best way for me to look after my mental health.

It is wonderful to hear Naomi say:

> I am incredibly proud that I can get on and enjoy my life now with nothing holding me back.

To conclude

As this chapter demonstrates, the part that exercise and sport play in eating disorders is very important and can also be extremely contradictory. On one side of the equation, the ultra-competitive environment of sport can be one factor in the development of an eating disorder, despite athletes being seen by the general public as being at the pinnacle of physical health. Furthermore, excessive exercise can be a tactic employed by those with eating disorders in order to burn more calories.

As Naomi Cavaday concludes by saying:

> My sport had some negative impacts as well as positive. Tennis was a big reason for me to get healthy, and it was a big reason for me to lose weight in the first place. It was not the sport that made it worse, but more the environment which could have been a lot healthier.

However, on the other side of the equation, I personally

believe that doing some closely and highly supervised exercise with an experienced trainer can actually benefit those with an eating disorder during their recovery by giving them back a little bit of the life they enjoyed before the illness took hold. It is okay for carers to acknowledge that if their loved one is very sporty, that drive and determination they have previously used to win can be a really positive force in motivating them towards recovery from an eating disorder.

Chapter 12

Eating disorders and the media

Caring effectively for an eating disorder sufferer takes hard work, determination, perseverance, patience and compassion from everyone involved. It is essential, where possible, to provide coherent and consistent support to counter the destructive force of the illness.

Any cracks in that support strategy could let the eating disorder find its way in, so it is crucial that you, the carer, do everything in your power to make sure that does not happen. However, one of the things that could infiltrate your support network and potentially undo all your hard-won progress is – the media.

When I talk about the 'media' this includes newspapers, magazines, TV but also websites, social media, bloggers and influencers. They are omnipresent in most of our lives. Many of us simply could not function without them and at times they can be a valuable source of information. However, when it comes to the portrayal of body image and eating disorders, the media as a whole is a veritable minefield (and something which I could probably devote an entire book to, on its own!).

People have their own opinions about whether the positive impact of the media (raising awareness, highlighting support and, in terms of responsible bloggers and influencers, being a source of empathy and understanding) outweighs the negatives.

Chapter 12

It may be helpful to understand just what a potential minefield this is by explaining the most extreme viewpoints. In the red corner we have the people who claim that eating disorders are intensely private, emotionally driven mental illnesses, so it would be irresponsible to claim that factors such as our celebrity-worshipping culture, airbrushing, fashion and irresponsible 'influencers' could possibly be at their root. In the blue corner we have those who argue that it is impossible to ignore increasingly unrealistic and artificially enhanced beauty paradigms, fuelled more and more by social media and other media platforms, and that the immense pressure to conform to these is enough to drive anyone to an eating disorder.

Jamie, who has suffered from anorexia and depression, sheds some light on how he thinks the media can influence people:

> I feel media pressure has a big part to play in some cases; magazines these days are full of diets, fitness, photo-shopped pictures etc etc. 'How to look like this' is a common headline in today's media, but as we all know each one of our bodies, bone structure, facial features are genetically different, unless of course you're an identical twin. The more edited, unrealistic pictures are published, the more people are likely to strive to try and imitate them.

The truth, of course, lies somewhere in between. While there are increased incidents of orthorexia (an obsessive drive to eat only certain foods or follow a 'pure' diet – see page 63) being reported, the vast majority of eating disorders still do not have as their genesis a desire on the part of the sufferer to match up to celebrities and models. However, in many cases the media can provide a catalyst in the creation of body-image issues which can lead to eating disorders, as well as providing an obstacle to recovery.

Eating disorders and social media

A filtered world
By Samantha Crilly

It's hard to tell these days what is really real
Whether a smile in a photo is how one really feels
A laugh captured in a slight second
Was it a human reaction or just beckoned
The colours of the world once looked so true
Yet all the filters now wash away the world I once knew
It's been taken to somewhere unreachable, out of our grasp
Even the ones living it struggle to make it last
I still can't remember the point, when a photo for myself
Then become one for everybody else
> *I can't remember when I thought this world doesn't look bright*
> *enough*
I'll edit it here and there, how much can I bluff
> *And the first time I thought I need to filter my face*
Trying to hide my flaws which I used to embrace
Well everyone else's looked so much better than mine
I had to keep up with society, you know, keep in line
But you soon realise when you get in the queue,
There is always, always someone in front of you
Always looking like they have a better life
But often their back would be stabbed with a knife
Trying to carve the perfect life for everyone to admire
How many 'likes' can they hire?
But we all know 'likes' will one day expire
Our lives spent worrying about how many likes everyone else is giving us
We would have lost our time with everyone living our lives with us
A photo used to be a pure memory taken for one's joy,
But now it's become everyone's guilty toy,
I once asked my grandma what she thought of this world

Chapter 12

She said, 'It has lost all the purity it once held'
A true picture is a memory in the heart
It was pure, just for you, now that was art.

The internet can be a valuable source of help and encouragement for sufferers and carers alike, linking them to people enduring similar situations throughout the world and creating a mutually-supportive, positive online community. However, the internet's ability to unite like-minded people can be both a blessing and a curse. While few of us could function without it, it can, at times, be unregulated and should be used with the same degree of caution that you would use – and advise your loved ones to use – in the real world.

In general terms, people are still divided on whether social media and the internet as a whole are a good or bad thing and that is truer than ever when it comes to eating disorders, which is something I am going to explore in the next section of this chapter.

The good

Just a decade or so ago, people trapped in a destructive and obsessive cycle around food might have felt like they were the only one battling in this way and they might have struggled to know what they could and should do to try to move forward. Nowadays, simply typing a few words into Google will introduce them to a whole community of help, support, understanding and empathy – immediately, right when they need it, without having to make an appointment, go on a waiting list, or even venture outside their front door. As quickly as they can type the website address into their browser, the internet will take them to the blogs of people who have recovered from eating disorders and show them stories of those who have gone on to live and love in a way they can only imagine when they are stuck in the maelstrom of an illness such as anorexia, bulimia or binge eating disorder.

That kind of support is absolutely invaluable and many recovered eating disorder sufferers will credit that access through the internet as a key part of their journey to rehabilitation.

Hannah, who is now recovered from an eating disorder, says:

> I found the media very helpful in recovery as I came across other recovery accounts. I would read them for hours; I even messaged a few with questions They'd post what they ate or over feared and it would inspire me too. The gym accounts also helped me as I wanted muscles and a bum like them and I couldn't get that without eating and gaining.

It can also be a lifeline for the carer and their families. They, too, can often feel isolated, and the internet can introduce carers to a community that cares and understands, in a way that even their closest friends can find hard. The advice available online can help them know what to do and what to say, and above all give them an incredible insight into what their loved one is going through. Where would any of us be without being able to search online and find that we are not alone in whatever is troubling us or those we care about?

The internet and social media also allow both carers and the person they are caring for to keep connected with friends. For those struggling with a mental illness like an eating disorder, this can be a very important reminder of the life that exists outside the illness they may find themselves imprisoned in. It can be all too easy to be completely overwhelmed by an eating disorder so that a life outside becomes difficult to imagine. Staying in touch with friends on social media provides that tunnel of light to the outside world and, if sufferers are connected with people they perhaps knew in happier times, it can remind them that their life was once very different – and that it can be again.

Through blogs, social media and positive chatrooms, anyone

can share their experience. They can provide the insight of real people in real situations and give people the 'virtual hug' they need when the going gets tough.

The bad

Sadly, there is a negative and very dark side to the internet and social media. For every positive, inspiring, supportive post, there is usually one that is unhelpful, undermining and sometimes dangerous.

There are many different environmental factors that may contribute to disordered eating habits, and now social media is close to the top of that list. Used by individuals of all ages and backgrounds, accessible from their handbag or pocket 24 hours a day, it has begun to play a larger role in the influence and development of eating disorders.

Helping your loved one discriminate the good from the bad, the life-changing from the life destroying, is another crucial thing you can try do to help them on the road to recovery.

Thinspiration websites

'Pro-ana' or 'thinspiration' websites that promote extreme weight loss as a positive and desirable aspiration are at the extreme end of 'the bad', but for those who go online perhaps searching for weight loss advice or looking for affirmation that their feelings are 'normal', they can be a very real and present danger.

Why are they so dangerous? Where do I start? These now-illegal websites promote weight loss at any cost. They are set up, run and contributed to solely by people who suffer from severe eating disorders. However, rather than helping one another towards recovery, these sites aim solely to fuel and perpetuate eating disorders.

Charliee tells us of her experience:

> I remember having so much 'thinspiration' saved on my phone, photos and quotes. I was also guilty of using pro-ana websites. To help with my recovery I have now deleted all of them and have blocked the websites too.

What makes them even more dangerous is that they disguise themselves as an acceptable and, indeed, supportive place to turn to for help. Despite pro-ana sites now being totally illegal, they still exist. It is just that now they masquerade under the identity of a 'support network' or 'journaling group', and in doing so they can actively lure those simply looking for weight loss advice into eating-disordered behaviour.

The sites claim to 'understand' the confusing and destructive feelings which categorise the early stages of anorexia nervosa. They will then convince sufferers that what they are feeling is natural and healthy, and that the existence of these feelings makes them superior to anyone who is not suffering from anorexia. They will teach users how to fool medical professionals, their family and friends into believing that they are eating. They will share 'tips' on how to promote optimum weight loss. They spread the message that anyone trying to help the sufferer towards recovery is not acting in the sufferer's best interests, and that only they understand the true nature of anorexia nervosa and bulimia nervosa.

Users will post pictures of themselves in various states of emaciation. Other users will praise them when they have lost weight by writing encouraging comments and urging them to lose yet more weight. Some users will also post comments accusing them of being 'fat' (despite most being dangerously underweight) and tell them that they must try harder. Users will post their daily food intake, measurements, weights and BMIs.

Eating disorders can then become a game, with users competing against one another to eat the least, to purge the most effectively, to lose the most weight and to avoid medical intervention for the longest. For every bit of progress you may make in aiding your loved one towards recovery, these sites exist purely to unravel your hard work.

Owing to the fact that most pro-ana or 'thinspiration' sites claim to be a 'support network', they are very difficult to identify. As a carer it is therefore of the utmost importance that you are vigilant in spotting whether your loved one might be visiting them. One of the most obvious signs to look out for is the inclusion of photographs on the site. Genuine self-help networks, such as the forums on the *Beat* or *Men Get Eating Disorders Too* websites, will not allow users to post pictures of themselves online because these images can be triggering to other users.

The other obvious difference between a genuine support network and a pro-ana site is the inclusion of weights and measurements. All posts on genuine sites are checked by a moderator, who should remove anything referring to how much users weigh, or their daily food intake. This will be stated in their 'users' policy' which can be found on the site itself. Referring to weight or BMI, in particular, is not tolerated by most genuine organisations, because eating disorders are inherently a competitive illness and users will usually try to 'out do' one another.

A discreet sign to look out for is if your loved one suddenly begins to wear a red bracelet. Often, these websites encourage users to wear a red bracelet as a signal to other people within the 'pro-ana' community and, equally, as a reminder not to eat during periods of temptation. Pro-mia (websites which promote bulimia) are far less common, but encourage their users to wear a blue or a purple band.

Negative influencers

Search for 'diet tips' online and you will soon be drowning in the weight of 'advice' from so-called experts, many of whom now air their views online via video. Many may indeed be genuinely informative, based on scientific evidence and offering responsible and informed knowledge to the website's millions of users. Sadly, it can be hard to know who those responsible vloggers are amid the ocean of unqualified and sometimes potentially dangerous advice.

The popular vlogging and video platforms provide a very simple stage for both the well-intentioned but unqualified influencer, as well as those who intentionally intend to promote dangerous eating behaviours to the wider public, often targeting the most vulnerable. Like pro-ana sites, it is easy for those with negative intentions to promote their 'wares' through social media.

The various social networking sites should also be handled with caution. While of course these sites themselves do not have any intention of promoting eating disorders – and indeed some have banned many of the most inflammatory phrases that point to users promoting eating disorders, including 'anorexia', 'pro-ana' and 'thinspiration' – these sites can present an easy and instantaneous way for sufferers to share potentially damaging information.

There is justifiable concern that social platforms could be more harmful than pro-anorexia websites, as they are more accessible and have a much wider reach. On the one hand, eating disorder sufferers may actively seek out or attract other people with the same illness, both within their real and their cyber lives. This can significantly hinder their recovery, because sufferers could 'normalise' their behaviour by surrounding themselves with other people who behave and think in the same way.

But almost as worrying is the insidious creep of negative influence that these sites can have on a person's life. For those who struggle with body image and/or low self-esteem, constantly scrolling through 'perfect' photos from friends, celebrities and models can greatly exacerbate that negative cycle that they find themselves in. The presentation of a perfect life with photographs of 'gorgeous' people enjoying great times, can be intoxicating to many, especially impressionable youngsters. For those already struggling with low self-esteem, it can be all too easy to start believing that if only they looked like that, they too would be happy and enjoy the same influence as the 'stars' of many of the social media platforms.

Juliet, who is in the early stages of recovery from anorexia nervosa, says:

Social media can have a negative impact on all of us, whether we realise it or not. These days I've found that the pressure from social media is less about an emphasis on being skinny but rather on being strong, fit and appearing to look in peak physical condition; all good things but just as dangerous when taken to the extreme. It can appear as if everyone these days is a personal trainer, everyone spends hours in the gym honing their abs, ensuring their bum looks as peachy as possible and sculpting their arms so that they look perfect. You can't go on your phone without seeing images of beautiful people adorned in gym leggings and a crop top with six packs peeping out, holding a water bottle in their hand and talking about their latest work out or new healthy, balanced diet plan.

This then leads to a pressure on everyone as we feel that this is the new normal. We feel as though we all need to dedicate hours to the gym, feel as if to fit in and be normal we need to look like a fitness model. Most of the people we end up idolising are in fact normal people who have turned to the gym lifestyle and made some seriously impressive results, fuelling the feeling of inadequacy even more as it leaves us feeling devastated that we cannot achieve this 'ideal body'. This promotion of 'health' and perfection is taking over the social media scene and whilst 'strong not skinny' may seem less sinister than the pro-ana and 'thinspo' side of the internet, 'fitspo' can be just as dangerous to our mental health and how we view our own bodies.

If those 'influencers' (the clue is in the name) then start promoting a certain way of eating (and 'clean eating' in particular is rife on social media at the time of writing this book), it is easy to see why many would see this as a desirable lifestyle to follow. Unfortunately, these same people who promote a particular food or exercise regime rarely have any qualifications for doing so, nor academic or scientific backing for their claims.

Paige, who is in recovery from anorexia nervosa, says:

> I feel bad about myself when the media state what foods we should or shouldn't eat, or what foods are 'good' and 'bad'. I think you can have things in moderation but the way the media portray it seems as though we can only eat specific food otherwise we are eating the wrong things.

What we need to remember is that this presentation of perfection, whether it's how they look, where they holiday, or who they surround themselves with, is deceptive. Despite how 'perfect' someone's life may appear, everyone has their upsets and battles – they just do not choose to show that side. Their photographs are likely to have been touched-up and had filters applied, and the bad days they inevitably will have had will have effectively been erased from their personal history. These people may not have deliberately dangerous intentions, but for those at risk of eating disorders and other mental illnesses, their false presentation of a perfect life combined with the negative self-perception of those with crushingly low self-esteem may be a recipe for untold damage.

Paige goes on to explain how the portrayal of the 'perfect' life on social media makes her feel:

> I am trying to get better and avoid listening to what the media says and make my own choices, but sometimes it is unavoidable. I feel this especially with how I should look instead of my own personal taste. I feel I should have a great body, exercise all the time, eat the perfect diet and travel the world whilst also having a good job and a brilliant relationship. In reality, these things aren't easy to have and/or balance, but they

> are constantly pushed in our faces and I feel this adds a lot of
> pressure into my life.

Parents and carers can often feel powerless in the face of the onslaught from social media. While, indeed, the pull of social media is incredibly strong, there are nevertheless still things that carers and their families could do to counter its effects. Sometimes it can feel like another battle but setting strong boundaries for online use can be vital. Debbie says of her struggles in setting boundaries:

> Both my children aged 14 and 17 have trouble sleeping, suffering from insomnia. When I was a child I always slept through the night well. I got an iPhone 6 three years ago and have realised I have become addicted to it, always checking if I have messages and looking on Facebook whenever I get the chance. I'm 52 and it's drawn me in! What chance do our children have? They keep their phones in their room not wanting to miss anything, claiming they need the alarm to get up in the morning for school. I seriously believe they affect my children's sleep and have requested phones stay out of their bedrooms, but the objections are so great it's as if they actually can't breathe without their phones on charge near them overnight. They refuse to do it. I think small LED lights disturb our sleep too. I cover my alarm clock with a towel! I'm middle aged and menopausal – I'm not supposed to sleep! But what about our children? They should be sleeping well to be able to learn at school and develop and grow!

Age limits exist on social media sites for good reason (for most sites the minimum age limit is 13), and you may want to think carefully about your own loved one's individual maturity, mental strength and toughness before you allow them to have accounts on these sites. It is also vital to keep the channels of communication open with them, and to counter the images and influences they are exposed to with a reminder of the unreal side to social media. Even while watching TV, discuss whether what you are seeing is really like real life. If you suspect your loved ones might be particularly susceptible to the unhealthy influence of social media, it might be helpful to start talking about that with them. Suggest that they replace the sites and accounts that bring them down with ones that inspire. Have a look with them to find people to follow that make them happy, not miserable or anxious. Encourage them to follow people who post inspirational messages, and seek out role models that inspire through their good works or incredible attitude.

Richard Styles, head of Year 10, tells us his thoughts:

> There is an unfortunate stereotype to which young people nowadays have an unprecedented access. That is, they are seeing, perhaps several times a day, images from those in the public eye whose bodies have been photo-shopped or half-starved or both, and are feeling a terrible pressure to conform to impossible shapes. A Google search for 'beautiful woman' returns pictures only of a specific size – 'zero'. It is this false representation of bodies in the media which must be addressed if we are to see a decrease in the number of sufferers. Parents and teachers, too, must ensure that young people are directed towards role models who represent values and virtues that outshine ten-fold a person's dress size or bicep circumference: integrity, honesty, kindness, ambition, respect.

Away from social media, you can talk together about the things that make you smile. Ask your loved one about the good things that happened in their day, the acts of kindness they noted or the surprising things that made them smile. Consider keeping a positive diary, either as a family or individuals, to arm you all against the negative influences that surround us today more than ever.

And above all, remember you are not powerless. Yes, the pull of the internet and social media is strong, but the love and caring of close, real-life relationships can never be replicated online.

Chapter 12

Bullying

With the rise of social media has come a shocking rise in body-shaming and bullying, and with as many as 65 per cent of people with eating disorders in America saying that bullying contributed to their condition,[81] the scourge of the online world is something we should be rightly concerned about.

The particularly worrying thing about bullying on social media is that it can feel as if there is no escape from it. Without wishing to minimise the pain of bullying in real life, at least in the days before social media, people could go home from school or work and have a break from their tormentors. With social media, bullies can now victimise the vulnerable 24 hours a day, seven days a week. Cyberbullying can leave people feeling there is nowhere they can hide as every time they access social media they have to face unkind comments and criticism; threatening or aggressive messages. Cyberbullies often aim to sabotage friendships and encourage groups of people to exclude or abuse someone for usually very trivial reasons. At their worst, cyberbullies actively encourage people to hurt themselves or even take their lives, and sadly tragedies have occurred.

While social media sites state that bullying, abusive behaviours which include harassment, impersonation and identity theft are banned, sadly this kind of behaviour still continues to proliferate on most of the popular social media platforms. Users of one of the platforms, for example, can post photos and comments that simply 'disappear' after a few seconds. Those few seconds, repeated over hours, days and weeks, if negative, can have a devastating effect on people's lives.

It can be very hard for someone who is being bullied to see a way out of this torment, but there are things that they and their loved ones can do. Simply by talking about cyberbullying takes some the power out of it. If you suspect that someone you care about is being bullied online, try to broach it with them or suggest they talk to someone else. Encourage them to use the 'block' function available on most social media to prevent further bullying from taking place. Most sites now have a system to report abusive or inappropriate messages and many will take action against users who repeatedly abuse rules. Use these systems and report bullying messages and remind the victim to try not to respond to bullying messages, and instead to delete or ignore them.

Eating disorders and the mainstream media

By mainstream media, I am talking about the newspapers, magazines and TV programmes that are woven into the fabric of everyday life and which, even in the digital era, exert a huge influence over what people believe and how they act and behave.

Danny Bowman, director of Mental Health at Parliament Street, tells us of how the pressure of the images in the media led him to a dark place in his younger years, where he was using social media for up to 10 hours per day:

> Unfortunately, the effect of the media and social media had an extremely detrimental influence on me. It made me believe I wasn't good enough in my younger years and amplified feelings of guilt, insecurity and fear. This led me to a very dark place, a place in which my confidence was rock-bottom and the belief I had in my own future diminished because of the crushing pressure of the bulky magazines, full of images of what I could look like instead of being happy with how I did look.

Danny goes on to say:

> I believe society puts immense pressure on not just me, but all young people, to be a certain way, look a certain way, wear the best clothes, and become the reflection of what society deems as acceptable. The pressure from friends is a side effect of the

> growing level of importance society puts on appearance. This is deceiving people into thinking if they do not look a certain way their life will be a failure.

It is easy to see the media as the enemy, but that is not always the case. The media represents a great diversity of organisations and individuals, and there are many journalists, television producers and editors working ethically to effect positive change in eating disorders and body image and how they are reported.

However, there can be serious issues in terms of how eating disorders are reported. Unrealistic advertising, air-brushing, and irresponsible reporting and body shaming are still far too prevalent and the influence they exert continues to be very concerning.

I'd like to share the results of a survey I commissioned, designed to explore the effect the media has on people's mind-sets and lifestyle choices.

Of all the people that took part, 92 per cent believed that the media encourages unhealthy lifestyle choices. However, this does not prevent an overwhelming majority of almost 89 per cent claiming they have been made to feel bad about their own appearance by something they have seen in the media. Eight in 10 of them agreed that the media or their friends put pressure on them to look a certain way.

To attempt to gain an insight into the apparent anomalies in the thinking of young people, I interviewed Tom, Ed and Louis, all young adults. They explained that, while the media may affect each individual to a lesser or greater extent depending on how vulnerable to media messages that person is, those influenced by the media then go on to inflict their views on their peer groups.

Ed said this:

> The media affects certain people, then they affect others; for example, they feel pressure from their friends.

We can see from this how any potential damage from the media is magnified, so any research might not be accurately reflecting how influential the media is. The young men also, paradoxically, claimed to be aware of airbrushing and unrealistic imagery within the media, but admitted to attempting to emulate an 'ideal' body type, anyway.

The boys said:

> When you see airbrushed abs, etc. it makes you strive harder. It still plays on your mind, even though you know airbrushing has been used. When I look at images of men on the front of health magazines, with defined, rippled chest and abs, I know that's what I'm aiming for.

We can see here, worryingly, that images in the media promoting aspirational beauty could, in fact, even be cartoons, and young people would still attempt to emulate them. It would be remiss to blame celebrities for this. They are at the mercy of their industry, and it is an industry which sadly often demands a warped version of 'perfection'.

Bobby Davro, who has enjoyed a long career in show businesses since the early 1980s, and is the father of three daughters, says:

> I do believe that the pressure to look good within the media can, and has, led to certain celebrities going beyond the normal dieting parameters and this has led, in some cases, to bad health. All celebrities have egos and some are greater than others. Many celebrities become role models to the young and I believe it is their moral responsibility to care about how they look and behave. However, only the media industry can really address this and achieve a fair balance.

British actress and former anorexia sufferer, Gemma Oaten, says:

> It was so very difficult for me to go public with my illness. It's a double-edged sword. I want to leave all this behind me and live my life, but then the life I have chosen puts me in the public eye. I can't have it both ways. Acting makes me happy. It's all I have ever wanted to do and it's never been a decision. I hope I am strong enough to deal with the echoes of my past but I will never hide from it.

Actress Mikyla Dodd echoes this:

> The media plays a huge part in projecting images of how people should look, and yet the images are seldom untouched by a computer. The pictures of people with no make-up on, having a normal day and wearing baggy clothes are portrayed as negative, rather than just normal. There is so much pressure on society to be glamorous and a perception that beauty is in some way connected to being slim or, worse still, super-skinny.

Body shaming

Look at the newsstands on any given day and on their front covers certain magazines will be openly body-shaming celebrities, purely on the basis of a bad photo or, as Mikyla says, a 'normal' day. These headlines might scream about 'My weight battle' by one soap actor, or 'My bikini diet' by a reality show star. The message that readers pick up is clear – that weight and what you look like matter, and skinny is 'best'. It is a message that is false, wrong and hugely damaging for those with already shaky self-esteem. That is not to say that these kinds of headlines or articles are the cause of someone's eating disorder (we know that the causes are usually a much more complex combination of factors), but could they play a part in triggering disordered eating behaviour? Of course.

We know our brains can be influenced by the environment in which we live and the media holds up a magnifying glass to this society which appears to prize body image above so much else.

The growth of a celebrity culture where young people at the peak of physical health are either idolised for their perfect bodies or criticised for their physical failings creates a powerful influence that is unhealthy for many and toxic for a vulnerable few. Furthermore, being surrounded by these idealised images when your own body image is distorted by a mental illness reinforces the shame that someone with an eating disorder may feel about themselves.

A carer's role is key here. Try to find ways to counter these messages, to talk openly and often about how these stories in the media may not be telling the truth. If you can, try to point out that when we see celebrities groomed to within an inch of their life and squeezed into skin-tight gowns, they will have had hours – possibly days – of help to get them looking like that, and then the photo that appears in the press may have been airbrushed. In other words, these images are not a realistic idea for those of us living in the real world, and to try and attain something like this is to strain fruitlessly towards a false ideal.

The same narrative should be used to counter the sleek images of perfect models used in advertising campaigns and fashion articles. Whether the pictures are of very slim female models, or men with bulging muscles and an abdominal six-pack, the images are only very loosely based on reality. In many cases the models may have followed a disordered eating pattern themselves to get to the size required to even take part in the photoshoot.

As Zuzanna Buchwald, model, wellness mentor and mental health advocate, openly tells us:

> I was a professional athlete before entering the fashion industry and had a significant muscle mass. The muscular body was not the body type I was expected to have by my agency so I was asked to get rid of my muscles by refraining from exercise and not eating (so I didn't replace the muscle with fat). The thinner I was, the more jobs (better paid and more prestigious) I would book and the more praise I would receive from my agents.

They then will have been primped and preened to enhance their natural beauty, and using all the most high tech tools, their images may have been airbrushed, altered or have had flattering filters applied. And yet, even though most people know all this, these pictures still manage to make people feel they do not measure up.

There are changes afoot. More ex-models and celebrities are playing their own role in countering the extreme standards their industry sets, bravely speaking out about their own battles with eating disorders or body image issues which their work has exacerbated. For them, experiences of anorexia and bulimia among their friends and colleagues in the modelling industry are all too common. What is more, they tell how unhealthy weight loss is all too often admired in their business, even though the models themselves may be unhealthy, weak and unhappy.

Victoire Dauxerre, a former model, tells us more of her experience in the industry:

> Modelling was the trigger point of anorexia for me. I was a slim, determined young girl. When I was scouted as a teenager I had no dream of becoming a model, but I wanted to be the best in whatever I would do. They constantly repeat to you that you have to be a size zero if you want to be chosen for the job and applaud you when you lose weight, so the message is clear: the thinner, the better. This is how I fell into anorexia. The fashion industry loves you down to the bone.

Eleni Renton (director of Leni's Models), sums up the changes which need to be made within the industry when she says:

> The media distorts what the average person thinks they should look like. We are no longer seeing this just with models, but with Hollywood celebrities and reality television stars. Ultimately, the most important thing should be for fashion, and all of the media, to portray health.

Thanks to these people speaking out, and a small but significant fightback from the public against this 'thin ideal', we are starting to see changes occurring. A few pioneering fashion labels are insisting on using healthier role models in their campaigns, and the fashion industry itself is starting to take some responsibility for the problem. In 2016, for example, France passed a law requiring models to present a medical statement when applying for jobs within modelling, stating that they are medically stable and able to work.

One of those pioneering fashion labels is the women's fitness brand Sweaty Betty; Tamara Hill-Norton, founder and chief creative officer, says:

> At Sweaty Betty our mission is to empower women through fitness and beyond and we aim to reflect this when casting models. I always look for fun girls who embody our brand values and live a really balanced lifestyle. We look for muscle tone rather than waist measurements and ask each girl what physical sports they love to do. Recently we've had an athlete who is training for Olympic high jump, a rock climber and a martial arts expert. On top of this, I attend every shoot personally and we all eat lunch together, before ending the day with a cocktail (obviously).

Awareness is growing in the mainstream media too. Although some pockets continue to body shame and place undue emphasis on the importance of weight, others are starting to acknowledge more the part their own publication may play in the mental health of the nation. Powerful campaigns, including Heads Together, spearheaded by Princes William and Harry, have pushed mental health to the top of the media agenda in recent times and, although eating disorders are not always explicitly included in that, any progress in the reporting on mental illness can only be a good thing.

Since 2011, the charity Beat has asked journalists to abide

by its media guidelines. The charity acknowledges the positive effect the media can exert, saying: 'Reporting eating disorders honestly, truthfully and with compassion for those affected makes a tremendous difference. It helps overcome the stigma and shame many people feel – making it easier for them to accept the treatment and support they need to beat an eating disorder.' The charity also makes clear that some reporting can be very damaging. The guidelines asks reporters not to include the specific weights of eating disorder sufferers, or use pictures of their emaciated frames when at their lowest weights. The charity urges reporters to reflect the complexity of eating disorders in their articles and not to focus on the specifics of what a sufferer ate or how they hit such a low weight, as those details could act as an encouragement or even be interpreted as an instruction by those at risk of eating disorders. Many journalists and publications abide by these guidelines. Sadly, some still do not.

Beating Eating Disorders has also contributed to new guidelines that have been drawn up looking into how mental health issues as a whole should be reported on.

Mental health campaigner Natasha Devon, who drew up the Mental Health Media Charter, explains more:

I describe myself as an activist (simply because 'campaigner' is increasingly used to label those who raise awareness of issues, which is of course both valuable and needed, but I prefer to lobby for solutions and change). One of the main focuses of my activism is mental health. I have created projects which aim to change laws, improve service provision and examine the way education policy impacts the wellbeing of young people, all with the ultimate goal of improving the mental health of the nation. Part of my passion for this comes from having first-hand experience. I have an ongoing anxiety disorder and have survived seven years of bulimia nervosa in my late teens and early 20s.

You probably have built some sort of image of me in your mind as you read that; now let's see if it changes when I tell you a little more… For three years, I had a monthly column on the last page of *Cosmopolitan Magazine* (called 'The Last Word'), of which I was immensely proud. I continue to write for, amongst others, *Grazia* and *Women's Health*. I love having fun with fashion, worked as a part-time model whilst getting my degree almost two decades ago and am absolutely obsessed with make-up (seriously, if you added up all the time I've spent browsing the shelves of Boots in my lifetime it would be years).

Can you reconcile the two people described in the above paragraphs? They are each equally and unequivocally me. Yet, as I travelled the UK delivering talks in schools and at events about mental health, body image and social equality, one of the commonest questions I would be asked was 'how do you reconcile all this with working for glossy mags/being on telly/the fact that your eyebrows are totally fleeky right now?'

Over time, I began to see myself as a bridge between worlds. I knew that the publications I worked for were filled with intelligent, kind, creative people who got into journalism because they wanted to make the world a better place. I also knew that the end result was often making the public feel worse about themselves. I could see that often the media was portraying mental illness in unhelpful ways, but I also knew how much power it had as a force for good.

Of course, when it comes to eating disorders, imagery is paramount. Triggering 'before and after' pictures often used to illustrate eating disorder stories in magazines and newspapers can not only perversely incentivise people currently struggling; they also encourage the public to believe that the illnesses are all about weight. This couldn't be further from the truth – eating disorders are mental illnesses which begin and end in the mind. As a student of English, I was also hyper-aware of the power of language. Words matter – they shape not only social attitudes but our internal belief system. I found evidence, for example, that the continued use of the phrase 'commit suicide' was discouraging people with suicidal thoughts from seeking help, because they thought it would somehow have legal implications (you commit a crime and it hasn't been a criminal offence to end your own life in the UK since 1961).

All of these considerations led me to create the Mental Health Media Charter, which I launched on World Mental Health Day in October 2017. It's seven simple guidelines for anyone who wants to ensure that the way they are speaking, writing or portraying mental health issues is responsible, genuinely educational and doesn't perpetuate unhelpful stereotypes.

Of course, many charities have their own media guidelines – I believe the Samaritans is considered to be the gold standard and Beat have an extensive list of dos and don'ts when it comes to eating disorders. However, I noticed that these organisations were often being deferred to and misrepresented when media were criticised. When a reality TV star appeared on a daytime show and essentially gave a glamorous-sounding 'how to' guide to anorexia, the presenter who interviewed her responded to the subsequent social media outcry by insisting that they had adhered to Beat's guidance. When a broadsheet was roundly criticised for its reporting of the death of a celebrity by suicide, it issued a statement claiming that it 'worked closely with the Samaritans'. I felt that responsibility was being absolved, charities were being scapegoated and that the entire process needed more transparency.

The charter is a page in length, is displayed in full on my website along with a comprehensive list of the media outlets that have pledged their support. I also enlisted the help of artist Ruby Elliot (better known as Rubyetc) to create a 'stamp' so that organisations could display their membership of the charter on their pages, websites and social media. Our followers can (and do) often refer to these in order to supervise media outlets and remind signees if they slip, because everything is out there for the public to see.

I was wary of treading on anyone's toes, so I involved Beat, the Samaritans and Mental Health First Aid England to be my partners in creating the charter, which was first and foremost based on a survey I undertook of people affected by mental illness, whether directly or via a loved one, of what they found most and least helpful in terms of media reporting. To date, more than 50 outlets and individuals have pledged, including Countdown's Rachel Riley, Sky News' Stephen Dixon, *Heat* and *Happiful* magazines, *Planet Rock*, the *Times Educational Supplement* and the *Eastern Daily Press*.

Given my professional history, I was particularly proud that the first publication to sign was *Grazia Magazine*. When I saw their beautifully worded and completely appropriate tribute following the death by suicide of Kate Spade on their inside front page, in the context of many other media outlets which were getting it so wrong, I shed a tear.

The charter is very far from all-encompassing, but it is making a difference to the landscape of mental health reporting. Whilst I did want media to be held to account, I didn't want the campaign to turn into a witch-hunt, which would in turn perhaps deter new signees. I was therefore very careful to emphasise in the charter's mission statement that the guidance only calls for those who sign up to do their best. We all occasionally make mistakes, and this is particularly likely in a large organisation or a hectic news room. That is entirely forgivable. What is not forgivable is knowing what's appropriate and safe and choosing wilfully to ignore it.

You can read the charter and see the stamp by visiting my website, natashadevon.com. If you'd like to help the cause, please write to your local news outlet, or any publication to which you subscribe, asking them to join up.

To conclude

As a carer, the internet can be your friend or your foe. It is certainly no coincidence that the meteoric rise in eating disorder diagnosis has mirrored the increase in access to the internet. However, the internet is also invaluable in uniting people with a genuine desire to get better and those who can help them on their way.

The official advice is that pro-ana websites should be reported to Google, who then prevent the site in question from showing up in any internet search. However, many people believe that there is little value in doing this, since the site will simply change its name and URL, or that five more sites will pop up in place of the one which has been removed. Reporting pro-ana websites also forces them to become more subtle and sneaky in their techniques, making them all the harder to distinguish from genuine support forums.

It is, of course, a matter of personal choice whether or not to report a pro-ana site. However, the most important consideration for any carer is, if possible, to prevent sufferers from using these sites at all. If you do find your loved one visiting a pro-ana site, you should initially have a look at what they have written in the forum or on their blog. It may provide a crucial insight into how they are currently thinking, and allow you to stay one step ahead of their illness.

You then need to turn your attention to why they are doing this, in the hope of preventing them from using the pro-ana site any further. You may choose to introduce them to a genuine forum so they can interact with people who can provide an alternative and healthier way of thinking. You might also opt to apply 'parental controls' to the sufferer's computer, which prevent sites which use certain words from being accessible. You may also choose to ban the internet altogether, depending on how old your loved one is and what your relationship is with them.

It is worth remembering, however, that the internet is not an entirely bad influence. There are individuals and organisations both online and offline who want to help sufferers towards a healthy mind-set and future, and their positive influence should not be disregarded. You may find that these publications, sites and internet users contribute to your own network of support, providing ways and means of helping your loved one towards recovery which you are unable to do yourself.

The important thing is not to feel that you are powerless compared with the might of the media. Yes, the influence it exerts is strong, but as someone who cares deeply for a person battling disordered eating, your strength and energy also hold huge sway. At times it may feel as if you are swimming against the tide, but please do not give up. With your persistence and love, that tide will one day turn. Do not be afraid to 'take on' the media yourself. By that I mean you should not be afraid to limit your loved one's access to the internet and talk to them about what they are seeing online. Counter the images they see there with your own narrative, explaining that what we see online or in mainstream media is only part of the story, and a story is often glossed over or skewed to make it more attention-grabbing or to exert a particular influence.

As with all elements of effective caring, in this instance, knowledge is power. Simply being aware of the existence of the dangers that lurk online, in particular, and being vigilant in checking for signs of what your loved one is accessing is better than having no knowledge of them at all. I hope that this chapter has given you some insight into the role social networking sites, the internet and mainstream media can play in both helping and hindering recovery from eating disorders.

What is recovery?

From my own personal and professional experience, I have learnt and believe that recovery from an eating disorder is not only possible, but also sustainable. Throughout this book, I hope I have helped you to understand and believe that recovery is achievable and have given you some of the tools to help you, your loved one and your family, move forwards towards that goal.

However, what is sometimes not always clear to both the sufferer and their carers is knowing when they have actually reached that place of 'recovery'. It can be confusing to understand what recovery actually looks like, and sometimes friends and family can become fixated on the idea that recovery is their loved one returning to the person they were before they became ill. Often, the sufferer was not happy in themselves before the eating disorder came into their life; often or not the 'recovery process' can encourage the person suffering to find out who they really are, and this is usually not the person they were before they became ill.

Looking back, before I had any understanding of eating disorders myself, I can remember saying to Samantha: 'We will know you are better when you are back to eating that big chocolate sundae at TGI Fridays!' Little did I know how unhappy and insecure she was within herself at the time she was doing that. Her recovery took her on a journey to find who she really was and, more importantly, like what she found. As she approached the end of this journey, I got a 'newer version' of my wonderful girl, one with more emotional depth, confidence, humour and humility than I could ever have imagined. So, has she recovered from her eating disorder? A resounding 'yes'. (We never did go back and have that chocolate sundae at TGI Fridays!)

Recovery is not the finishing line you get to at the end of a race. It is a process to go through and an understanding to arrive at. It is an acceptance by the sufferer of who they are and how they want to live, and it is rarely achievable without a lot of effort, support, perseverance, determination and hard work, through set-backs and obstacles, often over a number of months and possibly years.

It is also – and I cannot stress this enough – a completely individual goal. It is a unique journey for everyone who has had an eating disorder, and 'recovery' will look different for each and every one of those people. Some will know they have recovered when they never have another eating disordered thought. Others will acknowledge those thoughts are still there but be able to control them through the coping mechanisms they have acquired, taking all the power out of those thoughts so they no longer have the effect they once did.

For some it will be about body image and reaching a point of acceptance of who they are and what they look like. Others will say that being able to enjoy a meal 'normally' with friends or family is their recovery milestone. For some sufferers, accepting that those destructive thoughts may not fully go away but being able to live with them and control them is a good form of recovery. For others, feeling stronger than the eating disorder is a real marker. Some may eventually be able to reach a place where the eating disorder no longer plays any part in their life, where it feels like it happened to someone else.

Some of the contributors to this book were keen to help you, the reader, understand what recovery looks like and means to them. Their stories show some of the different guises of recovery, but there are many more. Recovery is, as I say, a unique place for each eating disorder sufferer, which can only be reached when that sufferer finds the right path for them.

Ways others have recognised recovery

Accepting you have changed:

> A lot of people think recovery is going back to how you were before the illness. Even I did, but I soon came to realise that for a lot of sufferers this is not the case; think about all the experiences and challenges in life you may face, you are never completely the same when you come out the other end. Mental illness is no different; the soul will always still be there, but it would have grown, strengthened and changed a little, and learn to accept that things may a bit different, but isn't that part of life? – Samantha

Eating with less anxiety:

> Recovery for me is certainly not going back to the person I was before the disorder because I had issues with over-eating and was overweight before I started with restrictive behaviours. For me, it's about being able to eat in social situations and not have anxiety around it, not constantly be thinking 'Are people watching me eat? Or judging whether I am eating too little, or too much?' It's being able to make healthy food choices but also being able to have a treat when I want one, without thinking I need to binge, or purge. It's eventually, one day, not needing to keep a food journal in order to keep the thoughts about restricting from taking over. It's being able to have a relaxed relationship with food, instead of an anxiety-filled one. I've not gotten all the way there yet, but I try to celebrate every interaction I have with food that isn't full of anxiety, and the ones that are, I try not to punish myself about. – Evelyn

Being stronger than the eating disorder:

> Recovery to me is being able to go out for dinner last minute, being able to enjoy whatever I want to eat and whatever I want to wear (including a bikini) without that critical voice in my head. Recovery is choosing what I want to eat without worrying about the calories and knowing that I can silence that voice. Recovery is Hope being louder than the manipulative anorexic voice. – *Hope*

Feeling like it happened to someone else:

> My recovery ends with me being much happier and stronger than I was before. It was a nine-year process. I thought I would have to manage the illness in some way for the rest of my life, but that is not the case. It now feels like it happened in a different life time and I have no symptoms or thoughts at all about it. It is quite remarkable. – *Naomi*

Understanding yourself better:

> For me, recovery is a long journey into self-discovery. It's not going back to your old self but finding out who your true self is. I listen to myself. I do what I love with the ones I love and I try not to judge myself. I would never do that with friends, so why would I do it to my soul? Little by little, I hope I allow my true self to come to life. – *Victoire*

Being yourself:

> For me, recovery is coping. It's about perspective, space to breathe and an understanding that it will get better. Recovery is about enjoying being yourself rather than trying to be something else. – *Dave*

What is Recovery?

Persevering and finding freedom:

> For me, recovery is about experiencing a level of freedom. It's not necessarily being symptom free. Also, recovery is about perseverance and using what you've gone through to help others. – *Tara*

Moving on:

> The term 'recovery' gives me a sense of thinking before realising I had disordered eating and was a sufferer, that everything was good, but truth be told it wasn't. For me, 'recovery', or as I like to think of it, 'moving on', is taking the good and workable bits of everything and using the eating disorder part of me as a siren or warning sign that things aren't as smooth as they could be. By doing this, I know I need to take stock and move on in a way that is good for me at that moment in time. This process is always ongoing, and it can be hard to remember that at times, but it works. Just don't put a time limit on it!
>
> I feel that using the term 'recovery' basically undoes everything I went through and the stronger person I became as a result of my journey because there's a sense that I am now fixed. The thing was I was never broken to start with; I just knew ways that were not the best for me. I wasn't aware they weren't the best for me at the time and now I know they were. It's like a tool box; before I only had a hammer and a flat-headed screwdriver, but now I have so many more tools in my tool box, it is now a tool chest. So now I can adapt to things so much better than before! – *Will*

Finally, this is from a mother, Melissa, about her daughter, Kate:

> I shall never forget the afternoon I was in our sitting room, and I heard my daughters laughing as they messed around with the sprinkler in the front garden. It was an enormous shock, the sound of them playing together, because it was a sound we hadn't heard around our home for months. That's when I

understood how far we'd come in Kate's recovery. She was so much better, she could actually forget herself and enjoy playing again.

Another marker in her recovery was the fact that we could eat meals out together, and at home, and in unfamiliar places on holiday. We could finally sit with absolute confidence that Kate would be able to choose something she liked to eat, and that she would eat it, and there wouldn't be a whole lot of stress to go with it.

Finally, my husband and I nearly fell off our chairs when she fancied a bit of chocolate. We had resigned ourselves to the fact that our child would probably never eat sweets, desserts or chocolate ever again, which made us feel sad. How wrong we were. Never resign yourself to anything.

To conclude

Melissa's final sentence really does sum it up: Never resign yourself to anything. Recovery from an eating disorder is possible. It is also personal. Recovery will look different to each and every sufferer and their loved ones. Recovery rarely means getting 'back' the person you had before, but their experience will have made them wiser, stronger and more empathetic to others. With recovery, they will look forward rather than back, embracing a future rather than harking back to the past.

Recovery is not easy, but it is achievable. Never resign yourself to anything.

Conclusion
From me to you...

Over the last decade I have watched my beautiful daughter, Samantha, struggle, gain control, and thankfully conquer her eating disorder and OCD, so I can honestly say without hesitation, there is a light at the end of the dark tunnel for most people living with a mental illness and those caring for them. These powerful and controlling mental illnesses were so entrenched in my daughter that I did not think it possible for her to make it out the other side... but she has. She is free from those crushing, all-consuming shackles and is now chasing her dreams, having just completed a degree in stage and media and graduated with a 2.1. Samantha is doing and experiencing things she herself, and none of us, ever dared to think possible. I can honestly say, she is the happiest and healthiest I have seen her for many years and every day she challenges herself, taking positive strides towards a future she now knows she has, due in large to her utter determination and perseverance to free herself from the confines of mental illness.

I know that caring for someone with an eating disorder and OCD can be frustrating and exhausting, and can often seem like a thankless task, but please be assured, there is always a way forward. As I have said many times throughout this book, each and every sufferer is unique and so is their recovery; there is no one-size-fits-all, so finding a course of treatment that is suited to the individual and their loved ones is paramount. If one treatment does not work, do not be afraid to try another, and then another... It may take some time before you all find the right path to recovery, so please do not give up. You will find it, remembering always that long-term recovery is possible. Explore every avenue you can, ask the professionals as many questions as you need to, and do not settle until you are happy with the answers and choices you and your loved ones have made. Keep in mind that it is about the right recovery path not only for the sufferer but also for the family as a whole. Mistakes will be easily made, which is only natural – I made enough of them too – but for every one made, a valuable lesson can be learnt.

Do not be afraid to stand up to the eating disorder by staying positive and working together to tackle it; be prepared for the long haul as any recovery takes time, acceptance and under-standing. Patience will need to be exercised at every turn, for everyone involved; never lose sight of the fact that the person you love is still in there, trapped by the mental illness, waiting for your help to set them free. Your focus should remain entirely on what you can do for them – not what you cannot do for them.

There will also be times when you will need some down-time yourself, so make sure you take time out to catch up with your own friends or do something else you enjoy. Spending quality time outside of the restrictions of mental illness will help you to see things more clearly with renewed strength and focus, ready to tackle the next challenge that your loved one will face, as every hour of every day is different.

And what of the end of the journey, when your loved one has made their recovery? Where does that leave you? I should stress, here, that it is very common and completely natural to feel mixed emotions at this stage. Your life, which has previously been dominated by your loved one's illness, might feel a little empty, and sometimes, as their carer, you may have lost your own identity and direction. I know I did. At this stage, I would highly recommend thinking about having some life coaching sessions, as they have given me a new lease of life and enabled me to look forward to a better, brighter future, not just for Samantha but for the family as a whole.

I sincerely hope that, with each chapter, this book has helped you gain a clearer understanding of this most devastating and sometimes totally misunderstood mental illness and given you the HOPE that eating disorders can be conquered. Never give up. Families, relationships and lives can be rebuilt. My family is living proof of that.

I will leave you with my guiding principle:

> The cure is in the recovery; there is no elevator – you have to take the stairs.

Yours with hope…
Lynn Crilly x

Kevin leaves you with:

> I have been around mental illness for years and as much as I have tried I still don't get it. What I do know now is that if it isn't treated and the sufferer doesn't receive help it's not going away and could manifest into something much worse! Thankfully my lovely Sam is back with us now, from wherever she was.

Charlotte leaves you with:

> Although, at times, it can be hard to come to terms with why mental illness chose your family and loved one to hurt, when I look back now, I realise that I wouldn't change anything, otherwise we wouldn't be where we are today. I do feel in the long run it has brought us all closer together, especially my relationship with my sister.

Samantha finishes with her words of HOPE:

I know and believe that everyone has the strength to beat their demons; it won't be easy; it will probably be one of the hardest challenges you will ever face, but one thing I can promise from the bottom of my heart is that when you come out the other side you will feel exhilarated with life, you will see beautiful things around you that you never noticed before and, most of all, feel an abundance of freedom and power in yourself. Trust me on this one – you will never, ever regret recovery.

Resources

Charities

SANE

www.sane.org.uk

0300 304 7000 (4.30 pm – 10.30 pm daily)

SANE is a UK-wide charity working to improve quality of life for people affected by mental illness. SANE has three main objectives:

1. To raise awareness and combat stigma about mental illness, educating and campaigning to improve mental health services.
2. To provide care and emotional support for people with mental health problems, their families and carers, as well as information for other organisations and the public.
3. To initiate research into the causes and treatments of serious mental illness, such as schizophrenia and depression, and the psychological and social impact of mental illness.

SANE offers emotional support and information to anyone affected by mental health problems through its helpline and email services and its online Support Forum where people share their feelings and experiences.

Registered charity number: 296572

Beat
www.b-eat.co.uk
Helpline: 0845 634 1414

Beat is the UK's leading eating disorder charity and the largest of its kind in the world, supporting people affected by eating disorders and campaigning on their behalf. It runs telephone helplines, local support groups and a website with information, message boards and online chat. Last year the charity had direct contact with 250,000 individuals, and many, many thousands more through its website and the media.
Registered charity number: 801343

Men Get Eating Disorders Too
www.mengetedstoo.co.uk
sam@mengetedstoo.co.uk
Helpline: 0845 634 1414

MGEDT is a national charitable organisation that is dedicated to raising awareness and supporting the needs of men with eating disorders. Their website provides essential information that is specific to the needs of male sufferers and is an online platform on which men can get their voices heard by telling their stories and exchanging peer support in the online forum and live chat sessions.

Beyond the website, MGEDT reaches out to sufferers, carers and the general public in a number of engagement platforms whether these are via social media and blogs, outreach in the community or in the press/media. They also provide essential training to professionals working in the field.
Registered charity number: 1139351

Samaritans
www.samaritans.org
Tel: 116 123 (UK) / +44116 123 (ROI)

Resources

Samaritans offer a safe place for you to talk any time you like, in your own way – about whatever's getting to you. They are available round the clock, 24 hours a day, 365 days a year. If you need a response immediately, it's best to call Samaritans on the phone. This number is FREE to call.
Registered charity number: England and Wales (219432); Scotland (SC040604).

The Grace Dear Trust
www.thegracedeartrust.co.uk
Facebook: @gracedeartrust
Twitter: @GraceDearTrust1
Instagram: @gracedeartrust

The Grace Dear Trust is a Surrey-based mental health charity spreading and raising awareness around the county.

The Grace Dear Trust was set up in memory of Grace, who was a loving member of the Dear family and an amazing friend to many. She died in early 2017 after suffering from mental health problems for a number of years, in part falling victim to the inability to communicate her problems early enough or effectively enough to save her life.
'It's ok not to be ok'
Registered charity number: 1175955

SEED Eating Disorder Support Services
www.seedeatingdisorders.org.uk
hello@seedeatingdisorders.org.uk
Tel (01482) 344084
Help Line (01482) 718130
Resource Room 9.30am to 2.30pm daily

SEED is a group made up of ordinary people who have had first-hand experience of eating disorders in one form or another.

Their Secretary and co-founder, Mark Oaten, says: 'We feel it is important to share experiences with others and help in any way possible. We know from personal experiences how difficult it is to obtain professional help and assistance in overcoming eating disorders. We hoped that by starting Support and Self Help Groups we would be able to offer help and advice. Our services have developed well beyond that, as we strive to bridge the gaps and meet the needs of those affected by this devastating illness.' Registered charity number 1108405

Amigo Productions – founded by Gemma Oaten and Richard Lamberth
www.amigoproductions.uk

Amigo Productions, founded by Gemma Oaten and Richard Lamberth, supports eating disorder charity SEED by raising money through cabaret shows and corporate performing arts experiences, as well as through running workshops for people who have struggled with eating disorders.

Mental Health First Aid
https://mhfaengland.org
https://www.mhfaireland.ie
Aims to train one in 10 people in Britain and Ireland to recognise the signs of mental illness and to support those who suffer from it.

Contributors

Steve Blacknell
teeheesb@yahoo.com
www.steveblacknell.com

Danny Bowman – Director of Mental Health at Parliament Street
Twitter: @DannyBowman10

Resources

Zuzanna Buchwald – model, wellness mentor and mental
health advocate
www.zuzannabuchwald.com
Instagram: @zuzabuchwald

Dave Chawner – Stand-up comic, author and eating disorders
campaigner
www.davechawner.co.uk
Tel: 07791 884 543
Book: *Weight Expectations* published by Jessica Kingsley
Publishers

Dr Lizzie Croton – General Practitioner and NLP, Psy-TaP, TFT,
SIRPA and OldPain2Go therapist
Bournbrook Varsity Medical Practice
1A Alton Rd, Selly Oak, Birmingham, B297DU, UK
www.boundlessflow.co.uk

Victoire Dauxerre – author, actress, mental health advocate and
former model
Instagram: @victoiredauxerre
Book: *Size Zero: How I Survived My Life as a Model* published by
William Collins

Tom Fairbrother – long-distance runner and mental health
advocate
www.tomrunsten.com
Twitter: @fairboyruns

Tara Homsey – author and mental health and addiction
advocate
www.tarahomsey.blogspot.com
Book: *Not Mine Alone* published by Dorrance Publishing

Debbie Roche – Chairperson of Men Get Eating Disorders Too and author
www.noteduk.com
Book: *Anorexia: A Son's Battle, A Mother's War* published by CreateSpace

Hannah Rushbrooke – mental health advocate
www.aitchlouise.weebly.com

Hope Virgo – author and mental health advocate
www.hopevirgo.com
Twitter: @HopeVirgo
Book: *Stand Tall, Little Girl* published by Trigger Publishing

Professionals

Jeff Brazier – Life Coach, NLP practitioner, TV presenter
www.jeffbraziercoaching.com

Dionne Curtis DipIPch – Hypnotherapist, NLP practitioner and TFT practitioner
www.whatiftherapy.co.uk
dionne@whatiftherapy.co.uk
Tel: +44(0)7533149242

Russell Delderfield, PhD (Eating Disorders in UK Men)
University of Bradford
Tel: +44(0)1274 236 794
www.bradford.ac.uk/eating-disorders-and-men

Natasha Devon MBE – Mental health campaigner
www.natashadevon.com
Book: *A Beginner's Guide to Being Mental: An A-Z* published by Bluebird

Resources

Angela Di Benedetto BSc(Hons), MBAcC, MFHT, MSST – TCM
acupuncturist and sports therapist
www.angiestherapies.com
angie.dibe3@btinternet.com
Tel: +44(0)7779118851

Laura Forbes – Bodytalk practitioner
forbesla@icloud.com

Alison Fuller – Hypnotherapist and reflexologist specialising in
women's health
www.thehormonaltherapist.co.uk
info@thehormonaltherapist.co.uk
Tel: +44(0)7811123494

Tamara Hill-Norton – Founder and creative director of Sweaty Betty
www.sweatybetty.com

Jay Hurley – Personal trainer
www.jayhurleyphysiques.co.uk
jayhurley@hotmail.co.uk
Tel: +44(0)7774320855

Inspiration Awards for Women
www.inspirationawards.co.uk

Mark Jermin Stage School with Charlie Brooks (Surrey and Wales)
www.markjermin.co.uk
info@markjermin.co.uk
Tel: +44(0)1792 45 88 55
'A school where pupils are valued, where real confidence is
born and harnessed, and where ambitions are recognised,
encouraged and achieved.'

Catherine Kell Therapy – MA(Hons), DipHyp (Paediatrics), DipClHyp, Cl NLP, MNCH(Reg), CNHC Registered
www.catherinekell.com
info@catherinekell.com
Tel: +44(0)7376 388048

Kingston College of Further Education
info@kingston-college.ac.uk
Tel: +44(0)20 8546 2151
Kingston Hall Rd, Kingston upon Thames KT1 2AQ

Jenny Langley – author, Schools Mental Health trainer, New Maudsley trainer, Carer support co-ordinator and campaigner
www.boyanorexia.com
Tel: +44(0)7887 840470
Book: *Boys Get Anorexia Too* published by Sage publishing

Kevin Laye – DPsy psychotherapist and founder of Psy-TaP, published author and international trainer and speaker
For training www.psy-tap.com
www.kevinlaye.co.uk
cameltrain@aol.com
Tel: +44(0)7803 161021   Skype: Kevin.Laye1

Leni's Model Agency
info@lenismodels.com
www.lenismodels.com

Neil Long – Voice and confidence coach
www.becomefree.co.uk

Janine Lowe – Reiki Master teacher, Feng Shui consultant, NLP counsellor
www.janinelowefengshui
janine@janinelowe.co.uk

Resources

Facebook: Janine Lowe Coach Feng Shui Consultant
Tel: +44(0)7843620472

Renee McGregor – Performance and eating disorder specialist dietitian
BSc (Hons) PGDIP (diet) PGCERT (sportsnutr) RD SENr
reneemcgregor.com
Book: *Orthorexia: When Healthy Eating Goes Bad*, *Training Food* and *The Fast Fuel Book*.

National Centre for Eating Disorders
www.eating-disorders.org.uk
Tel: +44(0)845 838 2040
Open from 9.30 am – 5 pm Monday to Friday

Michele Paradise – Harley Street practitioner of NLP and Havening techniques and clinical hypnotherapist, published author, international trainer and speaker and wellness expert with Deepak Chopra
www.changeyourmindforgood.com
Tel: +44(0)7958607599

Debbie Pennington, CThA – Yoga and massage specialist
debcobb@hotmail.co.uk
Facebook: @yurtopiatherapies & @holisticmeadow

Leanne Poyner – Personal performance and life coach
leannepoyner@yahoo.com
Tel: +44(0)7868 650021

Tan Quddus – Personal trainer
Instagram: @tanqud

Resources

Martin and Marion Shirran – Gastric Mind Band
www.gmband.com
mail@gmband.com
Tel: 0034 951 311 591
Books: *Gastric Mind Band, Pause Button Therapy* and *Cruise Yourself Slim* published by Hay House.

Dave Spinx – Professional actor for over 30 years and founder of The Neston Drama Studio
Neston community and youth centre
info@nestoncyc.co.uk
Tel: +44(0)151 336 7805

Professor Janet Treasure PhD FRCP FRCPsych
www.thenewmaudsleyapproach.co.uk
Books:

- Treasure J, Alexander J. *Anorexia Nervosa: A Recovery Guide for Sufferers, Families and Friends* Second Edition. 2013. Published by Routledge.
- Schmidt U, Treasure J, Alexander J.*Getting Better Bite by Bite: A Survival Kit for Sufferers of Bulimia Nervosa and Binge Eating Disorders*. Second Edition. 2015: Published by Routledge.
- Treasure J, Smith G, Crane A. *Skills-based Learning for Caring for a Loved One with an Eating Disorder*. Second Edition. 2017. Published by Routledge.
- Langley J, Gill Todd, Treasure J. *Training Manual for Skills-Based Caring for a Loved One with an Eating Disorder* (in press)
- Schmidt, U, Startup, H, Treasure J. *A Cognitive-Interpersonal Therapy Workbook for Anorexia Nervosa for People with Anorexia Nervosa*. 2017 (submitted).

References

Chapter 1: What is an eating disorder?

1. Beat Eating Disorders. Statistics for journalists. https://www. beateatingdisorders.org.uk/media-centre/eating-disorder-statistics (Accessed 15 September 2018)
2. National Eating Disorders Association: Factors that may Contribute to Eating Disorders https://www. nationaleatingdisorders.org/sites/default/files/ ResourceHandouts/FactorsthatmayContributetoEatingDisorde rs.pdf (Accessed 17 September 2018)
3. The Center for Eating Disorders at Sheppard Pratt. What causes an eating disorder. https://eatingdisorder.org/eating-disorder-information/underlying-causes/ (Accessed 15 September 2018)
4. Shisslak, C.M., Crago, M., & Estes, L.S. (1995). The spectrum of eating disturbances. *International Journal of Eating Disorders*, 18 (3), 209-219.
5. Beat Eating Disorders. Statistics for journalists. https://www. beateatingdisorders.org.uk/media-centre/eating-disorder-statistics (Accessed 15 September 2081)
6. MGEDT (Men Get Eating Disorders Too). The facts. https:// mengetedstoo.co.uk/information/the-facts (Accessed 15 September 2018)
7. *The Guardian*. Eating disorders in men rise by 70% in NHS figures. 31 July 2017. https://www.theguardian.com/ society/2017/jul/31/eating-disorders-in-men-rise-by-70-in-nhs-figures (Accessed 15 September 2018)

Chapter 2: Anorexia nervosa, bulimia nervosa and over-eating

8. Blinder BJ, Cumella EJ, Sanathara VA. Psychiatric comorbidities of female inpatients with eating disorders. *Psychosomatic Medicine* 2006; 68: 454-462.
9. NHS Digital. Statistics on obesity, physical activity and diet: England 2017. 30 March 2017. SOURCEhttps://www.gov.uk/government/uploads/system/uploads/attachment_data/file/613532/obes-phys-acti-diet-eng-2017-rep.pdf (Accessed 15 September 2018)

Chapter 3: Other eating disorders

10. National Eating Disorders Collaboration, Australian Government Department of Health. Other specified feeding or eating disorders. http://www.nedc.com.au/osfed (Accessed 15 September 2018)
11. Turner PG, Lefevre CE. Instagram use is linked to increased symptoms of orthorexia nervosa. *Eating and Weight Disorders* 2017; 22(2): 277-284. https://www.ncbi.nlm.nih.gov/pmc/articles/PMC5440477/ (Accessed 15 September 2018)

Chapter 4: Recognising an eating disorder and seeking treatment

12. Beat Eating Disorders. Delaying for years, denied for months. https://www.beateatingdisorders.org.uk/uploads/documents/2017/11/delaying-for-years-denied-for-months.pdf (Accessed 17 September 2018)

Chapter 7: Eating disorders and other mental illnesses

13. MentalHealthScreening.org. The Relationship Between Eating Disorders and Anxiety https://mentalhealthscreening.org/blog/the-relationship-between-eating-disorders-and-anxiety (Accessed 17 September 2018)
14. Morgan C, Webb RT, Carr MJ, Kontopantelis E, et al. Incidence, clinical management and mortality risk following self harm among children and adolescents : cohort study in primary care. *British Medical Journal* 2017 ; 359 : j4351. doi.org/10.1136/bmj.j4351
15. The Children's Society. The Good Childhood Report 2018.

https://www.childrenssociety.org.uk/what-we-do/resources-and-publications/the-good-childhood-report-2018 (accessed 24 September 2018)

16. Koutek J, Kocourkova J, Dudova I. Suicidal behavior and self-harm in girls with eating disorders. Neuropsychiatric Disease and Treatment. 2016;12:787-793. doi:10.2147/NDT.S103015.

17. Beat Eating Disorders. The costs of eating disorders Social, health and economic impacts https://www.beateatingdisorders.org.uk/uploads/documents/2017/10/the-costs-of-eating-disorders-final-original.pdf (Accessed 17 September 2018)

18. Eating Disorder Hope. Bipolar Illness and Eating Disorders https://www.eatingdisorderhope.com/blog/bipolar-illness-and-eating-disorders (Accessed 17 September 2018)

19. National Eating Disorders. SUBSTANCE ABUSE AND EATING DISORDERS https://www.nationaleatingdisorders.org/substance-abuse-and-eating-disorders (Accessed 17 September 2018)

20. NHS. Causes of Post-Traumatic Stress Disorder.https://www.nhs.uk/conditions/post-traumatic-stress-disorder-ptsd/ (Accessed 17 September 2018)

21. Eating Disorder Hope. PTSD, Eating Disorders and Trauma https://www.eatingdisorderhope.com/treatment-for-eating-disorders/co-occurring-dual-diagnosis/trauma-ptsd (Accessed 17 September 2018)

Chapter 8: Eating disorders in men

22. Andersen AE. Eating disorders in males: Critical questions. In: Lemberg R, Cohn L, editors. *Eating Disorders: A reference sourcebook* 1998. Oryx Press Inc. p. 73-9.

23. Farrow CV, Fox CL. Gender differences in the relationships between bullying at school and unhealthy eating and shape-related attitudes and behaviours. *The British Journal of Educational Psychology* 2011; 81(3): 409-420.

24. Núñez-Navarro A, Agüera Z, Krug I, Jiménez-Murcia S, Sánchez I, Araguz N, et al. Do men with eating disorders differ from women in clinics, psychopathology and personality? *European Eating Disorders Review* 2012; 20(1): 23-31.

25. Andersen AE, Watson T, Schlechte J. Osteoporosis and osteopenia in men with eating disorders. *The Lancet* 2000; 355(9219): 1967-1968.

26. Winston AP, Wijeratne S. Hypogonadism, hypoleptinaemia and osteoporosis in males with eating disorders. *Clinical Endocrinology* 2009; 71(6): 897-898.

27. Woodside DB, Garfinkel PE, Lin E, Goering P, Kaplan AS, Goldbloom DS, et al. Comparisons of men with full or partial eating disorders, men without eating disorders, and women with eating disorders in the community. *American Journal of Psychiatry* 2001; 158(4): 570-574.

28. Shingleton RM, Thompson-Brenner H, Thompson DR, Pratt EM, Franko DL. Gender differences in clinical trials of binge eating disorder: An analysis of aggregated data. *Journal of Consulting and Clinical Psychology* 2015; 83(2): 382-386.

29. Turja T, Oksanen A, Kaakinen M, Sirola A, Kaltiala-Heino R, Räsänen P. Proeating disorder websites and subjective well-being: a four-country study on young people. *International Journal of Eating Disorders* 2017; 50(1): 50-57.

30. Sweeting H, Walker L, Maclean AM, Patterson C, Räisänen U. Prevalence of eating disorders in males: a review of rates reported in academic research and UK mass media. *International Journal of Men's Health* 2015; 14(2): 86-112.

31. Mehler PS, Sabel AL, Watson T, Andersen AE. High risk of osteoporosis in male patients with eating disorders. *International Journal of Eating Disorders* 2008; 41(7): 666-672.

32. Mitchell JE, Agras S, Crow S, Halmi K, Fairburn CG, Bryson S, et al. Stepped care and cognitive-behavioural therapy for bulimia nervosa: randomised trial. *British Journal of Psychiatry* 2011; 198(5): 391-397.

33. Cohn L, Lemberg R, editors. *Current findings on males with eating disorders*. Hove: Routledge; 2014.

34. Griffiths S, Mond JM, Li Z, Gunatilake S, Murray SB, Sheffield J, et al. Self-stigma of seeking treatment and being male predict an increased likelihood of having an undiagnosed eating disorder. *International Journal of Eating Disorders* 2015; 48(6): 775-778.

35. Murray SB, Griffiths S, Mitchison D, Mond JM. The transition from thinness-oriented to muscularity-oriented disordered eating in adolescent males: A clinical observation. *Journal of Adolescent Health* 2017; 60(3): 353-355.

36. O'Dea JA, Abraham S. Eating and exercise disorders in young

college men. *Journal of American College Health* 2002; 50(6): 273-278.

37. Forney KJ, Holland LA, Keel PK. Influence of peer context on the relationship between body dissatisfaction and eating pathology in women and men. *International Journal of Eating Disorders* 2012; 45(8): 982-989.

38. Mitchison D, Mond J, Slewa-Younan S, Hay P. Sex differences in health-related quality of life impairment associated with eating disorder features: a general population study. *International Journal of Eating Disorders* 2013; 46(4): 375-380.

39. Gueguen J, Godart N, Chambry J, Brun-Eberentz A, Foulon C, Divac Phd SM, et al. Severe anorexia nervosa in men: comparison with severe AN in women and analysis of mortality. *International Journal of Eating Disorders* 2012; 45(4): 537-545.

40. Norris ML, Apsimon M, Harrison M, Obeid N, Buchholz A, Henderson KA, et al. An examination of medical and psychological morbidity in adolescent males with eating disorders. *Eating Behaviors* 2012; 20(5): 405-415.

41. Fichter MM, Krenn H. Eating Disorders in males. In: Treasure J, Schmidt U, Van Furth E, editors. *Handbook of eating disorders*. 2nd ed. Chichester: John Wiley & Sons; 2003. p. 369-84.

42. Mond J, Hall A, Bentley C, Harrison C, Gratwick-Sarll K, Lewis V. Eating-disordered behavior in adolescent boys: Eating disorder examination questionnaire norms. *International Journal of Eating Disorders* 2013; 47(4): 335-341.

43. Musaiger AO, Al-Mannai M, Al-Lalla O. Risk of disordered eating attitudes among male adolescents in five Emirates of the United Arab Emirates. *International Journal of Eating Disorders* 2014; 47(8): 898-900.

44. Darcy AM. Eating disorders in adolescent males: A critical examination of five common assumptions. *Adolescent Psychiatry* 2011; 1(4): 307-312.

45. Rand CS, Wright BA. Thinner females and heavier males: Who says? A comparison of female to male ideal body sizes across a wide age span. *International Journal of Eating Disorders* 2001; 29(1): 45-50.

46. Lavender JM, Anderson DA. Contribution of emotion regulation difficulties to disordered eating and body dissatisfaction in college men. *International Journal of Eating Disorders* 2010; 43(4): 352-357.

47. Feltman KA, Ferraro FR. Preliminary data on risk factors and

disordered eating in male college students. *Current Psychology* 2011; 30(2): 194-202.

48. Klimek P, Murray SB, Brown T, Gonzales IV M, Blashill AJ. Thinness and muscularity internalization: associations with disordered eating and muscle dysmorphia in men. *International Journal of Eating Disorders* 2018; 51(4): 352-357.

49. Rodgers RF, Ganchou C, Franko DL, Chabrol H. Drive for muscularity and disordered eating among French adolescent boys: a sociocultural model. *Body Image* 2012; 9(3): 318-323.

50. Pope H, Phillips KA, Olivardia R. *The Adonis complex: The secret crisis of male body obsession.* New York: Simon and Schuster; 2000.

51. Mosley PE. Bigorexia: bodybuilding and muscle dysmorphia. *European Eating Disorders Review* 2009; 17(3): 191-198.

52. Pope HG, Katz DL, Hudson JI. Anorexia nervosa and "reverse anorexia" among 108 male bodybuilders. *Comprehensive Psychiatry* 1993; 34(6): 406-409.

53. Davis C, Scott-Robertson L. A psychological comparison of females with anorexia nervosa and competitive male bodybuilders: body shape ideals in the extreme. *Eating Behaviors* 2000; 1(1): 33-46.

54. Grieve FG. A conceptual model of factors contributing to the development of muscle dysmorphia. *Eating Behaviors* 2007; 15(1): 63-80.

55. Wichstrom L. Sexual orientation as a risk factor for bulimic symptoms. *International Journal of Eating Disorders* 2006; 39(6): 448-453.

56. Morgan JF. Male Eating Disorders. In: Alexander J, Treasure J, editors. *A collaborative approach to eating disorders.* London: Routledge; 2013.

57. Botha D. *No Labels: men in relationship with anorexia.* South Africa: Moonshine Media; 2012.

58. Wiseman MC, Moradi B. Body image and eating disorder symptoms in sexual minority men: A test and extension of objectification theory. *Journal of Counseling Psychology* 2010; 57(2): 154-166.

59. Baghurst T, Griffiths S, Murray S. Boys and girls prefer hyper-muscular male action figures over normally-muscular action figures: evidence that children have internalized the muscular male body ideal. *North American Journal of Psychology* 2018; 20(1): 159-169.

60. Hiraide M, Harashima S, Yoneda R, Otani M, Kayano M, Yoshiuchi K. Longitudinal course of eating disorders after transsexual treatment: a report of two cases. *BioPsychoSocial Medicine* 2017; 11(1): 32.

61. Diemer EW, White Hughto JM, Gordon AR, Guss C, Austin SB, Reisner SL. Beyond the binary: differences in eating disorder prevalence by gender identity in a transgender sample. *Transgender Health* 2018; 3(1): 17-23.

62. Murray SB, Nagata JM, Griffiths S, Calzo JP, Brown TA, Mitchison D, et al. The enigma of male eating disorders: A critical review and synthesis. *Clinical Psychology Review* 2017; 57: 1-11.

63. Burlew LD, Shurts WM. Men and body image: current issues and counseling implications. *Journal of Counseling & Development* 2013; 91(4): 428-435.

64. Ray SL. Eating disorders in adolescent males. *Professional School Counseling* 2004; 8(2): 98-101.

65. Delderfield R. Coming Out of the Food Cupboard: Supporting young men with eating disorders. *University and College Counselling Journal* 2013 (March): 13-15.

66. Corson PW, Andersen AE. Body image issues among boys and men. In: Cash TF, Pruzinsky T, editors. *Body image: A handbook of theory, research, and clinical practice.* New York: Guilford Press; 2002. p. 192-9.

67. Räisänen U, Hunt K. The role of gendered constructions of eating disorders in delayed help-seeking in men: a qualitative interview study. *BMJ Open* 2014; 4(4): 1-8.

68. Bartlett BA, Mitchell KS. Eating disorders in military and veteran men and women: A systematic review. *International Journal of Eating Disorders* 2015; 48(8): 1057-69.

69. Griffiths S, Mond JM, Murray SB, Touyz S. Young people's stigmatizing attitudes and beliefs about anorexia nervosa and muscle dysmorphia. *International Journal of Eating Disorders* 2013; 47(2): 189-95.

70. McLean SA, Paxton SJ, Massey R, Hay PJ, Mond JM, Rodgers B. Stigmatizing attitudes and beliefs about bulimia nervosa: Gender, age, education and income variability in a community sample. *International Journal of Eating Disorders* 2014; 47(4): 353-361.

71. Fernandez-Aranda F, Krug I, Jimenez-Murcia S, Granero R, Nunez A, Penelo E, et al. Male eating disorders and therapy: a

controlled pilot study with one year follow-up. *Journal of Behavior Therapy and Experimental Psychiatry* 2009; 40(3): 479-486.

72. Chambry J, Agman G. L'anorexie mentale masculine à l'adolescence. *La Psychiatrie de l'Enfant* 2006; 49(2): 477.

73. Russell L, Laszlo B. A group for men with eating disorders: when "lone wolves" come together. *Men and Masculinities* 2013; 16(2): 252-259.

74. Langley, J. *Boys get anorexia too: Coping with male eating disorders in the family*. London: Sage; 2006.

75. Roche, D. *Anorexia: A Son's Battle, A Mother's War*. CreateSpace Independent Publishing; 2015.

Chapter 10: Eating disorders in education and the workplace

76. National Eating Disorder Association. Bullying and Eating Disorders www.nationaleatingdisorders.org/bullying-and-eating-disorders (Accessed 17 September 2018)

77. National Eating Disorder Association. Bullying and Eating Disorders www.nationaleatingdisorders.org/bullying-and-eating-disorders (Accessed 17 September 2018)

78. National Citizen Service. Body Image – The Facts www.ncsyes.co.uk/themix/body-image-facts (Accessed 17 September 2018)

Chapter 11: Eating disorders in exercise and sport

79. Young SN. How to increase serotonin in the human brain without drugs. *Journal of Psychiatry & Neuroscience* 2007; 32(6): 394-399.

80. Penedo FJ, Dahn JR. Exercise and well-being: a review of mental and physical health benefits associated with physical activity. *Current Opinion in Psychiatry* 2005; 18(2): 189–193.

Chapter 12: Eating disorders and the media

81. National Eating Disorder Association. Bullying and Eating Disorders www.nationaleatingdisorders.org/bullying-and-eating-disorders (Accessed 17 September 2018)

Index

Abbreviations: AN, anorexia nervosa; BN, bulimia nervosa; OCD, obsessive compulsive disorder; OSFED, other specified feeding orand eating disorder.

Abbreviations: AN, anorexia nervosa; BN, bulimia nervosa; OCD, obsessive compulsive disorder; OSFED, other specified feeding orand eating disorder.

Abbreviations: AN, anorexia nervosa; BN, bulimia nervosa; OCD, obsessive
compulsive disorder; OSFED, other specified feeding orand eating disorder.

Index

Index

Abbreviations: AN, anorexia nervosa; BN, bulimia nervosa; OCD, obsessive compulsive disorder; OSFED, other specified feeding orand eating disorder.

Index

Abbreviations: AN, anorexia nervosa; BN, bulimia nervosa; OCD, obsessive compulsive disorder; OSFED, other specified feeding orand eating disorder.

Index

Abbreviations: AN, anorexia nervosa; BN, bulimia nervosa; OCD, obsessive compulsive disorder; OSFED, other specified feeding orand eating disorder.

Index

Coming soon...

Hope Through Poetry

By Samantha Crilly

Samantha has suffered, and recovered from, both anorexia and OCD and contributed to Hope with OCD, Hope with Eating Disorders and Hope with Depression, by her mum. Her poems about what it means to grapple with mental illness and overcome it – or not – give powerful support to fellow sufferers and unique insight for their families, friends and carers.

https://www.hammersmithbooks.co.uk/product/hope-through-poetry/

Coming soon...

Hope with Depression
A self-help guide for those affected and their families, friends and carers

By Lynn Crilly

Depression affects more than 300 million people worldwide from all walks of life, and can be a completely debilitating and isolating mental illness. Lynn Crilly speaks from personal and professional experience, having suffered depression herself, and provides much needed positive, practical answers, illustrated with observations and anecdotes from carers and sufferers themselves. This is a practical, supportive guide for anyone with this condition or helping someone with depression. It recognises that each person's illness and recovery will differ and having detailed knowledge and a full toolkit of treatment options is the way to empower each individual with hope for recovery.

www.hammersmithbooks.co.uk/product/hope-with-eating-disorders/